creative ESSENTIALS

THE ART OF **SCREEN ADAPTATION**

Top Writers Reveal Their Craft

ALISTAIR OWEN

creative ESSENTIALS

First published in 2020 by Kamera Books,
an imprint of Oldcastle Books,
Harpenden, UK
kamerabooks.com
Copyright © Alistair Owen 2020
Series Editor: Hannah Patterson
Copy-editor: Jennifer Steele

Extracts from *Hampton on Hampton*, edited by Alistair Owen,
reprinted by kind permission of Faber & Faber Ltd

978-0-85730-227-4 (print)
978-0-85730-228-1 (epub)

Typeset by Elsa Mathern in Sabon and Neue Haas Unica
Printed in Great Britain by Severn, Gloucester

Contents

Introduction

My first screenplay commission was an adaptation. By the time I had sketched out a screen story with the producer and was sitting down to start the script, the location had shifted from Devon to New England, the leads had aged from early teenagers to young adults, and the last third of the novel had been jettisoned. The novel didn't inspire me, so that wasn't a problem. But cut adrift from it, without the compass of the source material or a compelling alternative course, I wrote rubbish – and that *was* a problem. We had barely begun the second pass before I, too, was jettisoned. I learned some good lessons, though. Never adapt a book you don't love. Never accept a job just for the work. And never, ever, tell yourself, 'I'll fix it in the next draft,' because you might not get a chance to write one.

I subsequently turned out other, better adaptations – and my first rewrite; adaptation of a different kind. Even so, when Creative Essentials suggested I write a 'How To' book on the subject, I still had one key question: can I really tell other people how to adapt when I can't back it up with a produced adaptation of my own? The answer was no, I couldn't. What I could do, however, was assemble some of the best screenwriters in the business and ask *them* how it was done. So I did, and here they are: 12 writers, 22 case studies and one career retrospective, exploring adaptations of modern and classic novels, nonfiction books and stage plays, on film and television, in the UK and Hollywood. None of the interviewees has fewer than five produced adaptations on their CVs – and some of them have scripted a lot more – offering a unique and varied insight into the art and craft of adapting for the screen.

Each interview explores the writer's general approach to adaptation before focusing on two specific case studies – with the exception of the conversation with Andrew Davies, perhaps screen adaptation's most prolific practitioner, where I took the opportunity to couple the set questions with a broader tour of his extensive career. Otherwise, the set questions asked depend on the case studies discussed: fiction, or nonfiction, or both. The case studies were my choice in every instance, and were chosen to provide as wide and as recent a range of feature films and television series as possible – although I have deliberately not included plot synopses, in the hope that readers will be inspired to go on the same journey I made through the source material and resulting adaptations. I have, on the other hand, included interviews with two writers I have talked to previously – Hossein Amini (in *Story and Character: Interviews with British Screenwriters*, Bloomsbury, 2002) and Christopher Hampton (in *Hampton on Hampton*, Faber, 2005) – as both can claim significant adaptation credits since those books appeared, and both have had a considerable influence on my own writing over the years.

At this point, my thanks must go to all the interviewees for so generously giving up their time, and to their various agents and publishers (particularly Mary Mount at Penguin and Dinah Wood at Faber) for putting me in touch with them. Extra thanks to my first interviewee (chronologically if not alphabetically), Jeremy Brock, who helped me road-test the Q&A format and has remained an unfailing source of encouragement throughout. A big thank you to the entire team at Creative Essentials: Ion, Lisa, Ellie, Elsa, Jennifer, Clare and Claire – and my editor, Hannah Patterson, who enthusiastically embraced my adaptation of her original pitch. Thanks also to Bethany Davies for her invaluable transcription skills; to Rob Benton and Daniel Rosenthal for their insightful comments on the manuscript (twice over to Daniel for thoughtfully pointing Hannah in my direction in the first place); and to my book and screen agents at Sheil Land Associates, Gaia Banks and Lucy Fawcett, for all their efforts on my behalf while this project was under way. And a huge thank you, finally, to my friends and my parents – and especially to Louise Halfpenny, the best cheerleader any writer could hope for.

Alistair Owen
January 2020

Hossein Amini

Hossein Amini was born in 1966 in Tehran, Iran.

His screen adaptation credits include: *Jude* (1996, novel *Jude the Obscure* by Thomas Hardy); *The Wings of the Dove* (1997, novel by Henry James); *Drive* (2011, novel by James Sallis); *Our Kind of Traitor* (2016, novel by John le Carré); and *The Alienist* (2017, novel by Caleb Carr). He also wrote and directed *The Two Faces of January* (2014), based on the novel by Patricia Highsmith, and co-created and co-wrote the BBC series *McMafia* (2018), based on the book by Misha Glenny.

The Wings of the Dove was Oscar- and BAFTA-nominated for Best Adapted Screenplay.

APPROACHES TO ADAPTATION

Do you prefer to adapt material which chimes with your own work, or material which is completely different and gives you a chance to try out new things?

I like to do both. I think they're almost different challenges, especially doing them consecutively. After working on something personal, something I wanted to explore more deeply, the idea of going on an intellectual holiday by reading up on stuff that I don't know anything about is actually really attractive. Research has always been the bit I love most, learning about a completely new subject, and usually I'll choose assignments based on how interested I am in those subjects. Often they tend to be history, because that was something I studied and have always been quite passionate about. But if a sci-fi thing comes along and I like the idea of researching space and stars and the creation of planets, then I'll go, 'Yeah, that'll be fun.' I don't necessarily only think about the source material; sometimes the work around it is just as interesting.

Do you think adaptations involve a completely different set of creative gears to original screenplays?

Yes and no. For me, the research is equally important in both. With an adaptation, I'll always read 20 other books to inform what I'm writing. Likewise with an original, I'll probably read around it. In that way it's the same. There are a couple of adaptations I've done where the dialogue was there, scenes were there. That's almost a different gig, because that becomes about selecting and filleting and filling in the gaps. I generally tend to do adaptations where there's not a lot of scenes you can transcribe literally. Those interest me less, because I'm more interested in the combination of what the source material has and what I can bring to it as an individual, with my own experiences.

Do you always agree a mission statement or direction of travel with whoever has commissioned the adaptation?

Probably not enough, and as I've got more experienced I've tried to do that more, just to be sure of what they want. Certainly in the past I used to love the element of mystery and discovery in the writing process, but I've come unstuck a few times, so I tend to study whoever is commissioning me a lot more carefully now and to have useful discussions with them before starting.

Do you usually produce an outline or treatment before you start writing the script?

That actually relates to the last question. It's something I used to try to avoid doing, because it felt like writing something you already knew – and again I didn't want to lose that element of discovery, the excitement of a character surprising you or a scene coming out of nowhere. But more and more I've done the treatments, and I also prepare more before writing scenes. And you still get surprised. My scripts very rarely end up being that similar to the treatments, but at least I've got a road map – and someone else has had a chance to comment on that, so you can begin to learn what they want and what they don't want.

So the treatment becomes, if you like, the mission statement.

It becomes the mission statement, and it becomes a way of ironing out any differences between you before you start writing.

If the author of the source material is living, do you find it useful to have their input on the script?

It depends. The one great experience I had at the script stage was the le Carré, *Our Kind of Traitor*, where I worked with him well before the eventual director came on board. He was one of my literary heroes, so it was fantastic sitting with him for three days and going through the script. James Sallis on *Drive* was incredibly gracious. I didn't sit with him, but he was incredibly nice about the whole thing. Generally it's something I'd avoid in the writing process. It's not even the pressure from them, it's that you can start to feel a responsibility to them and, not necessarily for the best, be too faithful to their work because you like them too much. Caleb Carr, for example, on *The Alienist*. We had dinner after I'd written the pilot, and he has such a huge, inspiring presence that then, writing a couple of the other episodes, I felt him over my shoulder the whole time. He's pretty formidable.

Is it easier to navigate notes from directors, producers and script editors when you have a piece of source material to measure the screenplay against?

I'm not sure it is, actually, because after the first or second draft everyone who's involved in the adaptation tends to leave the book behind and it really becomes a critique of the script. Sometimes you'll go back to the book and say, 'Wasn't this a great piece that we missed?' or they'll go back and read it and say, 'We think this bit is useful,' but on the whole I find, certainly as an arbiter between director, producer and writer, it doesn't usually happen.

Have you ever started work on an adaptation and found it harder to adapt than you anticipated?

Every single time. I'll have an emotional reaction to a book, a moment where I feel, 'I can capture the essence of that,' but that's a much shorter reading experience. When you're actually writing it, day by day, it's hard to retain whatever that sensation, that feeling, that emotion was. Some days you feel it strongly and other days you don't. So the excitement of finishing a book and going, 'I know exactly how to do that,' often very quickly turns into a much harder slog.

Have you ever been offered material to adapt which you felt couldn't, or shouldn't, be adapted?

If I turn books down it's usually not because I think they're so great that they shouldn't be adapted. Almost never, because there's a challenge in taking on the great books. I mostly turn down books because they don't resonate with me personally, or I don't feel I can bring my own experiences to them – both emotional and life experiences, but particularly emotional. If I don't feel there's enough space for me in them, then it becomes more of a technical exercise, cutting some bits and keeping others, and that's not very interesting.

Are there any screen adaptations which you think are especially good or you particularly admire?

Anthony Minghella's adaptations of *The English Patient* and *The Talented Mr. Ripley*. He brought his own sensitivity and personality to both books, and transformed them from page to screen. They're adaptations but they're also originals, and could only have been reimagined in that way by an artist like Minghella. For me, they're classic examples of how adapted screenplays are no less an art form than original screenplays.

ADAPTING FICTION

Some writers try to include as much of the novel as possible by boiling scenes down to their essence. Others are more ruthless in editing it down to a sort of greatest hits, but being true to the spirit of it. Do you favour either of those approaches?

I got a bit burnt on my first adaptation, which was an adaptation of *Jude the Obscure*. On the whole the reviews were pretty good, but there were a few negative ones which said that it was a reduction of Thomas Hardy's great work – and in a way it was, because it was one of those books where the scenes were pretty much complete and it was a case of choosing the best ones, what you describe as the 'greatest hits'. After that, I tended to avoid books which were obvious adaptations. *The Wings of the Dove*, for example, had virtually no scenes that were written; it was all trains of thought and explained retrospectively, so I had to invent those scenes. *Drive*, similarly, had an incredible tone and a fantastic character, but the incidents in the script were often quite different to what was in the book, so again it allowed room for invention. So I try not to fall into the trap of the greatest hits, because I think that's the worst kind of adaptation, because it's never going to live up to the book. Whereas if you can turn an adaptation into its own story, which is inspired by the original book but not enslaved to it, then I think that's the best and certainly for me the most exciting way of writing.

If a novel has an unusual structure, would you try to reproduce that in adapting it?

Yes, because that's part of what draws you to the book – though it can also be one of the traps. I'm working on an adaptation of a nonfiction book about Hiroshima, *Shockwave*, which has a very holistic view, with lots of different stories. I thought the only way you could tell that story was to take every single aspect of it, from the pilots on Tinian to the politicians in Potsdam to the people on the ground in Hiroshima, and turn it into one of those multi-narrative stories. Similarly, there's a book I'm adapting called *A Terrible Splendor*, about a German tennis player in the 1930s, which is structured around a five-set tennis match, and after each set there are flashbacks to the lives of both players. I loved the idea of that structure, but I've had to make compromises because it was becoming too rigid and almost too neat, so in the end I've just kept the essence of it. But structure is one of the interesting things about telling a story, so I'd absolutely bear it in mind – particularly now, post-*Dunkirk*, when I think traditional, three-act, linear structure is more and more under siege anyway.

Do you try to avoid voiceover in adapting a first-person narrative, or do you see it as another tool in the toolbox?

I generally don't like voiceover. I feel that unless it's absolutely organic to the storytelling, it's best avoided. But then *The Thin Red Line*, which is one of my favourite films, uses it absolutely beautifully. So I'm not completely against it, but I'm certainly against it when it's used as a band-aid or a lazy way of getting inside people's heads: 'I don't understand this character. Can we have some voiceover?' I think there are more interesting ways of telling that in cinema.

Do you use the language of the novel in writing the screenplay, or do you put the whole thing in your own words?

I put it in my own words, but that's often affected by the way the book is written. *Drive*, for example, had a very terse, film noir style, and I followed that to a certain extent. And it's quite fun to write in different styles. Obviously with period – Thomas Hardy, say – you wouldn't write the stage directions that way, but even then I'd probably use a word which I wouldn't have used in a modern adaptation. But I don't think it really affects the writing that much.

And dialogue? If you like a line, do you tend to keep it?

Yes.

And what would you do if dialogue felt very literary?

Going back to *Jude* and *The Wings of the Dove*, one of the issues I had with literary, particularly nineteenth–century, dialogue was that it's often so wordy and elaborate that it's hard for an audience to follow. Sometimes that language becomes a pleasure in its own right, but what I've tried to do is to simplify it without being anachronistic. I haven't always succeeded, but that was the aim. I've worked on two adaptations set in nineteenth-century America, *The Alienist* and *Gangs of New York*, and there's an actual recording of an Irish guy talking in the Bowery; it was fascinating to listen to, but the slang was so extreme that you couldn't understand a word. So you have to make allowances for audiences.

Do you keep the novel beside you throughout the adaptation process, or do you try to internalise it and set it aside somewhere along the way?

Physically, I keep copies of the novel everywhere: one in my office, one by the bed, probably one in the bathroom. But what I tend to do is read it pretty thoroughly and with each draft go back to it less and less. Then towards the end I'll have another read just to see if there's any great nugget I've missed or forgotten about, or left out by mistake. Generally it's a love affair that cools off, I guess.

How much pressure do you feel when adapting a well-known and much-loved novel, knowing that you won't be able to please everyone with the finished product?

I don't really think about it while I'm writing. Maybe when the thing comes out. But I've noticed a change recently: critics and audiences will still be really brutal about a film, but it won't necessarily be because it didn't live up to the expectations generated by the book. Even on *The Alienist*, which had a very hard-core fan base, that fan base was relatively small compared to the other stuff which gets thrown at a film or TV series. That one got a few criticisms because 20 years had passed, and what Caleb Carr had done was so original that in that time other people had imitated it, so the series itself felt like an imitation of series which came before. So there were some comparisons to the book there, but on the whole I haven't had too many outraged people saying I've destroyed the book.

ADAPTING NONFICTION

You've said that research is the part of the process you love most. With a nonfiction adaptation how much use do you make of the author's research?

I'll look at the author's bibliography and find the books that are most interesting to me – but I'll also go through bookshops and look at lists on Amazon and so on. Because I'm so passionate about the reading, it's really exciting for me to do that. I wouldn't get a researcher to do it for me. A couple of times production companies have offered me researchers, and I've said no. I don't want to read the condensed version, I want to read the whole thing.

Do you approach a nonfiction adaptation in the same way as fiction, or does the strangeness of real events give you licence to experiment with, say, structure?

With the nonfiction books I've done, there has been so little to draw on in terms of specific events and scenes that they're almost like originals: you're inventing the story rather than reinventing it. So what I do much more with nonfiction is to plot it out and write treatments and do step outlines, because that inventing of the story is so critical.

Have you ever encountered events in a nonfiction book so strange that you couldn't use them in the adaptation because audiences wouldn't believe they were real?

On *McMafia*, Misha Glenny told us a story which wasn't in the book, about a mob boss whose hobby was dog shows, and we included that in the series, because even though it felt weirdly unbelievable, it had a surrealism which made it oddly credible. So you have to strike a balance between something being so big that it'll throw audiences and truth being more interesting than fiction.

How much responsibility do you feel towards historical accuracy when dramatising the lives of real characters?

A fair amount. With Hiroshima, I certainly feel a responsibility to try not to make the characters fit an argument. It would be very easy to paint certain people as war criminals because of that massive decision, but it was made in the context of a hatred of what the Japanese had done and a genuine desire to try to stop the war. That doesn't mean that I condone what happened, but I've tried to create three-dimensional characters with arguments back and forth. The tennis story is different, because it's an individual's life. I'll certainly stop myself being historically inaccurate if I feel it crosses the line too much, but at the same time you have to turn that person into a dramatic character. So again, it's a balance.

And would you continue to hold that line in the face of notes which told you that it was historically accurate but not dramatic enough?

I'd have to address that note. I'll still feel I can't go beyond the line, but it will make me question how I can make it more dramatic without being somehow untruthful to the reality. I quite like that challenge, though. What it tells me is that I've probably been too accurate, or I haven't been clever enough within that accuracy.

How do you set about finding the voices of real characters, especially if there is little or no written or audio-visual research material in their own words?

I'll read any stuff they've written or quotes they've given, but with all adaptations I need to find my own voice in their voices. I'll imagine what emotions they're going through, or try to draw on similar experiences I've had or put myself in their shoes in that situation, but their voices probably end up being closer to mine than they do to theirs.

Do you think that being based on a true story in some way gives a project more weight?

I personally don't, but the Academy tends to: you can judge by the number of actors who win Best Actor awards for portraying real people. I love history so I love writing it, but it's hard to argue that a true story has more weight than *Crime and Punishment* or *War and Peace*. I think fiction can be just as weighty philosophically, thematically and emotionally as true stories.

Are there any benefits which you think true stories definitely do bring to the table?

One of the great pleasures of adapting *McMafia* was that there was an authenticity to the tone, and that notion of authenticity is important to me. But something Peter Morgan does really well is taking those true stories and heightening them to the point where they become myth or comedy or great tragedy, so there are definitely two ways of looking at it. What draws me to true stories is the idea that this is the reality behind the news and the question of how to capture that, and one of the ways to capture it is to be as realistic as you can tonally.

CASE STUDY: *DRIVE*

US, 2011 • **Directed by** Nicolas Winding Refn • **Produced by** Marc Platt, Adam Siegel, Gigi Pritzker, Michel Litvak, John Palermo • **Screenplay by** Hossein Amini, based on the novel by James Sallis • **Cast:** Ryan Gosling (Driver), Carey Mulligan (Irene), Bryan Cranston (Shannon), Christina Hendricks (Blanche), Ron Perlman (Nino), Oscar Isaac (Standard Gabriel), Albert Brooks (Bernie Rose)

You've dabbled in film noir before: *Killshot*, from Elmore Leonard's novel; an unproduced adaptation of Dorothy Hughes' *In a Lonely Place*; and the noir elements which you brought to, or brought out of, *The Wings of the Dove*. But *Drive* feels like your most decisive step into that territory.

It's probably the one that's closest to the traditional film noirs that I liked, and also to the neo-noirs of Melville and the American films of the seventies. *Killshot*, with Elmore Leonard's humour, is a different kind of noir to *Drive*, which is very much that spare, samurai-type character in the middle of L.A. – which is such a noir city anyway.

The book is very aware of other books: it's dedicated to Ed McBain, Donald Westlake and Lawrence Block, and its narrator mentions, among others, George Pelecanos and Westlake's alter ego Richard Stark. The film, on the other hand, is very aware of others' films: Walter Hill's *The Driver* and Michael Mann's *Thief* in particular, along with John Boorman's Richard Stark adaptation, *Point Blank*. Were you

aware of all those reference points, both literary and cinematic, and how did you navigate between them?

I was very aware of those films. *Le Samourai* was another one and some of those Clint Eastwood westerns – the idea of The Man With No Name. But probably the film that influenced me most was *Shane*: the stranger who comes in and takes care of the family and leaves at the end. It's interesting, because I was probably more influenced by the references you just mentioned, from the late sixties and seventies, and Nicolas Refn, the director, was more influenced by the eighties. He brought a David Lynch stroke... who was the director who used to do those very colourful teen romance movies...?

John Hughes?

Yeah. Almost a John Hughes element to it. And also his influences in terms of exploitation cinema. So the combination of those two sensibilities means that the references are a bit crazy. And obviously it's set in Hollywood and the character is a stunt driver, so it's kind of a film about film.

Driver's job as a stunt driver was retained, but his screenwriter friend Manny was dropped. He's quite a prominent character in the book, not least as someone Driver can talk to. Did you feel the character was redundant, or simply too self-referential?

That was the first thing: it was a bit self-referential. And the idea of him having friends: I was more interested in the loner aspect. I also felt I could get some of those Manny elements into Shannon and combine the two characters: Shannon is a much smaller part in the book. But you're right, it was mainly my slight discomfort with the notion of a writer in this film noir world.

It's a short novel with a sparse style, very cinematic at first glance, yet it's probably the novel you've adapted most freely. What were you keen to keep in terms of tone and story, and what did you know you would have to change or lose?

I loved the central character. He's brilliantly described in the book. The slow pace at which he lives and his whole ambling nature, and then this sudden turn into violence. So the tone and the rhythm I totally kept. What it didn't have was a story that goes from A to B to C, and builds. It was more internal. So I knew I had to invent a story, which is why I spent quite a long time outlining it. But it was always informed by the brilliance of Sallis's characterisation of Driver, and also the fantastic tone. *McMafia* was the same: again, I followed tone most closely, I'd say.

Tone is so important in adaptations. How do you set about translating tone from the pages of a book to the pages of a screenplay, and guard that tone in the transition from the page to the screen?

I've always believed that stage directions are really important in a screenplay, because you're basically transcribing what you see, whether or not the director chooses to follow that. I've noticed more and more that screenwriting books say you shouldn't describe things because that's the director's job, but I find the only way you can capture tone is by describing atmosphere and describing characters' inner emotions. I'm interested in dialogue which isn't explicit, so I'll tend to write stage directions between lines of dialogue to capture pauses and unspoken reactions. The same with the description of a room, or the light. Those things are really important and the only way I can capture them is to describe them, which is probably why I tend to overwrite for some people's taste. I almost describe things the way you would in a novel, and that's going to be informed by the tone of the book.

The novel may have a sparse style, but it also has a discursive structure: flashbacks, not just to recent events, but to Driver's arrival in L.A. and his life before that – right back to his troubled childhood. Did you feel that a film called *Drive* required a more propulsive, straight-line narrative?

Yes, I did, and also it evolved over the various drafts. So in the early drafts, based largely on studio notes, there was a lot more exposition about Driver's past, even though there were no flashbacks. There was a constant note to make Driver more accessible, and it was something I resisted because I loved the idea of The Man With No

Name, the avenging angel who comes out of nowhere and you don't know anything about him. Then when Nic and Ryan Gosling came on, that was certainly what they were drawn to, so a lot of that exposition got cut out and the thing became sparse again. The final draft was almost closer to the first draft than it was to the second or third draft.

Driver talks slightly more in the novel, and we also have access to his interior life via the third-person narration. In the absence of flashbacks or voiceover, do you think that does affect his accessibility?

I think you write two drafts of a screenplay: one for the reader and one for when it gets made. When you're writing something to be read, dialogue is often helping tell the story. Then, when you get into it, the actors – someone like Ryan, who's brilliant about wanting fewer lines – will look at it and go, 'I don't need to say that,' or 'I can say that more simply,' and so it re-evolves. They also bring their face: it's as literal as that. The likeability and the persona of that actor, his face and his features with the camera up close, start to do a lot of the storytelling for you. There's a scene that was really telling, actually, the first time Driver faces off with his love interest's husband, Standard. In the script, I wrote an unspoken competition and tension between them, but Ryan played it almost as if he was unaware of why this guy should be jealous. There was an innocence about the way he played it, and that's a dimension an actor comes in and brings. However well-rounded the characters are, they're still on the page, so when all of those nuances come into it – in a face, in a gesture, in an expression – you need far less dialogue. That's why I think writers working with actors is an incredibly important part of the process. Nic was great at allowing me to do that, whereas other directors have been far more protective of their actors, and as a result I've felt I wasn't able to do my best work. He'd go off and do location scouts and be totally relaxed leaving the actors to give me notes. But some directors want to be there with you every second. And other directors just don't want you there at all.

It's Chapter 6 of the novel before there's any actual driving, and even then it's barely a two-page scene. You put Driver's first getaway right up front, nearly six pages in the script. Presumably you wanted to establish who he is and what he does as quickly and dramatically as possible?

We wanted to establish who he is and what he does, but there was also a rhythm element to it. The story takes a little while to unravel, and there's no real action after that until the violence kicks in halfway, so I felt I needed a very propulsive scene at the beginning: to give the audience a taste of what to expect, to tell them it was a thriller about a getaway driver, and to buy myself time to do 20 or 30 pages of character development.

And to establish Driver's world, the L.A. landscape he inhabits.

That's a classic case of where research was really important. There were three stages. The first one, before any actors or a director came on, was that producer Adam Siegel and I went to meet the security guy at Universal, who were at that point the financiers of it, and the first thing he said was, 'You can't get away from police helicopters.' So the notion of him being underneath a structure, both the tunnel he hides in and his destination at the Staples Center, came from that conversation. Then, when I arrived in L.A. to start work, Adam got me a driver – because I don't drive – to drive me around the areas near the Staples Center, so again that helped fire my imagination. And then, when I was actually writing the scene, I had a map of that area of L.A., so I was plotting it out street by street. I had so much material that it was a challenge *not* to make it six pages.

He's also listening to a basketball game on the radio during the scene, which helps guide you through it and adds another narrative element.

One of the dangers with action sequences, particularly car chases, is: what's the story? If the story is simply, he's getting away, there's only so much interest you can sustain in that. So the game helped create a sense of mystery, making the audience think: why's he listening to this, what's he up to?

The film was originally slated to be directed by Neil Marshall with Hugh Jackman as Driver – a very different team to Refn and Gosling. Did your approach to the material change accordingly?

That's when it was with Universal. I actually had some really good sessions with Neil Marshall. There was probably more horror in the script I wrote for him. For example, he wanted Driver to chop off someone's head at one stage. So elements like that, which I wasn't super-comfortable with, went fairly quickly. But the idea of Driver getting his revenge on Nino without using a weapon was Neil's. In the first draft he did it with a gun, and Neil said, 'He's a driver, he should do it with a car,' and Nic took that on board. Hugh Jackman was also a great collaborator and very gracious, but the idea of someone as good looking as him, in his late thirties, not having had any past relationships of significance was a bit of a stretch, so we needed more backstory in that version of the script. Ryan was young enough to have drifted off the street and be working as a mechanic. There was something more abstract about him, which meant he needed less backstory.

In the novel, Driver lives – though it's stated at the end that he's killed further down the line – and Irena, Standard's wife, dies. In the film, where she's called Irene, she lives and he's badly, possibly fatally, wounded. What was the thinking behind reversing the end points of those characters' journeys?

The Irene story evolved through a whole series of drafts. We had one with her son being taken away. We had one with the man ending up with the boy because the mother is dead. But in the end we went back to a fairy-tale structure: the man ends up on his own, the cowboy rides into the sunset.

Shane again.

Exactly. That was where the *Shane* influence came in. The script ended with him in the car and you think he's dead, then he opens his eyes and starts the engine. I think that's how Nic originally had it in the cut, and then they felt they had to add that extension where you see him driving. But for me it was keeping it a bit more mysterious:

does he live or does he die? And that was in keeping with my notion of him as the angel who comes in: is he a man, or is he a ghost?

Shannon is drawn from three characters in the novel: Manny, Driver's agent and a fellow stuntman, who's killed quite quickly in the book. You've also given him a different occupation – garage owner – and a brand new ambition – racing stock-cars. Again, what prompted those changes and additions?

The stock-car idea came from the fact that the book didn't give us a plot, so we had to invent one – and when I say 'we', it was mainly with Adam Siegel, who was the producer on the first iteration. The idea of the friend who sees what a genius he is behind the wheel and wants to make something of that was probably influenced by the character of the coach in the first *Rocky* movie. He has these big dreams and is someone things have never worked out for, and is also like the stock character you get in a lot of film noirs, the slightly run-down buddy who was often played by those great character actors. He was very much a type, but he did help bring Bernie Rose into Driver's world. Bernie was one of the characters I loved in the book, and I wanted them to have a moment of peace before they went to war, so I needed to engineer a meeting between them. So from Shannon's stock-car dream came the idea of Bernie putting money into it and the fact that they had a past, and that started to draw these characters together. There aren't a lot of links between the characters in the book, and that's quite hard for a screenplay. You need to identify the secondary characters from the beginning in order for them to pay off at the end, whereas Bernie comes in really quite late in the book.

Do you think you managed to be true to the tone of the novel?

I certainly felt I'd captured it in the script, and I think Nic brought a whole other level to it in the way he directed it.

A lyricism.

Absolutely. The book and the script are probably closer to those seventies thrillers, with the very hard-core tough guy, but Ryan brought an innocence to the character and Nic brought a surreal, sort of magical quality to the film, and those three things meshed really well.

And do you know what James Sallis thought of the finished film?

One of the most gratifying things I've had in my career was how full of praise James Sallis was for the film. Adam was very good about keeping him included every step of the way. He didn't want to read anything, but he was very supportive. He's a poet as much as a novelist, and I hope the film brought more recognition to his work. I'm a huge fan, so it was a really happy experience in that sense.

CASE STUDY: *McMAFIA*

UK, 2018 ▪ **Directed by** James Watkins ▪ **Produced by** Paul Ritchie ▪ **Created by** Hossein Amini & James Watkins, based on the book by Misha Glenny ▪ **Written by** Hossein Amini, James Watkins, David Farr, Laurence Coriat, Peter Harness ▪ **Cast:** James Norton (Alex Godman), David Strathairn (Semiyon Kleiman), Juliet Rylance (Rebecca Harper), Merab Ninidze (Vadim Kalyagin), David Dencik (Boris Godman), Aleksey Serebryakov (Dmitri Godman), Sofya Lebedeva (Lyudmilla Nikolayeva)

Nonfiction adaptations are very popular at the moment, both in film and TV, with their factual basis usually one of the selling points. It's more unusual for a nonfiction book to be turned into a fictional story, which is what you and James Watkins did with Misha Glenny's *McMafia*. Was that always your pitch, or did you consider sticking more closely to fact?

I actually pitched it as a film to Working Title seven years earlier, where I took four of the stories and wanted to tell a *Traffic*-type version of it. But by the time it came around again as a TV series, that approach didn't feel right. It felt like it had been done. *Traffik*, the original TV series, did it. *Babel* did it. So we had to find a new way to do it that would incorporate the scale and tone of it, and we came up with a completely new story which was like a spine for other stories to be attached to.

Not only did you turn nonfiction into fiction, you also introduced some film genre elements: the final confrontation between Alex and Vadim reminded me strongly of the ending of Michael Mann's *Heat*, and the series as a whole has clear echoes of *The Godfather*. Were those reference points in your mind from the start as you created the new storyline?

Heat has always been a massive inspiration for me: the notion of two enemies who meet at one stage as friends – the same as Bernie Rose and Driver – and who, in a different world, could have been friends. And *The Godfather* was also a huge inspiration – inevitably, when you tell a story of an ordinary person sucked into a world he's trying not to get into. So, structurally *The Godfather* was the biggest influence: the anti-hero that the audience initially sympathises with, then his descent. But spiritually I'd say it was *Heat*: the love/hate relationship between these two antagonists.

You mentioned the TV series, *Traffik* – and the film version, *Traffic*. Did you look to those for inspiration?

Certainly the original TV series: the idea that you could jump from country to country and that all these things link. But that was several different stories, whereas ours is more linear and has a central character running through it.

The book traces a network of gun runners, drug smugglers, people traffickers, money launderers and cyber criminals in Bulgaria, the former Yugoslavia, Russia, Israel, the United Arab Emirates, India, Nigeria, South Africa, Canada, Colombia, Japan and China. How did you decide which perpetrators, victims and locations of organised crime you wanted your fictional story to focus on?

If you want to compare it to *Game of Thrones*, it felt like the two big kingdoms in the modern crime world were the Russian mafia and the cartels, so that informed some of it. The Lyudmilla story, about human trafficking, was really interesting, so that meant finding stories for Israel which would tie in. Prague is the gateway from Russia into Eastern Europe, so that became inevitable. And we always loved the India storyline. So it was almost like choosing our favourites and building a story around that, though obviously there had to be credible links between them.

Were there any stories or characters in the book which you wanted to include in the series, but didn't have room for?

Not really. That's what's odd about the adaptation: there are probably only four pages from the 400-page book that have been used directly. But what is used enormously is Misha's tone, which is there throughout.

At least one story idea used in the series wasn't in the book when it was first published in 2008, but is described in the updated edition: remotely hacking into a port computer system to manipulate the records of shipping containers. Were there other new elements which you needed to research and introduce to reflect the growing sophistication of organised crime in the ten years since publication?

Absolutely. It's probably the adaptation I've done the most research for because it's so sprawling, and Misha was a very important part of that. I read half a dozen books on the internal politics of the various factions in Russia, and talked extensively to Misha about that. And we also talked to a lot of experts whom Misha introduced us to, so that informed the story as much as the book did.

With any story set in the world of crime, you have to address the question of relatability: why should the audience care about these characters when all they do is lie, cheat, steal and kill? What was your answer to that, or did you not consider it a problem?

It was hard for me to consider it a problem, because I've always loved those kind of characters. But I'm very aware that a large proportion of the audience don't necessarily, and relatability is a massive factor in not just commercial, but also critical success. One of the reasons we cast James Norton was because his persona as an actor is fairly likeable, and the idea was that you keep the audience on board with him for as long as possible before he starts doing the dark and dirty stuff. But it's a story about criminals. And personally I find Vadim really likeable because he's human. The challenge was always, how do you take the hero and make him the villain by the end, and how do you take the villain and make him the one everyone sympathises with, and that may be an experiment that turns off a large part of your audience. The other disadvantage we had was that it was about 'the one per cent': rich people. Some of the reviews suggested that it was self-important and wasn't about the real London. But what was really interesting to me was the idea that gangsters are gangsters maybe 5 per cent of the time and the other 95 per cent they're exactly like us: they're having family issues, they're taking their kids to school, they're doing all those everyday things. And that means a slower pace, because you're dealing with the mundane as well as with action. There probably wasn't enough incident in it for some people, but I think that's closer to the real world of these criminals than a lot of crime series that do focus on the action.

Glenny talks to a lot of people on the other side of the fence, those tracking and trying to stop the gangsters. But the forces of law and order play almost no part in your story, except where they are colluding with the criminals. What was the thinking behind that decision?

The idea was to save the law and order element for a second series: to focus on the rise of someone in the mafia world in the first series, then change perspective and come at the same characters from a different point of view, building that world gradually over the two series.

How did you arrive at an eight-episode structure for the series, and does each episode have its own three-act structure?

We arrived at eight because if you're telling the story of someone who goes from relative innocence to a pretty dark place – and you're taking in all these other storylines as well – six just felt too short. Six is more like a mini-series, it almost enforces a single propulsive story, and we wanted this to feel larger, closer to those ten-part series the Americans do. What I didn't realise – because I came to TV from film, where the most important thing is what you leave the audience with – is that reviewers only really review the first couple of episodes; they very rarely review the series as a whole. In our case, maybe one or two reviewed the whole series, and they were more positive than the ones who just reviewed episodes one and two. So I probably didn't pay enough attention to how each episode has to be totally satisfying in its own right. I almost wrote the first two as you would the start of a feature screenplay, which is the set-up, forgetting that the critics are going, 'It's too slow,' and the audience is going, 'I'm going to watch something else.' On *The Alienist*, one of the things the studio hammered away at was the importance of the pilot. I rewrote that episode half a dozen times, then they got other people to rewrite it, then they did reshoots of it, because they understood how much weight it had to take. Having done two shows, I'm now much more aware of that – and of what you talked about, a clearer structure within each episode. If in film the last act is the most important, I'd say in TV, pragmatically, the first act is the most important.

In his foreword to the new edition of the book, Glenny talks about participating in the writers' room with you, James Watkins and the other writers you brought in: Laurence Coriat, David Farr and Peter Harness. What was his, and their, contribution to the overall story and structure?

His contribution was the research, the detail. He was like an authenticity filter: when the rest of us were sitting around chatting, he'd come in and we'd say, 'What would happen in this situation?', or 'Do you think this scene is credible?' James and I had already outlined the story, not in huge detail, but enough to know where we were headed, so a lot of that work had been done. Then we refined that in the writers' room in terms of each writer's episodes. The interesting thing about the other writers was that each one brought their own particular skill set to it: David is brilliant at structure and storytelling; Laurence is more character-based; Peter's skill is in the quirky and surreal. The problem is that you end up with a real Frankenstein of a beast, because everyone's styles are so different – which is why I had to go through and rewrite all eight episodes. That's in no way devaluing the other writers' contribution, it's just that they're very in demand and you only have access to them for a limited amount of time, so when you end up with something which doesn't quite gel because they weren't really working together, you need to overwrite with a single voice.

David Farr was the writer of another globe-trotting BBC TV series featuring a large cast of morally compromised characters: John le Carré's *The Night Manager*. Was that also in your mind in terms of its scope and approach?

Anything which strays into the contemporary spy genre is inevitably going to be compared to that, and I think we suffered from the comparison. What David and Susanne Bier did brilliantly with *The Night Manager* was the glamour and excitement, and people were expecting something like that in *McMafia* and didn't get it. Having done a John le Carré adaptation, I consciously wanted to avoid that propulsive, heightened form of storytelling. It's very much the le Carré world, and I love that world, but we were trying to do something different: slower, more grounded – and more difficult.

Did you learn anything from writing series one, apart from the importance of the first act, which you plan to carry through into series two?

I'd say our female characters were weak, though in our defence I'd argue that's always been true of the gangster genre. It's easier, and more organic, to have people on the law and order side be women. I know that violent mafia women exist, but if you read up on it there are very few of them. It's the same problem with a war story: it's hard to find interesting, active female characters without somehow forcing them into the narrative. If you're going to do that, you need to choose stories that are actually about them. But we can do better than women as girlfriends in series two, I think.

Even though the book is ten years old, the series seemed to catch the zeitgeist in terms of Britain's relationship with Russia. The title itself is now used by the British press as a term for wealthy Russians, particularly in London.

It's also used to describe a certain kind of post-globalisation corruption. The traditional mafias have reinvented themselves as part of the global economy, and now include facilitators, governments, intelligence agencies. We took that idea and ran with it, which hurt us in one sense, in that it had traditional mafia story undercurrents, but wasn't what people were expecting in terms of gunfights and so on. However, it did capture the zeitgeist-y idea that this is how crime now works, that it's much closer to banks and corporations. You could argue that the thesis of Misha's book was in some ways the most powerful thing about it, and some of that found its way into the series, which is what led to people writing about it.

Jeremy Brock

Jeremy Brock was born in 1959 in Malvern, Worcestershire.

He co-created the BBC series **Casualty**, and his original screenplays include: **Mrs Brown** (1997); **I Am Slave** (2010); and **Diana & I** (2017).

His screen adaptation credits include: **Charlotte Gray** (2001, novel by Sebastian Faulks); **The Last King of Scotland** (2006, novel by Giles Foden); **Brideshead Revisited** (2008, novel by Evelyn Waugh); **The Eagle** (2011, novel *The Eagle of the Ninth* by Rosemary Sutcliff); and **Dark Crimes** (2016, article *True Crime: A Postmodern Murder Mystery* by David Grann).

The Last King of Scotland won the 2007 BAFTA award for Best Adapted Screenplay.

APPROACHES TO ADAPTATION

Do you prefer to adapt material which chimes with your own work, or material which is completely different and gives you a chance to try out new things?

I tend not to examine what motivates me to choose work, and only post-rationalise the choices I've made. Every choice is governed by whether I'm moved by the ideas inherent in the work, whether it's public domain or an adaptation. If you look back it's usually something to do with identity, often to do with faith – my father was a vicar and I'm an atheist, so those conflicts are internalised. The intricacies of familial and human relationships, and the detail of how we love and fail to love, would be, I think, what drives me. But like I said, I tend not to know.

Do you think adaptations involve a completely different set of creative gears to original screenplays?

Yes and no. With a novel you're adapting something that's already been imagined: another writer has done the work of creating narrative structure, character dynamics, internal and external tension, and plot. But once you internalise its narrative and its dynamics, your relationship with the material is the same as if you were writing an original. You read and re-read the book, then at some point in the process you put it to one side and treat the material as if it's your own, until you re-emerge as the person who adapted that book. So the initial approach is different, but for a period of time I think it's the same.

Have you ever been offered material to adapt which you felt couldn't, or shouldn't, be adapted?

Yes, but recalling specific projects is tricky. I've just been offered something, and of course I can't really talk about it. It's a short story that was in the *New Yorker*, by an extremely famous British author, and I just don't believe the short story can stretch to a full movie. So that's a straightforward choice to do with dramaturgy and whether the piece has the legs. Sometimes I've said no because I feel the subject has been worked to death. World War II: lots of potential adaptations of biographies and historical fiction still come my way, and I turn those down on the grounds that I don't have anything fresh to say about that period. I'll always look at the material in case there's an interesting detail, because God and the Devil are in the detail, and if it's really extraordinary then I'll think carefully about it. But sometimes film gets a bit stuck, because film tends to follow the zeitgeist. Commercial cinema particularly tends to be reactive rather than proactive. Indie cinema is where you're going to find the new approaches to adaptation. So sometimes it's subject, sometimes it's, 'How the hell are you going to adapt something which is ten pages long into a full movie?'

Do you always agree a mission statement or direction of travel with whoever has commissioned the adaptation?

Well, they've usually hired me because they've got an idea of what I'm going to deliver, and that's what they bring to the room when they sit down with me for the first time to discuss it. I don't think there's a mission statement per se, but often in those early conversations you agree an approach and then if they're good producers they leave you alone with it. I'm sure you'll hear this from others, but for the first draft you're God, and for every other draft your power diminishes according to how close you get to production.

Do you usually produce an outline or treatment before you start writing the script?

Always. The challenge in adaptation is 80 per cent structural. When you compress a novel into a three-act film, you have to think carefully about what you leave out and what you hold on to, and I don't think you can free-form on that, you have to have a structure. So it's about acknowledging the difference between the two media, and in the treatment being really disciplined and bringing intellectual rigour to the process of reduction and recalibration.

Do you try to get your outline or treatment to a certain length?

If I'm hitting more than ten pages, I'm nervous and I probably edit the treatment. I can guarantee that every page of prose you write is going to expand into ten or more pages in the script, so if you're hitting ten pages in a treatment you're already at 100 there. So ten would be the maximum. If it's an original I might go up to 15, but that's because I'm explaining the nature of the characters and their relationships to one another, so there's a whole load of guff I write which is an attempt to protect the piece of work from producers going, 'What the hell?', because they don't have the comfort of a novel. The reason adaptations are still so popular is because they're a security blanket, because there's the knowledge that somewhere out there are a million people who read the book.

If the author of the source material is living, do you find it useful to have their input on the script?

No, and I'll give you an example of where that was honoured. I adapted Sebastian Faulks's novel *Charlotte Gray*, and Sebastian was quite brilliant at offering encouragement, while stepping back and acknowledging that the media are bespoke and singular. He understood that whatever gifts he has, and they're massive, belong in a different medium. We had to pitch for it with six others, and for whatever reason he chose us. He then wrote me an email when he'd read my screenplay and an extremely touching letter after he'd seen the film, but other than that he left me alone, which I appreciated because you can't micromanage the transition between novel and film. The novelist has to trust the screenwriter's instincts.

Charlotte Gray was a World War II project. Why did you make an exception for that one?

Well, it was a World War II project at a time when I hadn't made the decision that World War II had been done to death. So that's my short answer. But it's a very good question. There was something about Charlotte morphing into another person that I found really interesting. Identity, and shifting identities, fascinate me, as they do many people, but I'm particularly driven by a desire to explore how you work out who the hell you are in any given situation. Where do you end and where do other people begin? Where, in Charlotte's case, does her mission end and her emotional relationship with this guy in France begin, and how does she deal with the necessary compromise that's going to smack up and hit her? I love those sorts of tensions, and I think audiences are always drawn first and foremost to the emotional conflict and interaction between characters. That remains true even of massive-budget movies. In the end, when you listen to audiences leaving the cinema, they're talking about people. And it's true of adaptations, too, however large the canvas.

Is it easier to navigate notes from directors, producers and script editors when you have a piece of source material to measure the screenplay against?

No. I would say having a piece of source material to measure the screenplay against is more complex than working with either public domain or original material. It offers too many opportunities for avoidance disguised as 'loyalty to the original', and unless you're careful it can cast a shadow over the production once directors and actors get hold of the novel and – with just days before shooting – say, 'I was reading the novel again last night and I loved the way that….' If adaptation is often about choosing what to leave out, conflate or render in cinematic equivalence, then having an extant document on which the work is based makes you a hostage to fortune.

Have you ever started work on an adaptation and found it harder to adapt than you anticipated?

Brideshead Revisited. But we'll come back to that.

Are there any screen adaptations which you think are especially good or you particularly admire?

I particularly admire Emma Thompson's adaptation of *Sense and Sensibility* because it feels so authentically Austen-like and avoids the self-conscious archness of other attempts on her work. The screenplay of *The Godfather* by Mario Puzo, Francis Ford Coppola and the great Robert Towne – *Chinatown* is possibly the greatest original screenplay – is flawless in its pacing. It's a really good example of great plotting – much misunderstood – superb character development and a masterly control of tone. In the wrong hands, it would be pastiche.

ADAPTING FICTION

Some writers try to include as much of the novel as possible by boiling scenes down to their essence. Others are more ruthless in editing it down to a sort of greatest hits, but being true to the spirit of it. Do you favour either of those approaches, or does it depend on the material?

It will depend on the material, but I would say the latter is the most effective way of approaching the difference between the two media. The big difference between novels and films is that the novelist is able to step inside any character's head or become God's eye and look down on the whole. A film can't do that. Film has a hunger for forward momentum and cannot go inside. It doesn't matter how tight the close-up, you're still outside. A novelist can internalise, externalise and create a relationship between the language and the reader. In a film, the relationship is between the audience and the characters, and how the characters manifest their emotions. It's far less intellectual than the process of reading a novel, which starts here [*points to his head*] and then goes there [*points to his heart*]. You sit in a cinema and it can go straight there [*points to heart*]. That's the beauty of it. But novels can give you the illusion that they're cinematic, particularly if they're powerfully written. I adapted Ian McEwan's *Enduring Love* for a Hollywood studio, long before it became the movie directed by Roger Michell, and that's a good example of where the brilliance of the writing can be deceptive. The opening chapter, where a man clings to a balloon as it rises into the air, is one of the greatest openings in modern fiction, and you're beguiled and left breathless by it, but actually what follows that firework of an opening is a much more novelistic novel than you might have thought. So I fell foul of that, because I was quite a young writer at the time – and I was also setting it in America, which was a mistake. The east coast, MIT, it made sense but it still didn't work, and it didn't work because I was trying to adapt the book's style when I should have been adapting its essence.

If a novel has an unusual structure, would you try to reproduce that in adapting it?

No. I think film is ruthless and it doesn't forgive you if you don't adhere to certain rules. There are exceptions, but they're exceptions to the rule – and the exceptions are Charlie Kaufman and Charlie Kaufman.

You're thinking of *Adaptation*.

I am thinking of *Adaptation*, which is an extraordinary piece of work. Charlie Kaufman is, for me, one of the greatest screenwriters there ever was and ever will be, and while we're on it, *Adaptation* is one of the greatest 'fuck you' adaptations, and for that reason I love it, but you can't do that unless you're Charlie Kaufman. There are reasons why films have rules. They have rules not to be a bastard, but because great writers and directors have tried and tested things out. The reason Billy Wilder and his co-writer, I.A.L. Diamond, were so successful is because they worked fucking hard on structure, and on structure that worked for film. The moment in *Some Like It Hot* when Marilyn Monroe walks down the railway station and is goosed by the steam from the train, the first moment the boys have seen her when they're dressed up as women, that moment required Wilder and Diamond to dial back through the entire first act to create the time jump that allowed for that cut, which is one of the loveliest cuts in cinema. That's structure. That's adhering to the rules, which means the audience has to be comfortable with where they're being taken, and have enough information without it feeling expositional, to make that time jump and enjoy it and feel it's as delicious as the authors did.

Do you use the language of the novel in writing the screenplay, or do you put the whole thing in your own words?

Always in my own words. Having said that, I'm not sure that there won't be passages which find their way in, but the longer I've been in the business the less I do that. It's extremely rare to find a line in a novel that's compressed enough to warrant inserting straight into a screenplay. Screenplays are all about compression, about finding the most boiled-down version, the version that tells its story with the least possible exposition. Novels don't need the least possible exposition. If the novelist chooses to expostulate on water in a glass or the meaning of the universe, we'll sit patiently with them because we're dazzled by their erudition. Ian McEwan comes to mind again.

The intricacies of brain surgery, say, in his novel *Saturday*.

If you're Ian McEwan, you can do that. If you're making the film version, you're not going to have a fuck-off chunk of voiceover talking about brain surgery, because it won't work.

Unless, possibly, you're Aaron Sorkin. I don't know if you've seen *Molly's Game*...

I'm really glad you mentioned *Molly's Game*, because I think it's been under-noticed. Now there's an example of great adaptation, because it's unapologetically intelligent, unapologetically verbal and unapologetically fast. A bold, brassy adaptation, beautifully directed.

Do you try to avoid voiceover in adapting a first-person narrative, or do you see it as another tool in the toolbox?

It is another tool in the toolbox, but I avoid it because of the impact it has on an audience. I think it does the opposite of what you might expect: I think it takes them out of the film instead of drawing them in. You might think it's going to help because it'll bring the novel into the film, but actually it's a device that says to the audience they're watching a movie. You're not suspending your disbelief when you're aware of the voiceover talking, unless it's handled with great care. If you're asking the audience to forget themselves for two hours in the dark of the cinema, you want to find a way of having the interaction between the characters reveal whatever information the voiceover was intending to. So what's the exception? It's probably the bravura Aaron Sorkin voiceover, or...

The Shawshank Redemption? You can't imagine that film without voiceover.

No, you can't. That's another good example. And that, too, is an extraordinary piece of work. But I guess the very fact that we're talking about films which are so renowned is an indication that you have to be at the very top of your game. I think *Molly's Game* will go down as a really great movie.

How much pressure do you feel when adapting a well-known and much-loved novel, knowing that you won't be able to please everyone with the finished product?

Well, here's something I learned after I adapted *Brideshead Revisited*. You can't please everyone, and if you try to you'll fuck up, so what you do is hold on to the rule of thirds: a third of the people may like it, a third of the people will be indifferent, and a third of the people will hate it. If you hold on to that rule you can grow old in this job, which is my aim.

CASE STUDY: *THE LAST KING OF SCOTLAND*

UK/Germany, 2006 ▪ **Directed by** Kevin Macdonald ▪ **Produced by** Andrea Calderwood, Lisa Bryer, Charles Steel ▪ **Screenplay by** Peter Morgan and Jeremy Brock, based on the novel by Giles Foden ▪ **Cast:** Forest Whitaker (Idi Amin), James McAvoy (Nicholas Garrigan), Kerry Washington (Kay Amin), Simon McBurney (Stone), Gillian Anderson (Sarah Merrit)

What attracted you to adapting Giles Foden's novel?

I actually took over the screenplay from Peter Morgan. Peter had written an extraordinarily powerful adaptation, but wasn't able to see it through because he was overwhelmed by work on other projects. My long-time producer Andrea Calderwood, who'd worked with me on *Mrs Brown*, said, 'I want you to bring yourself to this screenplay and the challenges that Kevin is having as director.' So I came in about a year before we went into production and worked very closely with Kevin Macdonald on my version. But, interestingly, one of the things they asked me to do was steer clear of the book.

You must at least have read it?

Yes, I did – though I'm not sure I told them I did. But the many drafts I went through were freer of the book than any other adaptation I've done, and ironically it's been one of the happiest and most successful experiences as an adapter I've had. I don't know what that tells you.

Did your approach to the material differ from Peter Morgan's?

Not consciously. It was never stated what they thought I would add to the material, but I understood that I had been hired to bring to bear my interest in the psychology of relationships and the dynamic between characters, primarily the complex duality between Nicholas and Idi Amin. When we won the BAFTA for Best Adapted Screenplay, Peter was incredibly positive and generous about my contribution. It was actually a classic Hollywood job, in the sense that he'd done his work, then I came in and did mine. That's how almost all 'collaborations' take place. If you see two names on the screen, you might assume that the writers worked together, but that's very rarely the case.

Did you see the story in terms of genre, and if so which genre?

If you asked Kevin he'd probably say thriller. I'm not sure I quite think that way. I was just busy being mesmerised by Nicholas's relationship to Idi. I suppose it would have to be political thriller, but it wasn't a post-it on my wall.

It's certainly paced like a thriller, particularly in the second half.

I remember Kevin saying to me, 'I need an opening which gets Nicholas to Uganda fast,' and I came up with the idea that he's spinning a globe and goes – thunk! I don't think any of that is in the novel, and it took an insane amount of time to write it. But once you'd got it, you knew that you'd done the cinematic trick and pulled off a moment of intense compression that tells an enormous amount of story. Because it's not just that he does that and then you cut, it's the manner in which he decides on that country. It's so random. That tells you so much about the unpreparedness of this sex tourist. You write for finding moments like that. Or for finding lines like 'It's not flying, it's falling with style' in *Toy Story* – a line that I'll forever wish I'd written.

Picking up your point about compression, it's almost halfway through the novel before Nicholas takes up his job in Kampala as personal physician to Amin. In the film, his bus journey to the hospital in

Mbarara is dealt with in the opening title sequence, and he's on his way again by the end of act one.

Yes, and there's a very simple reason. Film will not tolerate exposition. Film requires that you learn along the way as you're investing in a character and whatever dilemma they've been put in. Nicholas isn't in a real dilemma until he meets Idi. Nicholas is having a whole series of illustrative experiences in the novel that show how Uganda is, but illustrative experiences in film just don't hack it. You can have so many and then everyone is like, 'Just tell me some story.' And what is story, if not plot? And what is plot, if not something happens and then as a result of that something else happens? It's *King Lear*. It's *Hamlet*. Hamlet finds out that his uncle killed his dad, bang, you've got your story. Until he finds that out, it's just a bunch of weird shit going on. Plot is just story, and story requires narrative, and narrative is consequential, not sequential. Where film fails more often than at anything else is that it creates sequences of scenes that have no narrative connection, no consequence. You watch a scene and go, 'You could have cut that and nothing that comes after it would have changed.' For me, adapting novels is often, crudely, about acknowledging that a brilliant novelist can afford to piss about and spend three chapters telling me shit about the world that doesn't advance the plot one jot, but a film just can't do that.

The first title card in the film is 'Inspired by real people and events'. Did you therefore move closer to the facts in writing your version?

Yes. The facts interested me, so I wasn't shy of researching whatever public domain evidence there was for what existed in Peter's screenplay and for what I wanted to invest in this project. Ever since *Mrs Brown*, I've loved research. It's an element of the work that I consider an honour. How many jobs in the world are there where you're given a tertiary education in Ugandan politics circa 1973? So research was a big and important area in my work.

To what extent did you feel a responsibility to accuracy, in terms of the time, the place, the political context and, particularly, the real people portrayed?

I can't remember worrying unduly about that. I remember being fascinated by someone who has just left home and gone out to reinvent themselves, and their relationship with this patriarch who could appear to be one thing and actually be another; that graduation from a naïf to someone who's fully cognisant of how much horror they've stepped into, but as with *Macbeth* they're so far in that it's as hard to go back as it is to go forward. There's a scene where Nicholas is trying to get hold of his passport and his house has been turned over, so he rushes back to Idi and Idi says, 'Uganda embraces you,' and you can feel the air freeze around him. That was a central scene for me in the writing: the feeling of Idi's power at that point and Nicholas being trapped, like a monkey in a cage – because he was accused of being his 'white monkey'. I can't remember whether that's in the novel or whether it's in the public domain, but I suppose what I'm saying is, true to the spirit not the facts, driven by that central relationship.

Amin has several long speeches in the novel, but in the film, especially early on, those speeches seem much more eloquent.

There's a very good reason why: for the first flush of Nicholas's seduction, Idi should be as eloquent, cogent and charismatic as possible. I could see no good dramatic reason to reveal him as clumsy, inarticulate or unattractive. There's no journey then. This is a film about the seductive quality of evil.

Staying with seduction, two characters in the novel – Joyce Merrit, wife of the doctor who runs the hospital in Mbarara, and Sara, another doctor at the hospital – have been combined in the film into a single character – Sarah Merrit – who feels a strong attraction to Nicholas, but won't allow herself to be seduced by him. In other words, she acts as a thematic mirror to him.

Absolutely. That was completely intentional. It's important to say that some of these fundamental decisions were made by Peter, but I remember writing and rewriting and re-rewriting the attempted seduction of Sarah by Nicholas, and what made it difficult was that you needed to feel like he wasn't a complete idiot. This guy has been shagging away on a bus, but now he's turned up at the hospital and he's messing about playing football and he's not really taking it very seriously – in his head, he's on holiday. But this total waste of space needs to have sufficient charisma to make that feel like a struggle for her, because why would it be a struggle otherwise? Why would she even give him the time of day?

There's an earlier scene which helps set that up, the scene where Nicholas meets Amin for the first time, after Amin has hit a cow and crashed his car. For a start, Nicholas shoots the cow to put it out of its misery – which also helps make him less passive and more empathetic – then he takes off his Scotland football shirt because Amin wants to give it to his son. The combined effect of those actions is an assertive masculinity which Sarah is obviously struck by and contrasts with her rather earnest husband.

Completely. And I can't take credit for that scene, because that's Peter. But this is an interesting point. I worked on every single line of every single page, and some of the changes were radical and some were surgical, and that difference is true of adaptation too. You're constantly in a dance between a radical and a surgical relationship with the material as you adapt it into this new format. Thinking about it now, that's one of the most challenging balances you have to strike. Most of the time you're doing it through instinct. How muscular should I be, how delicate should I be? Should I leave it alone and trust that it works, should I find a way of gently teasing it out? So in some ways, with *The Last King of Scotland*, I felt like I was adapting an adaptation.

The scene where Nicholas meets Amin does several things at once, and so does the scene where he tries to seduce Sarah. Her rejection of his overtures is part of what motivates him to accept Amin's.

Completely. His sense of rejection and his confusion.

But she also represents his last link to goodness and morality. Once he cuts loose of her, he's adrift, he just doesn't know it yet.

And he'll come to realise it too late when he's mired in evil. But there's a moment later where he sees her through a bus window, and

I remember that was an important moment to capture, because you feel how trapped he is – and there it is, that's goodness right there, and he's lost it.

In the novel, Nicholas receives a message appointing him as Amin's doctor, then simply leaves for Kampala. In the film, Amin invites Nicholas to Kampala and makes the offer in person, then Nicholas returns to Mbarara before deciding to accept it, making it a more gradual pulling away.

That just felt so much more cinematic. You need Idi to be the seducer, and you need to make the expression of that seduction as experiential as possible and not have it be second-hand.

You didn't use voiceover in the film and you also didn't use captions, apart from the one about real people and events. Were you deliberately dropping the audience into a situation they didn't entirely understand, reflecting Nicholas's experience?

Yes. There are occasions when it's useful to have the audience be one step behind, and this is a really good example of that. Let them catch up, trust them to use their eyes and their ears, have them hold Nicholas's hand and walk alongside him and experience things as he does. That's why it's important that Idi is articulate and rumbustious and funny. It's all a bit Trump-ian, but then it stops being self-parodic and just gets darker and darker and darker – until, at the end, Nicholas is being strung up and tortured.

The novel increases in tension as it progresses, but it remains a character study throughout. The film becomes more of a thriller as it goes on, seducing the audience and then turning on them in the same way Amin does to Nicholas. Did you have that transition in mind from the start?

I'd say that was a conscious exercise. I probably wouldn't have framed it as elegantly as you have; I'd probably just have thought that we needed to make this jangling, kaleidoscopic world of Idi Amin as loud and vivid as possible, and only at precisely the right moment should you feel that turn. I talked about the scene between Idi and Nicholas. It's happened long before then. Nicholas knows before he knows. He knows that bad shit is happening. The terrible moment when he finds out that a guy he's shopped has been murdered is his realisation that what's going on is very, very dark. With a script like this – and I suppose it is a thriller – you're in the business of peeling away the onion layers and revealing information only where it's most powerful. A very different kind of writing to *Brideshead*.

Well, *Brideshead* maintains a steady pace, whereas...

This tightens up and tightens up and tightens up, until by the end you're going at a furious pace and you're complete gripped and all you're thinking about is whether Nicholas will get out alive, never mind with his conscience intact.

You could argue that his realisation of what's going on happens earlier, in the scene at the airport following the assassination attempt on Amin. Yet he still informs on Amin's minister after that scene, despite knowing what Amin does to those who cross him. It almost feels like the two scenes are the wrong way round.

That's a good point. I remember the moment you're talking about and I think there may have been some argument about it, but I can't remember why the information was revealed like that. It might have worked better the way you described it. I'm not saying that to sound modest, I'm saying it because it speaks to a really important point about this whole process: you don't always know. You give it your best shot, but the translation between the two-dimensional screenplay and the three-dimensional film is to some extent an improvisation. You have to have faith in your director and – something else which is really important – faith in your actors, who imbue your lines with meanings and emotions you didn't think were there. And that's different, too, from the novel. In a novel, the relationship between the reader and the characters is entirely direct. In a film, it's mediated by the actor and their lines. That adds a whole extra element to the potential impact it has. We're watching an actor interpret the lines, creating a dynamic on screen that we then reinterpret, inferring certain things about the story, about the character, about the relationships. What actors do in the process of adapting a novel is key. They're adapting as well.

The scenes preceding the assassination attempt do several key things simultaneously: the gift of the car puts Nicholas deeper into debt with Amin; the drive to the airport gives them a personal moment talking about Amin's epileptic son; and the assassination attempt itself turns Nicholas into a killer when he has to mow down a man with the Mercedes to allow them to escape. Were you consciously trying to pack all that in, or is there an element of good luck in so many elements cohering?

Both. I worked on that and worked on that and worked on that, and I honestly don't know what's me and what's Peter in any of those elements, and that's fine, that's as it should be, because your job is to simply dive in, lose yourself and try to render each moment as effectively as you can. It's a sweet spot when you hit it, when you know that a scene is carrying so much weight and so many themes but doing it lightly, when nothing feels ponderous or expositional and it just races towards its apogee. But on the whole you don't really know, you just look back and go, 'That was good. I got away with that.'

In the novel – drawing on real events – one of Amin's wives, Kay, has an affair with a Ugandan doctor and ends up dead from a botched abortion. In the film, the affair is with Nicholas and the unborn child is his, which gives him something he doesn't have in the novel: a desire to kill Amin. In fact, in the novel, killing Amin is the one thing Nicholas resists, either because he's too much in thrall to him, or because he's too much of a coward, or because it's his final remaining principle. Either way, it's a significant change in terms of his character.

Yes, and I remember having conversations about that with Kevin and Andrea. And it seems to me even now a really important change to make, because not only does it give the last third traction, but it shows that Nicholas is maturing and changing. It's a huge shift for him to make, and it's important that he makes it. It's important that it's his affair with Kay, not a third party's affair. It's important that his reaction to that horror is to say, 'I have to take action.' And of course he, in turn, is found out and the whole thing accelerates from that moment. But it's really important that Nicholas invests himself and takes a risk. A novel can afford to be at one remove, to make a thematic extrapolation about loyalty or principle. Whereas in a film you want something more visceral and direct, because that's what film feeds off and at its best does so powerfully: just puts the man in the room and says, 'Right: now do something about it, you idiot.'

That's *Hamlet* again, isn't it?

It's *Hamlet*. It takes him four fucking hours, but he gets there in the end.

CASE STUDY: *BRIDESHEAD REVISITED*

UK/Italy/Morocco, 2008 ▪ **Directed by** Julian Jarrold ▪ **Produced by** Robert Bernstein, Kevin Loader, Douglas Rae ▪ **Screenplay by** Andrew Davies and Jeremy Brock, based on the novel by Evelyn Waugh ▪ **Cast:** Matthew Goode (Charles Ryder), Ben Whishaw (Sebastian Flyte), Hayley Atwell (Julia Flyte), Emma Thompson (Lady Marchmain), Michael Gambon (Lord Marchmain), Patrick Malahide (Mr Ryder), Joseph Beattie (Anthony Blanche)

You've described *Brideshead Revisited* as 'one of the finest books in English'...

Okay, let's talk about that. Let's talk about the fact that you approach a masterpiece, whatever the hell that means, with fear and trepidation. It was offered to me by Ecosse Films, who I'd worked with on *Mrs Brown* and *Charlotte Gray*, but when they first approached me with *Brideshead Revisited*, I turned it down. There was already an extremely accomplished screenplay by Andrew Davies, and I also felt the shadow of the television version, which stands in memory as one of the great pieces of event TV. So I was really nervous about that hurdle, and even after I took the job I'm honestly not sure we overcame it. I think we were hobbled by the 'compare and contrast' that the audience did, and I wish in retrospect that I'd been more cavalier with the material and dealt with the book as if I was a virgin to it. Of course, that's impossible, because of its iconic status, which meant that there was a kind of reputational undertow holding me back from doing the thing I should do best, which is, as I said, to disappear into the novel and re-emerge owning it. You have to own it. And you have to be quite blunt and egocentric about that.

But with *Brideshead*, I didn't feel the freedom to move around the material as loosely as I would if I were adapting a contemporary novel. I didn't have the same fear when I approached *The Last King of Scotland*, not because Giles Foden's novel isn't a great work, but because it didn't have that huge status.

How did your take on the book differ from Andrew Davies's adaptation?

I remember thinking Andrew's adaptation was brilliant, and if I remember correctly he'd used as a device the idea that Julia is talking to Charles on board the ship and that conversation is a constant running through the film within its own timeframe, while the rest of the film is a series of flashbacks seen through the prism of their remembering – their revisiting, if you will. In conjunction with Ecosse and the BBC, I decided that the novel was too important to be altered to that degree. The solution as I saw it was to adhere more closely to the structure of the book. The problem with adhering more closely to the structure of the book is that the book is gargantuan. So my choice was taken with the best will in the world, because I thought the novel demanded and deserved to find a more direct equivalent in film, but the direct equivalent in a two-hour film is too reduced. So it may well be that Andrew was right and I was wrong, and we'll never know precisely because of course his version never made it to the screen in that form and was therefore never tested. But that was the big change I made.

You did retain some of the structure you described, though, because the film uses a double flashback device: it starts in 1943 with Charles returning to Brideshead, then goes back to the ship in 1935, then goes back further to 1925, before looping around to 1935 and finally ending in 1943 again.

I'd forgotten that. That will be me holding on to an element of Andrew's idea. But it's hard for an audience new to the story to make that double leap back. If you think about the title *Brideshead Revisited*, the book is about the in memoriam nature of lost youth, of love and youth remembered, and how much of that is accurate and how much is really grief. These things are really hard to translate.

The novel also starts with a double flashback: from Charles at Brideshead in the 1940s, to Charles on his way to Brideshead for the first time with Sebastian in the 1920s, to Charles in London before he goes up to Oxford. The film reverses the order of those scenes, establishing Charles's claustrophobic life in London before the glories of Oxford open up to him.

You need the claustrophobia. You need a sense of what he's running away from, so you understand what he's running towards. There's a beautiful shot in the movie where he first sees Brideshead, and the car goes over the hill and the music swells, because that's the relationship he's having with this moment. I don't think that would be the same if you'd seen nothing of where he belonged prior to that, because he'd just be one of that crowd and how would you know he comes from a different background? The rules of film demand you set context for your central characters, otherwise the audience is going to spend the first 20 minutes trying to catch up: why is he so in awe of this, why is he so surprised? As I said earlier, sometimes it's useful to take the audience a step back and not have them catch up, but you've got to know why you're doing that, and here there seemed to be no good reason for it.

In terms of what Charles is running towards, there's a suggestion in the film, which might simply be drawing out of the novel something which is...

Implicit. That's a very interesting issue. Go on.

Sebastian says to Charles: 'You're not in anybody's gang. That's always been your problem.' Lady Marchmain says to him: 'You just want to be liked.' And Anthony Blanche says to him: 'There really is no end to your hunger.' None of these lines are in the novel, but together they seem to suggest that, consciously or not, a lot of the things Charles does, including becoming involved with Julia, are driven by a desire to be master of Brideshead.

What you're talking about now is a classic difference between novels and cinema, in that the novel can imply and the reader can infer in a way that characters in films have to reveal through dialogue or through their actions. Those lines that you quoted, Anthony Blanche's line in particular – 'Is there no end to your hunger?' – lines like that, delivered as questions, are the cinematic equivalent of what Waugh can do through long passages of discursive and sinuous prose. A film doesn't have the luxury of time or going inside characters' heads, so you have to find other ways of capturing that. I like the way film can boil it down to a single line, to someone asking a rhetorical question. You know Anthony Blanche doesn't expect an answer.

In his preface to the 1959 reissue of the novel, Waugh defines its theme as 'the operation of divine grace', and that doesn't seem to be what the film is about. In the novel, Charles is an agnostic; in the film, like you, he's an atheist. In the novel, he's newly converted to Catholicism at the end; in the film, he's still in flight from faith at the end. That shift away from Waugh's theme has a huge effect both on the shape of the story and the fate of the characters, so it's a considerable alteration to the novel.

It is, and you're reminding me now of the unconscious drives that had a massive impact. I probably intellectualised it to myself as: a modern audience will not accept the central premise of the novel; what they will relate to most closely is the coming to terms with grief, the reconciliation between the experienced and the remembered – which is the human experience. If I was being difficult about this, I'd say that faith can have many manifestations; it doesn't necessarily have to be religiose. It can be manifested as faith in someone's love for you, faith in their essential integrity and authenticity. The moment when Charles goes to Morocco to see Sebastian springs to mind. I don't think I consciously set out to be that cavalier, though you're right to remind me that I was.

Another major change in the film is the love triangle between Charles, Julia and Sebastian, which isn't present in the novel, or isn't present to the same degree. The scene in Venice where Sebastian sees Charles kissing Julia is entirely new, and though it provides a clearer reason for something which is slightly opaque in the novel – Sebastian's decline into alcoholism – it shifts that reason away from Catholic guilt and towards romantic disappointment. In other words, the script draws various threads of the novel into a more understandable, more

commercial whole, but the changes it makes mean that, after a fairly faithful first half, the film basically goes its own way in the second.

Yes, it does. The axis on which the second half shifts is a moment that's not in the book, which has to do with human emotion in its raw state, not with extrapolated guilt. Film struggles with the internal and always will. Plus, I think what drives Sebastian has to be yearning, sexual and emotional, as well as guilt, whether that's acknowledged by Waugh or not. What holds an audience's attention isn't an esoteric thesis about faith, it's the agony of a young person seeing their dream shattered. Even if they half-knew it wasn't real, until then they could hold on to the delusion. From that moment on they can't, and they're set on a catastrophic path of self-destruction. So for me that moment was incredibly important and, weirdly, I didn't have any trouble changing the novel. And the more I talk to you about what I did, the more I realise I was going my own way more than I remember. Another thought which comes to mind, a theme which interested me, is the relationship between Sebastian, Julia and their mother: her power to both lift up and destroy, to shape and damage her children's prospects for a healthy and balanced future, which is so tightly allied to her faith and Catholicism.

Lady Marchmain struck me as being more austere and autocratic in the film than in the novel.

More matriarchal – she's a matriarch par excellence. I think the mother, the id in all of us, is a really powerful place to play, and the way I could most easily represent the power of a realised faith was through the way she expresses that faith in relationship to her children. It's suffocating. Catholicism is not a milky, Sundays-only faith. It is forever and it is in your DNA. So yes, she's more matriarchal, and that was because I felt she could embody the authority of an all-seeing, all-knowing God.

Charles, as a character, presents two big problems for any adapter: passivity and selfishness. Your adaptation makes him both more proactive...

An active participant in the narrative, yes.

...and more 'relatable'. For example, the scenes where he tells Julia he's going to settle things with Rex, which he doesn't in the novel, and where he cleans up Sebastian's vomit rather than letting his college scout do it. He also has children in the novel, but when he leaves his wife for Julia we never hear about them again. In the film, he and his wife have no children. So there's a sense of making Charles more sympathetic to try to keep the audience with him.

Yes, and I think this is an example of cultural shifts around the novel. Let's be clear: if you're making a commercial film, you're making a film for a wide audience. Culturally, now, someone with Charles's solipsism isn't your natural protagonist. Some of his behaviour in the novel is so self-centred that you're only staying with him because of the novel's brilliance. Also his passivity isn't such a problem in the novel because he's part of the novelist's controlling imagination. In the film, you don't have that relationship, where a novelist can step back and narrate around a character. That character's relationship with the audience is direct and immediate, and unless they're holding the audience's attention either through their empathy or their charisma, then you're in trouble and you'll lose the audience – and it's the hardest work in the world to get an audience back. So part of what was driving the changes wouldn't even have been conscious, it would just have been a need to find a way of making his behaviour seem, as you say, relatable. I noticed you put invisible inverted commas around that word, but actually I think it's perfectly justified, because if you're asking people to pay ten quid to watch someone who belongs to a culture that's already historical and therefore at one remove from their lives and then is behaving like an ass... you know?

Talking of narration, voiceover was used extensively in the TV adaptation, but only sparingly in this one: two passages in the script, reduced to one in the film, spoken by Charles in the opening scene...

How interesting. I'd forgotten there were two. Did they bookend?

Yes.

That would be my style, yes.

How early did you decide to avoid voiceover to that extent – or had Andrew Davies already made that decision?

I don't remember Andrew's version well enough. It may be that he'd already made that decision, or it may be that when I addressed the material I felt that, apart from taking you in and taking you out, voiceover wouldn't work in a film which was going to be such an intense, boiled-down version of the book. I asked if they bookended because they're the two moments in a film where you're conscious of the process. At the beginning the voiceover is saying, 'I know you're settling into this, but I'm just going to introduce you to me or some ideas.' And at the end, equally but in mirror, it's saying, 'We're leaving now and I'm going to draw out this theme.' I'm interested that the second one didn't make it, though I can't remember why. It was probably deemed irrelevant because it had already been explored, but I wouldn't have been part of that decision because screenwriters are in a strange relationship with the finished film. Incidentally, whether it's an adaptation or an original, I would like to say that screenwriters are the only people in the entire process who deal with infinite possibility. Everyone else, including the director, is in the business of interpreting a *prima facie* document. Not always noted.

Interestingly, the final line of the single passage of voiceover...

Was it from the book? I'm wondering if I lifted the book at that point.

Well, the line I noted was, 'Only one emotion remains my own: guilt.'

I think that's me.

It's a very bold statement, though, and in tune with Waugh.

Yes, because one of the things which has always interested me – as the fallen son of a vicar – is the imagined original sin, the thing that makes us flawed, the thing we are always in flight from. That guilt is what moved me in the book and why I wanted to have a go at it, and that guilt is manifested by Charles primarily in relation to how he handled himself with Julia and Sebastian and less to do with his own relationship to faith, which for Waugh was obviously central.

I was approaching it from a more viscerally human, flesh and blood point of view, because that's what drives me.

So if you were summarising Charles's journey, summing up what he's learned, it would be the extent to which his needs clashed with the needs of others...

And potentially damaged others.

...and the way in which, while trying to satisfy those needs and without necessarily meaning to, he treated others very badly.

Yes. That's absolutely right. That is the extrapolation I would make about Charles in the film – but not Charles in the book.

How do you feel about the film now – revisiting it?

I was proud of the work before the work became a film, but the film didn't catch the zeitgeist in the way I hoped. I remember Emma Thompson saying, 'You've managed what I thought wasn't possible, which is to draw the novel down to its essence.' Flattered, I marched forward, and I think she wasn't just being kind, I think she believed that, as a lot of people did when they read the screenplay. But here's a thing about screenwriting: there's a fibre-thin relationship, so easily broken, between your ambition for the screenplay and its eventual realisation. You take a piece of paper and put it through an industrial process in order, finally, to put it on a screen so that it can have an intimate relationship with its audience. It's a very strange arc that a film goes on. That's not an excuse, by the way. I'm not excusing the failings in the screenplay. I'm just trying to tell you why I think some elements of my ambition for the screenplay didn't quite make it.

Moira Buffini

Moira Buffini was born in 1965 in Middlewich, Cheshire.

As a playwright, her work includes: *Gabriel* (1997); *Silence* (1999); *Loveplay* (2001); *Dinner* (2002); *Welcome to Thebes* (2010); *Handbagged* (2013); and *wonder.land* (2015).

Her screen adaptation credits include: *Tamara Drewe* (2010, graphic novel by Posy Simmonds); *Jane Eyre* (2011, novel by Charlotte Brontë); *Byzantium* (2012, from her play *A Vampire Story*); *Viceroy's House* (2017, books *Freedom at Midnight* by Larry Collins and Dominique Lapierre, and *The Shadow of the Great Game: The Untold Story of Partition* by Narendra Singh Sarila); and *The Dig* (2020, novel by John Preston).

She also co-created and co-wrote the ITV series *Harlots* (2017–2019), inspired by the book *The Covent Garden Ladies: Pimp General Jack & The Extraordinary Story of Harris' List* by Hallie Rubenhold.

APPROACHES TO ADAPTATION

Do you prefer to adapt material which chimes with your own work, or material which is completely different and gives you a chance to try out new things?

The latter, I think. I have to empathise with the work in some way, but it can be so different in form and tone from my own work and

I find that a great pleasure. You learn such a lot about writing by getting inside another writer's work, by seeing the world through their eyes – and you bring yourself into that as well, so if you think it's going to be a bad marriage you just shouldn't do it. I would never adapt a Henry James because I've never been able to finish one of his books, but I would love to adapt other writers who are really different from me, even people with quite different world views.

Do you think adaptations involve a completely different set of creative gears to original screenplays?

They're certainly easier. There's nothing harder in my job, in my opinion, than making up a story. It sounds so simple, but it's actually really hard. With an adaptation, someone else has done the hard work and you have the joy of taking that story and making it accessible to people in a different form. So it can be more pleasurable than, say, writing a play – though, at the end of the day, less satisfying.

Do you always agree a mission statement or direction of travel with whoever has commissioned the adaptation?

Absolutely. Films are collaborations. I'd never go off on my own and present a bunch of producers with something. You know you're going to be rewriting it a thousand times, so let's at least be on the same page at the start.

Do you usually produce an outline or treatment before you start writing the script?

I try really hard not to. I hate them. I just hate them. I want to win a prize for hating outlines most. I do them for television, because your episode is part of an ongoing narrative that other people have to write around. I get the point of that. For adaptations, I don't get the point. We all know the story. I can sit and tell you what I'm going to do, you can agree it and someone can write notes, but why am I wasting time when I should be doing what I've trained my whole life to do?

If the author of the source material is living, do you find it useful to have their input on the script?

Definitely. I'd hate to write an adaptation that the author didn't like or didn't approve of, and in both cases where I've adapted books by living authors – Posy Simmonds and John Preston – I've met and get on well with them. *Jane Eyre* is a different matter, of course, but I did try to channel Charlotte Brontë.

Is it easier to navigate notes from directors, producers and script editors when you have a piece of source material to measure the screenplay against?

Yes, though you quickly find that the notes stop being about the source material and start being about the film, so there's not really a lot of difference between notes on an original screenplay and notes on an adaptation. Certainly by the second draft it's becoming its own thing.

Have you ever started work on an adaptation and found it harder to adapt than you anticipated?

My own play, *A Vampire Story*. I thought that would be quite straightforward, but it's the hardest adaptation I've ever done. I had no objectivity on it whatsoever and my relationship with the author was really difficult. I didn't have the same feeling of confidence.

And the film, *Byzantium*, was made by a writer-director, Neil Jordan, with a strong voice of his own.

A lot of his ideas I absolutely loved, like making Ireland the setting. My background's Irish; why didn't I have that idea? So there are certain things that are great about working with another big creative force, but I think it was one of those occasions when you're both interested in different things in the same story – and at the end of the day he's a hard guy to fight your corner against. So then you have to make a choice: do you want to protect your sole vision, or do you want the project to get made? I wanted it to get made.

Have you ever been offered material to adapt which you felt couldn't, or shouldn't, be adapted?

Yes, and I've turned them down. I've twice been offered adaptations of brilliant documentaries, and I just thought, 'I can't take that on. My film won't be as good.' The documentary has profoundly moved me and those are the real people. How can a piece of fiction do any better? I've also turned down wonderful stories because I haven't, at the time, had the emotional resources to deal with them. The place you have to go to write a screenplay is sometimes so lonely and so dark and you know you've got to spend such a long time there. There have been several occasions where I've loved a story and been very affected by it and wanted to do it, but thought, 'That's too painful right now.'

Are there any screen adaptations which you think are especially good or you particularly admire?

There's a very long list – though often I've seen the film and haven't read the book because I'm not a great reader, especially of modern fiction.

ADAPTING FICTION

Some writers try to include as much of the novel as possible by boiling scenes down to their essence. Others are more ruthless in editing it down to a sort of greatest hits, but being true to the spirit of it. Do you favour either of those approaches?

It changes according to the material. In my first draft I try to be as faithful as I can and just say, 'This isn't really a screenplay: I'm going to adapt all the central scenes of the book, I'm going to keep the structure of the book and I'm going to write it as drama'. That brings up all the problems straightaway, and I really learnt that on *Jane Eyre*, because you get two-thirds of the way through the book and think, 'I can't introduce all these new characters 20 minutes before the end of the film – no one's going to care.' There are some novels where elements of the story that work in a poetic way as prose just don't have that film feeling, where you've got to tighten and tighten and tighten until you get to the climax. Films are very simple and it's often a matter of cutting down in order to let other things carry the weight. It's like John Preston's book, *The Dig*, which I fell in love with, which is this elegy on time and love and loss. How do you make it dramatic when the two central people in the book are desperately lonely and don't really have a relationship with each other? How do you make that work in order to bring that novel to a wider audience? It all comes from your own emotional and political and visceral response to the work. How has it made you feel? What has it made you think? What's the biggest, widest resonance of the book? That's how you have to approach it, and what you're trying to capture.

If a novel has an unusual structure, would you try to reproduce that in adapting it?

I don't really know how to answer that. I don't think the structure is the reason you adapt anything, it's the story within that structure and the characters who are tied up in that story. If the story is good, that's what you're adapting; the structure is just the climbing frame. I also think that some things simply aren't films. *Middlemarch* isn't a film, it's television. Some novels are just too big to lend themselves easily to film. Films are incredibly short and distilled. Writing *Harlots*, the television series, is like writing a three-dimensional dramatic novel – but that's what television is. I think it's about choosing your form: does this book lend itself to being a two-hour film?

Do you try to avoid voiceover in adapting a first-person narrative, or do you see it as another tool in the toolbox?

It depends on the source material. Maybe I'll read the thing and think, 'This has to be voiceover.' Mostly I try to avoid it. There are certain films, like *Badlands*, where the voiceover *is* the film: Sissy Spacek's voiceover in that is absolutely right. But usually, a film that starts with a wide shot of a house and a voiceover, I'm already asleep.

Do you use the language of the novel in writing the dialogue and stage directions, or do you put the whole thing in your own words?

I'll take anything that the writer of the novel gives me in terms of dialogue. The trick is to meld it seamlessly with your own, so it all has the same voice. The stage directions are always my own. I never lift prose description from a novel. That doesn't feel right for a film.

Do you keep the novel beside you throughout the adaptation process, or do you try to internalise it and set it aside somewhere along the way?

For the first draft it's right there, I'm all over it – until it's a dog-eared wreck, covered in stickers and notes. Then I set it aside. If I'm stuck, I'll go back to the book later on in the process. Sometimes it's good to go back to a scene several drafts down the line and go, 'Where was that scene in the book?' It's become so much its own thing that maybe you'll unblock something.

How much pressure do you feel when adapting a well-known and much-loved novel, knowing that you won't be able to please everyone with the finished product?

Particularly with *Jane Eyre*, you feel the weight of world literature on your shoulders. But in that situation I always try being myself when I first read the book. Teenage me: that's who I'm writing for. I'm not writing for critics or academics, I'm writing for that girl who's never read the book before. That's quite freeing. That's what keeps those sneering voices off your back.

CASE STUDY: *TAMARA DREWE*

UK, 2010 ▪ **Directed by** Stephen Frears ▪ **Produced by** Alison Owen, Paul Trijbits, Tracey Seaward ▪ **Screenplay by** Moira Buffini, based on the graphic novel by Posy Simmonds ▪ **Cast:** Gemma Arterton (Tamara Drewe), Roger Allam (Nicholas Hardiment), Bill Camp (Glen McCreavy), Dominic Cooper (Ben Sergeant), Luke Evans (Andy Cobb), Tamsin Greig (Beth Hardiment)

The first frame of Posy Simmonds' graphic novel is the advert for the writers' retreat which forms one of its primary locations, and the

first phrase of the advert is the title of Thomas Hardy's *Far from the Madding Crowd*. Did you go back to Hardy's works in adapting it?

I did read *Far from the Madding Crowd*, but Hardy is another novelist I couldn't adapt and that's the only book of his I can bear. I read about Hardy as well, and the more I read about him the less I ever wanted to adapt one of his novels. I actually can't remember whether Glen is a Hardy scholar in the book, but I thought, 'If he's a Hardy scholar I've got to know something about Hardy.' Basically, it's a flirt between Glen and Beth in the scene where he describes Hardy as having snow on the roof and fire in the cellar, and she finds it all so distasteful that Hardy married a younger woman and gave his first wife syphilis – and meanwhile her own marriage to the controlling guy who's having an affair with a much younger woman is falling apart around her – and you just think, 'This is great. This is all feeding the same beast.'

And what do you think the relationship is between the Simmonds and the Hardy?

Again, writing a good story is the hardest thing, and this is a great story – Bathsheba Everdene and her three suitors – and Posy has taken that and concentrated on the things she finds interesting. Two big British exports are heritage and literature, and she's taking quite a wry look at all that. She's essentially having fun with Thomas Hardy, and that's what I love about her, how deliciously tongue-in-cheek she is. You can almost see her smile as she writes. I think she's the Jane Austen of graphic novels. She has that same fantastic ability to send everything up whilst being true to people as well-rounded emotional beings.

The look and feel of the graphic novel seemed to me quite different to the look and feel of the film. The graphic novel struck me as subdued, measured, as dramatic as it is comic. Whereas the film is light and bright, pacy and jaunty, a romantic comedy with dramatic asides. Was there a particular tone you were trying to achieve?

I think you're right that the film is much more of a romantic comedy than the book, and I think in the first couple of drafts it was even more of a romantic comedy, simply because that's the market. So many of the films that I'd written in my early years as a screenwriter hadn't got made because they didn't fit into a market, they crossed genres. I wrote a horror film that never got made because it was northern and social realist and funny and no one knew what to do with it. I wrote another film that crossed genres – it wasn't really a romance, it wasn't really a drama, it was both – and that didn't get made. Something with a child protagonist didn't get made. So I just thought, 'I'm going to write a romantic comedy and see if I can get that made.' And I'm so glad Stephen Frears found all that really boring and made a less genre film. It probably would have done better box office if it had stayed more in that romantic comedy genre, but at the end of the day it probably wouldn't have been as good a film. Frears found Glen much more interesting, he found the two girls, Jody and Casey, much more interesting – and actually, they are. He took it back closer to Posy's book, which is why I think he was the right director for it.

In a regular novel, each reader forms their own impressions of the characters and locations from the author's descriptions. In a graphic novel, that work is done for you. What impact did the visual nature of the source material have on the way you adapted it?

Huge. The graphic novel was always around on set, everyone who was involved had a copy, and I think we recreated it wonderfully. The film is so faithful to Posy's world. Even down to the names of the hens, the Buff Orpingtons. I just got fixated on Buff Orpingtons; I thought they had to be in the screenplay. Posy gave me all that: she'd researched everything. I knew Derbyshire really well, where *Jane Eyre* is set, but I'd never been to Wessex before, and when I got down there I thought, 'Bloody hell, that's exactly what Posy's drawn.' I inhabited that world in my head for months.

The graphic novel isn't just visual, it's verbal too: there's obviously dialogue in the cartoon strip, but there are also accompanying passages of prose – mainly first person narration by Beth, Glen and Casey, interspersed with, as it were, un-narrated sections showing Tamara, Nicholas and Andy. How important was point of view in your adaptation?

In the novel, Tamara is always talked about, isn't she? She's the other. And that's great. But in a film, if you're not inside your lead character, if you're not seeing the world through your protagonist's eyes... I mean, I'm sure there is a version of the film where Tamara is the other, but I think it's colder, and I think you ultimately have to care about her. She can't be that unlikeable. She's more of an enigma in the novel, and women like that can be very interesting but often fail to be so in films. They did them really well in the 1940s, but if you try to write that kind of enigmatic woman now you just think, 'Who are you writing that for?' It's difficult.

The Tamara portrayed in the script and played by Gemma Arterton does feel more developed than the Tamara in the graphic novel – smarter, sassier, more proactive, more professional – and therefore more sympathetic.

I think Tamara is probably more sympathetic in my adaptation. There's obviously more of me in her than in Posy's Tamara, and of course Gemma is such a sympathetic presence, and I think both of those things contributed to her being more likeable. And maybe I just wanted to like her more. Maybe I was more inclined to like her than her three suitors. I probably did take her side more, and try to understand her as a messed-up young woman in that situation – like, why does she go for Nicholas, why doesn't she go for Andy? I thought she wouldn't go for Nicholas unless he was her only port in a storm – and, at that point, he is. It's one of those really bad things you do that feels good at the time and you hate yourself for afterwards.

A device Simmonds uses a lot is a character reflecting on recent events: a page or more in the form of a thought bubble while doing the cooking or taking a walk in the fields. The film also uses flashbacks, but for memories further in the past. Did you feel that it was better to keep the action as much in the present as possible?

Yes. If you had too many timeframes, it just wasn't clear. I think we tried them, and there's also one first-person direct-to-camera scene.

I was going to ask about that: it's the scene where Beth talks to the audience about Nicholas while baking a cake. Why did you decide to use that device at that moment?

Frears suggested it one lunchtime and I said, 'That's breaking the fourth wall, there's nothing else in the film like it, are you sure it will work?' and he said, 'Why don't you just try it?' So I went off and wrote the scene, came back and gave it to him, and he looked pleased and took it away and shot it. That was a really good day, writing that scene and getting it shot and going, 'That actually really works.' Sometimes you can overthink things, but I didn't have time to overthink that. One thing to say about *Tamara Drewe* is the speed of the production. Alison Owen [*producer*] gave me the book to adapt in autumn 2008, and by September 2009 I was on set and it was being shot. Everything fell into place very quickly, which is unusual. Most films take years, as I've subsequently learnt. So a lot of it was written on set, on the hoof, really instinctively.

Although the film is seen through Tamara's eyes in a way the graphic novel isn't, in terms of point of view your adaptation is as much an ensemble piece as anything else.

Yes, I think so. And I loved the ensemble nature of it. Because it's so Jane Austen-y, I sort of thought, 'I'm the omnipotent author like Jane Austen, I've got the joy of eight characters here, and I'm going to try to get inside everybody and write them much more equally.' So the girls are as important as Glen, and Glen is as important as Tamara, and the audience is the confidante of all eight characters. I think that's how I view everything, actually. I'm the audience. I'm the audience and in that cake-baking scene Beth is confiding in me.

The film follows the overall structure of the graphic novel: four parts for summer, autumn, winter and spring. What narrative significance do the passing seasons have?

It does give you a sense of time passing. Most film stories unfold really quickly, and to have a much longer narrative played out over a year is quite unusual. It had its own challenges as well, not least in trying to keep upping the narrative ante in this longer timeframe.

Films usually operate at a very fast pace unless they have virtually no story.

The ending of the film is somewhat softer than that of the graphic novel: Jody doesn't die and Glen gets together with Beth – though Beth is confronted more directly with Nicholas's death. What was the thinking behind those changes?

Really early on, in that meeting I described where you say what you're going to do, one of the first things I said was, 'I think this film only has room for one death, and I desperately don't want that to be Jody' – and Posy was in agreement with that. Jody represents one of the girls who dies in *Far from the Madding Crowd*, I can't even remember the character's name, and Posy was happy for me to reprieve her. Those two kids have got these shit boring lives, they're looking at all these educated middle-class people who've got so much more than they have, and I really wanted them to end on a high – and they do, they get exactly what they want, they get quality time with their superhero.

It does mean, though, that the life lessons which Casey learns from Jody's death in the graphic novel don't apply in the film.

No, they don't. Jody is the other in that relationship, she's seen through Casey's eyes, but to make those two characters fit into the ensemble, it can't be Casey's story. In the novel, Casey is reflective, so she doesn't do as much. Film is all about character through action, and Jody is the active one, the one who does, so she takes on more significance. So Casey becomes Jody's sidekick. But I think that it is one of the losses.

You also lose the scene in the graphic novel where, despite their differences, Tamara, Beth and Casey console each other over a cigarette around the kitchen table after Nicholas and Jody's deaths.

It's definitely lighter because Jody doesn't die, but then *Far from the Madding Crowd* is the only novel of Hardy's that doesn't have a miserable fucking ending. It just about allows Bathsheba and Gabriel Oak the peace of the fireside, and I think you can just about allow Tamara and Andy a happy ending in *Tamara Drewe*. Tamara hasn't burnt her boats, there's still enough in her to like. She's really lucky, but I think she knows it.

In other words, Tamara becomes the one who learns the life lesson?

Yes. In the novel, she's been through all this shit, but she's still using Andy to cover Nicholas's baby. She remains the same, whereas in a film if your protagonist doesn't change you're in a lot of trouble.

CASE STUDY: *JANE EYRE*

UK/US, 2011 ▪ **Directed by** Cary Joji Fukunaga ▪ **Produced by** Alison Owen, Paul Trijbits ▪ **Screenplay by** Moira Buffini, based on the novel by Charlotte Brontë ▪ **Cast:** Mia Wasikowska (Jane Eyre), Michael Fassbender (Rochester), Jamie Bell (St John Rivers), Judi Dench (Mrs Fairfax), Sally Hawkins (Mrs Reed), Freya Parks (Helen Burns)

There have been numerous previous adaptations of *Jane Eyre*. What did you think you could bring to it that would be new?

I'll tell you how I came to do it, because it's a job I really chased. I had a play at the Almeida around 2007, and Abi Morgan [*playwright and screenwriter*] was at the bar one night and we got talking. I said I was looking for another film and she said, 'I think the BBC want to do an adaptation of *Jane Eyre*,' and I said, 'I have to do it!' It was like this fire came through me. So I went in to meet Alison Owen and Christine Langan [*former Head of BBC Films*] going, 'I have to adapt *Jane Eyre*!' I didn't come to it with any fear that I couldn't do it. It was such a visceral feeling that I had to be the person to do it – because I loved the book. That book has been a friend all my life. It's one of those books you can turn to when you're having a really shit time. Just like it's always sunny in Pemberley, Jane Eyre is always having a more intensely worse time than you are, and somehow her amazing fortitude gets you through. So I started talking about the book and why I love it so much, and it became a meeting about how we all loved this book, and we carried that enthusiasm into all the meetings that followed. But we had to convince quite a lot of people who were saying, 'Why do *Jane Eyre*?'

And what was your answer to that question?

It's a wonderful story. It's also an important story, a radical story, written by someone who society regarded as having no value. Jane Eyre is Rochester's social inferior – she's a woman with no money, he's the lord of the manor – but she regards herself in her living soul as his equal, and by the end of the book he acknowledges the absolute truth of that and they achieve a proper harmony. Some people say that Charlotte Brontë had to emasculate Rochester. I think Rochester deserves that punishment for lying his head off for the whole book and for trying to use a young girl as his harlot. But Jane is aware of her own self-worth and she refuses. She refuses to be treated like most women were treated and like many still are, because she knows she has a soul as valuable as Rochester's. So it's still an important story. And it's a radical book in terms of its form as well. It's one of the first books to have a child narration. Charles Dickens subsequently nicked that for most of his books. I just think it's brilliant.

In some ways it's a very cinematic novel, full of detailed descriptions of people, places and seasons. How much did those guide you when you were conceiving the film's characters and locations?

The scene where Jane is taking the post to the village and Rochester comes by on his horse: I was so in that landscape when I was writing the scene, and in the book it's a wintry landscape so that's what I wrote, and then of course in production you can't do it. You've only got so many weeks and you have to compromise. But what's important about that walk is how intensely alone she is and how creeped out she is and how restless she is, because what Charlotte Brontë is actually giving you with that landscape is Jane's emotional state and those are the things that you try to keep. In the first draft I wrote the most ridiculous detailed descriptions of rooms and crystal glassware and all this kind of stuff. I've got so economical in describing things now that people keep asking me, 'Please can you write more?', because it's only the absolute necessities of a scene that end up on the page.

Another extraordinarily detailed aspect of the novel is the lengthy conversations between Jane and Rochester, which are sometimes so high-flown as to be hard to follow. How did you set about turning those into believable, understandable dialogue scenes?

Well, you see, I didn't find them hard to follow. I really loved them and I really loved writing them. They're like swordplay, they're like skirmishes, and they're some of my favourite scenes in the whole thing. Also, as a playwright, I'm not afraid of the long scene, I'm not afraid of the scene of scale. Sometimes I think, 'I'm going to write the play of this scene,' and that's what I did in those Jane and Rochester fireside scenes. They're such play-like situations. They're still, which is so rare in a film, and they're surrounded by darkness, which is what you get in the theatre.

The film unfolds in flashback from the point where Jane flees Thornfield Hall, and there are two good reasons for that choice: the fact that, as you said, a number of new characters – specifically St John Rivers and his sisters – would otherwise enter the story late on; and also the fact that, without flashbacks, you would have to open with young Jane before moving on to an older actor, which would make the story very stop–start. And you can't cut the school scenes, at Lowood, because they're so important.

The school stuff is really important: it shapes who Jane becomes. The flashbacks acted like Jane's memories and they became very economical and distilled. You don't have to tell the whole narrative. You can say: what are the really important things about Lowood? Well, it's that relationship with Helen Burns. And how do you tell that and make it as moving as it has to be? How do you tell the relationship with Mrs Reed? Who is Mrs Reed? So there's the script, and then there's the next layer, the further distillation which comes in production. Even when you film what you think is a distilled script, you find it's massively overwritten and you need far less. I've found that in every film I've done, and I've found the same with television: how little you actually need to tell the story. Actors bring depth and emotion to lines in a way that never ceases to amaze me, and you find you need fewer words.

Jane's friend Helen, who dies of TB at the school, is more of a presence in the script than the novel, almost like a guardian angel, guiding Jane away from Thornfield and later leading her back. Did you conceive of her as being an actual ghost?

The book has such a spiritual dimension to it: the voices on the moor; the great dog with the red eyes; Jane hearing her mother's voice coming to her; her dreams that have such meaning. Peoples' real lives are so constrained and yet their spirits are huge and their imaginations are as epic as the landscape. How do you bring that into the film? How does Jane carry her past with her? Helen Burns as her guardian angel seemed to do all that in a really visual way – but none of it ended up in the finished film. We shot it, but at the end of the day we cut it, because having written and shot it we found that it was there anyway without having to show it. We didn't need it. But I'm really glad it was there in the script and I'm really glad that we shot it, because everyone knew that was the feeling we were trying to capture in the film and I think, cinematographically, it was there.

Most of the supernatural elements in the script are absent from the finished film, in fact – though strangely I remembered them as being there, which must mean that the essence of them survived.

Oh, that's interesting. Again, there was a lot more written and shot that was cut out, because it just slowed the story down. We loved all the gothic stuff – a huge country house with an old lady, a schoolgirl, her maid, some servants, a governess and a madwoman in the attic: what's not to like? – but the pace was too slow for modern horror. The first cut was three hours and twenty minutes long. So those elements are there but they're there in their most distilled form, which is what you get in a good edit – and this was a brilliant edit. I was in the edit quite a lot, and I absolutely loved working with the editor, Melanie Ann Oliver. Editors are like writers, in a way: you begin a whole different process in the editing room. The structure changes. Things that you thought were incredibly important go out the window. You realise that you've written too much over here, but you haven't written some essential thing over there. I think we did two days of reshoots, or new shoots, on both *Jane Eyre* and *Tamara*

Drewe, and they were transformative: you realised how badly you needed that extra scene or two.

Something I noticed in both films is the way you combine two different elements from the books to create a third thing. For example, there's a girl at Lowood who has red hair, but she's a very minor character, and you've given that red hair to Helen, which makes her immediately visually distinctive. Do you deliberately look for those moments?

Yes, whenever you can. Again, it's distillation. You try to make every character and every scene do as much work as possible. In a novel, you can go off on all these amazing tangents. In a film, everything has to be adding to the emotional journey. There's not really room in a film to digress.

Similarly, and again during the Lowood sequence, you conflate two scenes from the novel: Jane dropping her writing slate and Helen being punished. In the film, Jane drops the slate deliberately rather than accidentally, to try to stop the punishment and draw attention away from Helen.

Because the scene can't just be Jane watching Helen get punished. It's about making the protagonist active in every scene.

The secret at the heart of *Jane Eyre* is so well known that there's an academic book named after it: the madwoman in the attic. In adapting the novel, do you approach it as if the audience doesn't know that, or are you obliged to navigate that knowledge in some way?

Jane Eyre doesn't know that, and the people who've never read the book don't know that, so again it comes down to: who are you writing this film for? And when you look at it from Jane's perspective, it becomes a perfect horror: he's locked up a woman in his house for over a decade and gone off around Europe shagging. Who cares about the rest?

The ending of the film, Jane's reunion with Rochester, is pretty speedy, but I noticed three deleted scenes in a row in the shooting script. Was the ending originally longer and more like the novel?

There'd been an ongoing conversation about the ending, and I remember writing the last couple of lines in one of the caravans on set. The ending I originally wrote was longer and more like the novel, by the fireside again, but Cary's instinct was that it should be much simpler and outside – and he was so right. Looking back on it, what I originally wrote was emotionally overwrought, and the simplicity of what we ended up with is really beautiful.

So do you feel that Rochester is redeemed in the film?

Yes, I do. In the age of Time's Up and #MeToo, he's a harder hero to like – he's certainly not the strong man Orson Welles portrayed in the 1943 version, where you get the feeling that his wife was really crazy and actually deserved to be locked up – but I do think he's redeemed. The other vital thing about Jane's position at the end, the revolutionary thing that makes her Rochester's equal, is her economic independence. She could not, and would not, go back to him without that. It was so hard to fit in all that stuff about the letter from Jane's uncle and the news of her inheritance, but it was so important that when she comes back to Rochester she's independent. St John Rivers is really important to the story, too: a good man who just doesn't understand love in the way that Jane does, who doesn't understand this awful, terrifying passion that she has for Rochester, and it's so brave of Jane to know that she'd never be happy with St John and to do the morally wrong thing and go back to Rochester in pursuit of her own happiness. Again, radical: women were supposed to do the morally right thing.

I've always understood the definition of drama to be character driving plot, whereas melodrama is plot determining character. Would you agree with that, and is *Jane Eyre* both at once?

I think it is. When I read it as a kid some of the scenes with Bertha Mason had me absolutely choking with fear. Then you read it again as an adult and you think, 'That's a little bit hokey.' And then when we came to film it, even though the actor who played Bertha was absolutely wonderful, it was just too strong a flavour – so again it didn't make it in. But it should always be character driving the story, and if the plot is feeling too much like plot, I just have to go back and embed it better.

Are you more aware now of the type of scenes which won't get shot, or will be shot and then get cut?

Yes. I'm also much more aware that when a director comes on board it's very important for them to feel ownership and confidence for when they go into production, so I'm always really willing to write a good director's draft. *Tamara Drewe* and *Jane Eyre* were shot back to back, my first two films, and the learning curve I went on was absolutely massive. When I stepped on to the set of *Tamara Drewe*, I'd never been on a film set before. For weeks I had this feeling of, 'I honestly don't know what the fuck I'm doing.' Fortunately, Alison and Christine and Stephen Frears were amazingly good teachers. On *Tamara Drewe*, Frears would say to me [*holds her finger and thumb a few inches apart*], 'That long,' and I knew he wouldn't shoot the scene I'd written, which was about a page-and-a-half, until it was that long, because he knew that was all the screen time it needed. What the director is really shooting is fragments, and it's so much better just to go, 'How can I distil this down to a tiny shot?' It's a wonderful puzzle and I find it so pleasurable.

Lucinda Coxon

Lucinda Coxon was born in 1962 in Derby.

As a playwright, her work includes: *Waiting at the Water's Edge* (1993); *Wishbones* (1997); *Nostalgia* (2001); *Vesuvius* (2005); *Happy Now?* (2008); *Herding Cats* (2010); and *Alys, Always* (2019).

Her screen adaptation credits include: *The Heart of Me* (2002, novel *The Echoing Grove* by Rosamond Lehmann); *Wild Target* (2010, film *Cible émouvante* by Pierre Salvadori); *The Crimson Petal and the White* (2011, novel by Michel Faber); *The Danish Girl* (2015, novel by David Ebershoff); and *The Little Stranger* (2018, novel by Sarah Waters).

APPROACHES TO ADAPTATION

Do you prefer to adapt material which chimes with your own work, or material which is completely different and gives you a chance to try out new things?

Writing original material and adapting are discrete processes for me. What it largely comes down to is that I write original material for the stage and I adapt for film and TV. I haven't written original material for the screen in a long time, not least because I've not had great experiences of doing that. But in terms of the material I'm attracted to adapt, it's very difficult to predict. Producers ask, 'What are you looking for? What do you want to do next?' and I never really know until I see it. I'm fortunate enough at the moment to be offered a great range of material, and a lot of it is really intriguing. It will sometimes be classic books, sometimes contemporary books, and I may really love them, but I mostly decline, either because I don't have the time, or because I think, 'Yes, I could adapt that, but so could a lot of other people.' If it's a thing that anyone could do, then why would I do it? You're attached to these projects for a long time, so it's got to be a situation where you feel the material needs you and you need it. In fact, the thing I'm going to do next is exactly what I wasn't looking for – a TV series, eight episodes – but when I read the novel I thought, 'Yes, I can live with this for two years. Or ten years, if that's what it ends up taking.' The book's humane and bittersweet, it's not too issue-y but it speaks to the time – and it's set in Rome, so I'm excited about a research trip! But then I'm often excited about the research trip, and don't actually make it until the writing process is finished. I was working on *The Danish Girl* for 11 years, but only went to Copenhagen when we were shooting.

Do you think adaptations involve a completely different set of creative gears to original screenplays?

No, not really. I mean, obviously you've got the gift of the material. I adapted *The Echoing Grove* by Rosamond Lehmann – the film was called *The Heart of Me*, because Americans never knew what a grove was – and that's an outstanding book, very rich pickings in terms of the underpinning it gives you. But with your own work, once you've got the material of the first draft, it's the same process.

Do you always agree a mission statement or direction of travel with whoever has commissioned the adaptation?

There's always a general conversation with producers about the book, but no matter how much you talk about the 'take', it's hard to know whether you're all imagining the same project. That's often not clear until it's too late. I actually think it's almost harder to be certain about the shared vision with adaptations than with original material.

Do you usually produce an outline or treatment before you start writing the script?

Not if I can possibly help it. Treatments are comforting for producers, but they're not always very useful for writers. I find them incredibly time-consuming to write, and in fact a lot of writers now have other people produce them. I'll often produce a summary of the book for myself, I'll break the book down, but I won't write an actual treatment. The occasions in the past when I have written very developed treatments have mostly resulted in a script that was just dead on the page. You start writing using the treatment skeleton and you're essentially just putting in the dialogue. You end up with something that ticks all the boxes and has all its turning points in the right place, but has no organic flow to it and is flat as a pancake. I'm mixing metaphors now, but you're flogging this flat pancake through draft after draft after draft and it just becomes a flat pancake with all the trimmings. But essentially it's still a flat pancake, and you'd be better off with something more alive and unpredictable. I understand why producers want treatments, and of course it's another way of trying to work out if you're talking about the same book, but in the end it's a terrible waste of time for many writers.

If the author of the source material is living, do you find it useful to have their input on the script?

I find it useful to have their blessing. If the author is living I always ask, 'Do you have any ambition to write this yourself?' and if they say, 'I wouldn't mind,' then I'm out. I don't want anyone looking over my shoulder in that way. If the material is factually based and you're dealing with a historian or a biographer that can be helpful, but fiction is a different animal, and I've been very lucky that the living novelists I've worked with have been terrifically supportive and hands off. So, for example, I couldn't have asked for better colleagues than Sarah Waters on *The Little Stranger* and David Ebershoff on *The Danish Girl*. I knew that *The Danish Girl* had been a great passion project for David, but when I went to meet him he said, 'You mustn't worry about me. If you sell your apartment you can't get upset when they put in a new kitchen.' The one I was most frightened about was Rosamond Lehmann, who wasn't living but was famously passionate about spiritualism. I used to think, as I was chopping out huge swathes of this very autobiographical book, 'Is Rosamond looking down at me, hissing?'

Is it easier to navigate notes from directors, producers and script editors when you have a piece of source material to measure the screenplay against?

I guess it is. I once worked on a World War II project, which involved a huge amount of historical research, and the producer's notes would include things like, 'Is there any way the Americans could come into the war a bit earlier, because it seems to take ages to get there.' One's eyes widen, you know? You're sitting in a meeting saying, 'Hmm... you're not the first person to wonder that. Churchill was quite exercised about it himself. But I'm sorry, the Americans really can't come into the war a bit earlier, they've just got to wait for Pearl Harbor.' I think, generally, when you're dealing with notes from producers and directors, you're always dependent on them being good on script – and that's not something you can actually take for granted. There are wonderful directors who are not very good on script and there are average directors who are brilliantly good on script: the two don't particularly go hand in hand. And there are wonderful directors who are not very interested in script development: they just want you to deliver it. Similarly, there are producers who hate development because what they love doing is making films, and there are producers who love development and then get cold feet when it comes to shooting it. You get a curious mix of different people, so it's not one size fits all in that respect.

Have you ever started work on an adaptation and found it harder to adapt than you anticipated?

Always. It's always harder than I anticipate. If I thought about all the problems, I'd never start. But I'm never interested in projects where I can see exactly what the process or trajectory will be. With *The Crimson Petal and the White*, I knew what the emotional arrow flight was, but then there was that huge trunk of material to deal with. And *The Little Stranger* has been interesting, because it's a sort of hybrid novel – it isn't horror, it's a psychological thriller with horror elements – so it's not a straight genre film. I can imagine a version where you said, 'Let's take this and make it into a pure genre piece,' but we haven't done that. The film has retained a lot of the ambiguity of the novel, including the unreliable narrator. I love an unreliable narrator, but an unreliable narrator in a film is very different to an unreliable narrator in a novel. The novel turns on a series of apparently supernatural events that are only reported and never seen, and of course in a film you have to make a decision about whether to show them. So another writer might well have pursued the genre version, but that wasn't something that interested me.

Have you ever been offered material to adapt which you felt couldn't, or shouldn't, be adapted?

Yes, actually, a book I absolutely loved – and I turned it down *because* I loved it and couldn't think of a way to do it without destroying it. It's a novel called *The Vintner's Luck* by Elizabeth Knox, and I still wake up sometimes thinking, 'Maybe I could do it in the theatre or as a ballet,' because I would love to work with it. It's set in France in the nineteenth century, and it's about a man falling in love with a male angel who he meets on the same day every year, so it's completely sui generis and structurally an absolute nightmare. I genuinely racked my brains thinking, 'Is there a way in?' and in the end I decided I wouldn't be able to forgive myself if I was the person who served up the dog's dinner of this book. In fact, Niki Caro [*writer-director of* Whale Rider] took it on, and I gather that didn't work either, and I just thought, 'If she can't do it, then maybe it can't be done.'

Are there any screen adaptations which you think are especially good or you particularly admire?

That's almost too big a question to address. But I can certainly remember the first time I even thought of screen adaptation as an art form, and that was after seeing Laura Jones's version of Janet Frame's *An Angel at My Table*, directed by Jane Campion. That would have been in 1990, I suppose, when I was writing for the theatre and just starting to develop some original material for the screen. It was such a brilliant and arresting piece of work. I can absolutely recall that moment of thinking, 'Okay, this might be an interesting way of collaborating...'

ADAPTING FICTION

Some writers try to include as much of the novel as possible by boiling scenes down to their essence. Others are more ruthless in editing it down to a sort of greatest hits, but being true to the spirit of it. Do you favour either of those approaches?

I think adapting fiction is pretty much a three-draft process. The first draft is working out how much of the book is going to make it into the screenplay. The second draft is managing the structure of what you've got and solving the problems of what you've cut. And the third draft is taking ownership of it as a writer – which can mean lots of different things. *The Echoing Grove* adaptation took great liberties with the novel, but it's such a wonderful book, and Rosamond Lehmann has such a strong voice, that when I was minting fresh dialogue for it I was fighting to make sure I was absolutely in tune with the existing dialogue. It's very particular – particular to a period and a place, but also highly idiosyncratic – and one of my happiest moments was sitting with the producer, Martin Pope, and the director, Thaddeus O'Sullivan, and them being unable to distinguish what I'd written from what had come from Lehmann. When *The Danish Girl* came out, I was doing a press tour with David Ebershoff and I had to ask him what was his and what was mine; I'd been working on the material for so long that I couldn't entirely remember. That's how it should be, really, that you're under the skin of it to that degree, but it's hard to achieve that until you've got the nuts and bolts out of the way at the beginning. I'm afraid that practical initial response on reading is hardwired into me now. I can hardly even look at a novel on holiday anymore without thinking, 'You could cut the brother. She doesn't need to have that friend. They wouldn't have a dog, it's too expensive.' It's terrible!

If a novel has an unusual structure, would you try to reproduce that in adapting it?

I think you've got to decide what the relationship is between the structure and the story. *Crimson Petal* is full of postmodern tricks and I retained as much of that as I could, but what made those flourishes easy to fight for was the fact that it's also got an enormously strong story motor. *The Echoing Grove* is probably the novel I've had to break down the most, because it goes backwards and forwards in time so often, and when I took it apart to try to figure it out I couldn't really get it back together again. The chronology didn't work and characters would turn out not to be old enough at certain points or too old at others, and in the end I had to say, 'Okay, if we're really going to bring this story to the screen, what's actually useful?' So we concentrated on the central love triangle and narrowed it down to, I think, two or three timeframes, as opposed to the twenty-seven or something in the novel – and people liked it and were mostly very complimentary about it. But there's easily enough material for another film in that book – or a five-part series, if you were doing it now. So that's the novel that I've had to attack most aggressively, but I'd probably never take on anything that was super-quirky structurally. I don't much like films that are fundamentally a trick.

Do you try to avoid voiceover in adapting a first-person narrative, or do you see it as another tool in the toolbox?

There's a great snobbery about voiceover because it's viewed as cheating – and sometimes it does get put on a film very late in the day to plug the gaps – but I'm interested in telling stories and audiences like being told a story. In *Crimson Petal* and *The Little Stranger*, you're being told a story by someone you probably can't believe, and that makes it more fun, so why wouldn't you have voiceover? It can be a hostage to fortune: you can find yourself in the edit, for example, and people are saying, 'Maybe we can put a bit more voiceover on it,' because it's the thing that's easiest to rewrite. It's also useful on occasion, being able to shuffle the pack of the voiceover. I have absolutely no compunction about it. I like it. I like direct address in the theatre, too. And when you think about a film like *American Beauty*, what would it be without that opening monologue?

Do you use the language of the novel in writing the screenplay, or do you put the whole thing in your own words?

It varies. The first draft probably has a bit of the original prose in it, then by the end much less. With something historical like *Crimson Petal*, Michel Faber had done an extraordinary amount of research – I mean, he was writing that novel for years and years and years – so there would be some quirky bits of Victorian detail that just had to be in. *The Danish Girl* has very little of the prose from the novel in it, but that was a slightly different process.

Do you keep the novel beside you throughout the adaptation process, or do you try to internalise it and set it aside somewhere along the way?

The latter. I read an interview with a writer – a wonderful writer who adapts really well – and she was saying that she loads the whole novel into Final Draft and then chisels away at it like a sculptor, so it begins as a 400-page screenplay and she just keeps cutting bits out. And I just thought, 'God almighty, that's terrifying.' I certainly couldn't do that, I have to make all the marks on the page on my own, but I was impressed by the chutzpah of it. For a moment I thought, 'Am I missing a trick here? Is that what I should have been doing all these years?' But that really wouldn't work for me. At the beginning I have to live alongside the book very closely. I had to rip *Crimson Petal* into four just to carry it around, because I didn't have a pocket or bag big enough to hold it. It felt very transgressive, breaking this book into pieces – and then I had to buy a new edition, because the pages started fluttering away. But I had to keep it to hand; I couldn't just do the surgery on a computer screen.

How much pressure do you feel when adapting a well-known and much-loved novel, knowing that you won't be able to please everyone with the finished product?

You hope people will like things, but if I'm honest, I don't really worry about it. A book and a film are different. Terrible books can

THE ART OF SCREEN ADAPTATION

make marvellous films, and sometimes wonderful books become terrible films, so you just hope for the best. What I was worried about, when I wrote *Crimson Petal*, was whether Michel Faber would like it. Michel and I have since become very good friends, but I had absolutely no contact with him until we'd shot it, so I adapted the book in the dark. It's a mighty piece of writing, and I was so under the skin of it that I felt very connected to him. It really mattered to me that he liked it. So I feel lucky: I wanted Michel to love it and he did. He was incredibly generous about it. But in terms of the public, the readers, what can you say? All you can do is cross your fingers.

CASE STUDY: *THE CRIMSON PETAL AND THE WHITE*

UK/Canada, 2011 ▪ **Directed by** Marc Munden ▪ **Produced by** David M. Thompson, Steve Lightfoot, Greg Dummett ▪ **Screenplay by** Lucinda Coxon, based on the novel by Michel Faber ▪ **Cast:** Romola Garai (Sugar), Chris O'Dowd (William Rackham), Amanda Hale (Mrs Agnes Rackham), Shirley Henderson (Mrs Emmeline Fox), Mark Gatiss (Henry Rackham Junior), Richard E. Grant (Doctor Curlew), Gillian Anderson (Mrs Castaway), Isla Watt (Sophie Rackham)

What was your initial reaction on reading this doorstop of a novel?

I'd been approached many years before about doing the novel as a film, and that didn't go anywhere. At the time, I was very unsure about it. My daughter was still very young, and I couldn't imagine going to L.A. with a two-year-old. I also couldn't imagine a studio making the film, because it's filthy in a proper, dirt-poor kind of way. And I was worried about the sexual politics of it, wondering whether the novel wasn't sometimes having its cake and eating it. So I thought it was brilliant, but I was nervous about it, and in the end Curtis Hanson was brought in as director and I was immediately out of the conversation. He brought his own writer in; they then had about 20 writers on it sequentially and never made the film. Fast forward almost a decade, David Thompson – who had been the executive producer on *The Heart of Me* – got in touch with my agent and said that he now had the rights, and would I think about looking at it again?

I still had the book, so I got it down and started re-reading it and about a quarter of the way in I thought, 'Okay, I know exactly what this is and I have to adapt it.' It was the same book, but a completely different experience, and the difference was not in the material, it was in the fact that by then my daughter was much older and I had learned that when you parent a child you have the luxury of, in a sense, re-parenting yourself – and I could see that in the book. I could see that the real centre of the novel was the love story between Sugar and her lover's daughter, Sophie. Their relationship was as complicated and terrifying and as full of passion and betrayal as any adult love story, and as long as I could deliver that, the project would sing.

Could you even conceive of it as a feature film now?

I don't know how one could do it as a film. We had to really cut it down, even with four hours of screen time to play with. A lot of secondary characters got a bit shaved and I would like to have had more time with them. I could have done a whole episode that was just Agnes Rackham's diary. But in terms of the main story I think it was a pretty rare thing, where we managed to give it a real engine, but also allowed breathing space around the story. In many ways, it was by far my most straightforward experience of adapting – or of writing for the screen at all. Mostly because the show was greenlit very quickly and there wasn't a lot of time for rewrites. Some things need a lot of reworking to get right, but I came into this at quite a pace, I knew what I was doing with it and I think there is a freshness about it which would have been lost in revisions.

When I took it on, having told David I absolutely had to do it, I sort of had panic attacks because I wasn't a TV writer at all, and I feared it was going to be one of those bloody awful, badly-lit period dramas we've all seen too many of. I called Martin Pope to share my fears, and he was just great. He said, 'You can't think about it like that. You've got to assume it's going to look like *Barry Lyndon* and have the performances from *The Lives of Others*' – which had just come out. It was brilliant advice. I thought, 'He's right. I've got to set the bar in such a way that it's impossible to make it look like one of those things. I've got to come in with the high style.' So I went into the writing process swinging an axe above my head, in that respect. Then Marc Munden came on board, who's a really fantastic director and no stranger to the high style, and he really got it and wanted to make something extraordinary. I remember him looking at the first two pages and saying, 'I don't want to do all that Dickensian shit. It's got to look like Mumbai,' and I thought, 'Yes, exactly.' I was very lucky with it and it was a very happy process.

The novel has the denseness and richness of Charles Dickens and Wilkie Collins, but also a frankness and explicitness they could only dream of, the ability to tackle head on subjects which they could only allude to. Did you capture as much of that as you wanted to, given the sensitivities of TV audiences?

When I wrote the first episode there was a rumble among the producers that the scene in the brothel was quite harsh. In fact, someone said, 'I was thinking the brothel would be more welcoming and sumptuous,' and I thought, 'Yes, that's the punters' point of view, and that's not what we're making. We're making it from the girls' point of view.' It's a place of constant danger and degradation, but also the only place they can call home. It's a place where people shit in a bucket because they have to, or where people pay to watch someone else shit in a bucket because they can. It's a place where anything can and will happen, and where there's no room for niceties. That seemed really important. I was very mindful that those scenes should not be titillating. I went out of my way to give the viewer no pleasure in that regard. Because what happens around those back streets is not beautiful. It should be clear that these women lived with a threat of violence over their heads constantly. The other thing I was pressured to tone down was Sugar's friend Caroline, the prostitute, having been beaten. The producers said it was an incredibly depressing way to start, and I thought, 'Yes, but that's the motor, and that's potentially Sugar's future: being beaten to death for fun by these vile middle-class men.' She has to operate out of that place of pain. Obviously I thought hard about the sexual content. But I think the really terrible frankness in the adaptation are the scenes with the children in, because it's a world of such terror that any time you see a child on that screen you're afraid for them, even though there are people trying to look after them – or imagining they're looking after them. In a sense, Sugar is a child: she's her mother's child, and her mother is her madam. It's a world where there are no grown-ups, there are just people who are bigger or richer or crueller than you. The little boy she leaves behind when she leaves the brothel; the betrayal of that boy is almost the hardest thing in it for me.

I remember David Thompson was somewhat squeamish about Sugar's psoriasis and used to note me on it, to the point where it became a kind of joke. He'd say, 'You think I haven't noticed that you haven't cut the skin condition, but I have noticed and in the end you'll have to cut it.' My response was: 'David, you might be right, I might have to cut it, but I haven't cut it yet,' and then we ran out of time and I didn't cut it. The psoriasis was a brilliant device for a character who has very few people she can talk to and who is unable to articulate her emotions verbally; having her skin flare up when she's under pressure is a fantastic barometer for her. I think it's also part of her appeal: it's disgusting, it's beautiful, it's unravelling, it's like lace, it makes her vulnerable and porous in the world. It's so many extraordinary things. I mean, why would you lose that? Anyway, that ended up being a battle I won, and David's been gracious about it since. It's fascinating the things that people are squeamish about. With *The Danish Girl*, the one note that I'd get endlessly was, 'Is there any way we can talk about Gerda not being pregnant without talking about her period?' and I said, 'There are only so many ways to find out that you're not pregnant!' I was sure it wouldn't be a problem, but it came up again and again – especially in America.

The opening of the novel has one of the boldest narrative voices I've ever read, a direct address to the reader which is both completely of its time and entirely modern. In the series, it's Sugar who takes us by the hand and looks us in the eye and leads us into this world – which is equally bold in its way.

I was always very determined and specific about that opening visual. That was always how those pages ran – with that set of images and

Sugar writing her story – and I don't think we changed it at all. In the novel, there's an omniscient narrator who introduces the story, then disappears halfway through, and it just becomes a free for all. Obviously that wasn't going to work for us, but I also wanted passionately for it to be Sugar's story. The beginning, with her plunging us into this confusing landscape as she's desperately trying to write her way out of it, seemed very important. And then when we arrive at the end, so much of her anger and confusion have left her, have been poured into this book that is finally jettisoned and she's on her way – without us. The ending of the novel frustrated people and there was a suggestion that, of course, I would find a less ambiguous way to end the series, and I thought, 'Fuck, no. We've seen this woman from every angle, she's had so little privacy. Sugar's entitled to keep the next chapter to herself. It's hers, not ours.' We did briefly talk about whether there would be some kind of sequel – what Sugar did next – and there was quite a lot of excitement around that, but for me, she has to disappear, into whatever the future holds. The idea at the end is that she says, 'Your money's run out. Time's up.'

The novel is in five parts: 'The Streets'; 'The House of Ill Repute'; 'The Private Rooms and the Public Haunts'; 'The Bosom of the Family'; and 'The World at Large'. The series is in four parts, compressing the first two sections of the novel into the first episode, then more or less following the shape of the book for the next three. Did that compression of the opening sections come from a desire to get things moving as quickly as possible?

That's probably about right. One of the things that made it a pleasure to write was that the four parts are very different. They're completely different landscapes, but all of them are dangerous. The streets and the brothel are dangerous, but living as a kept woman and being isolated is also dangerous. Then the third episode, where she moves into the house, is like a thriller – and the fourth episode, when she tries to cross back into those other worlds, is something else again. To have those four discrete worlds to play with was very good fun.

A screen adaptation gives you the chance to cross-cut and juxtapose scenes in ways which a novel may not. William showing Sugar the

burning lavender fields, for example, as Henry immolates himself while lost in lust for Mrs Fox. Do you feel at those moments like you almost get to improve on the novel?

Compression is often a bonus. You're experiencing something in a completely different timeframe when you're watching things on screen, and there's something hugely potent about that. There are lots of pleasures in that novel, and I hope that people saw the series and then went on to read the novel, but the truth is that you can sometimes deliver a different set of pleasures. The ability to work that way, not just with visuals, but with sound design as well, is a gift. *Crimson Petal* was a truly immersive watch because those elements were so strong. Marc and the designers really delivered an unusually rich sensory experience.

The novel doesn't teem with characters in the same way that Dickens' do, and in fact for such a big book a lot of it is quite contained, but you obviously still had to make some pretty hefty cuts. How did you determine what to keep and what to cut in terms of character and plot?

It was actually relatively simple, in that Sugar came first. Sugar's story was the most important thing, and her trajectory with Sophie, that terrible chain of mothers and daughters. That's why Agnes's diary, fabulous as it is, simply couldn't be a big feature. But Sugar's relationship with Agnes is so brilliant: by helping Agnes escape from her husband, Sugar simultaneously saves a woman in peril and gets rid of her lover's wife – just as she rescues Sophie by abducting her. You're so spoiled as a writer to be allowed that sort of ambiguity, to be working in a universe with characters who are so shifting and true. I really loved Sugar as though she were my own. I love that she's not cold and calculating, she's just a survivor, a human being trying to find a safe corner somewhere. I really think she's one of the great female characters. It's a great role and Romola Garai did a brilliant job of inhabiting her.

The novel positively drips with disgust at the way most of its male characters treat their wives and lovers – and women generally. It feels like you picked up that ball and ran with it – and it seems even more relevant several years on.

Absolutely. We're living at a time now where lots of 'nice' men feel tarred by the #MeToo brush and are angry about that. I think William Rackham knows just what they're going through: 'I'm a nice guy, I'm not like them.' And there's a moment in the story where you think he's really going to evolve and become the good guy, but of course that's impossible. His limitations are what they are, he's operating in the context that he's operating in, and it's a crazy fantasy that he might marry this prostitute, his mistress. Sugar responds to this betrayal with incredible speed and nerve, stealing the daughter he's not fit to look after and leaving him in a place of abject pain. But where and to what does she take that child? Is history going to repeat itself? Is she saving Sophie, or is Sophie going to be a prostitute in ten years' time? All that ambiguity, all those possibilities, are there in that ending, which just frays away to eternity.

CASE STUDY: *THE DANISH GIRL*

UK/US, 2015 ▪ **Directed by** Tom Hooper ▪ **Produced by** Tim Bevan, Eric Fellner, Anne Harrison, Tom Hooper, Gail Mutrux ▪ **Screenplay by** Lucinda Coxon, based on the novel by David Ebershoff ▪ **Cast:** Eddie Redmayne (Einar Wegener/Lili Elbe), Alicia Vikander (Gerda Wegener), Ben Whishaw (Henrik Sandahl), Sebastian Koch (Dr Kurt Warnekros), Amber Heard (Ulla Paulson), Matthias Schoenaerts (Hans Axgil)

I found this novel very moving but quite distressing: Lili's physical and emotional journey is so hard. How did you respond to it?

I'm embarrassed to say that the book sat on my desk unread for quite a long time, because on the first edition it said, 'The story of the world's first sex change'. That's not the language we'd use now – and it's actually not true – but it wasn't something I felt I was especially interested in. So the book hung around for a while and then after a nudge from my agent I started reading it, and it wasn't what I'd expected at all. I suppose the thing that really gripped me about it was this deeply loving marriage between two artists.

I was just fascinated by Einar and Gerda's shared trajectory, and by the sense of Lili as her own art project, achieved through their collaboration. Gerda's love for Lili and her willingness to embrace incredible change, and Lili's bravery in becoming herself – the courage and vision involved in the decision still astonishes me. But also the incredible modernity of their imaginations. Lili is so much more than the product of a surgical procedure, the 'sex change'. I have a painting from the set of the film of Eddie as Lili, and it always has a vase of lilies in front of it. I find myself sitting and looking at it sometimes, just wondering about her. I spent so many years trying to really understand and imagine her.

Lili's story has always had an ambiguous relationship with historical fact. David Ebershoff's novel is a fictional story inspired by her life, and he describes her own edited book of diaries and correspondence, *Man into Woman*, as a 'semi-fictional, hybrid biography'. He's also described how she worked on the manuscript in the last years of her life and was 'keen to tell her story, but also conscious of creating a myth about herself'. Adapting the novel, which itself drew on her book, what course did you set out to chart between fact and fiction?

Well, the novel tells the story from before they met and takes place over a much longer period of time. Also, Gerda is called Greta and she's American, and when I asked why, David was very straightforward and said, 'It was my first novel, and the idea of writing a woman at all was terrifying and the idea of writing a Danish woman was even more terrifying, so I thought if she were American it would give me a much more secure base to imagine her from.' There's also a character central to the novel who doesn't appear in the film at all, and that's Gerda's brother. I couldn't see why we needed him; he seemed to me to be extraneous to the story and to get in the way of that central relationship. I wasn't interested in the before and I wasn't interested in extra people, but David had done a lot of research, so I thought, 'Why would we tell the story if we're not going to tell the story? Let's take what's factual in the novel, and what David has so brilliantly imagined of the factual, and strip away everything else.' There are so many stories about Lili, but the facts are very slippery and she remains mysterious in lots of ways. I suppose I dealt with that by having my point of view in the film be Gerda's. I always felt it was Gerda's film in many respects: she's the audience's proxy, and I was behind her eyes a lot of the time. That role is a stealth lead, which is perhaps one of the reasons Alicia won the Oscar for it.

How much additional research did you do before writing the script?

I read a lot – *Man into Woman*, of course, and everything else I could find – and when I first delivered the script I thought, 'This is going to be a cinch to get together. The story is extraordinary, the roles are phenomenal, who wouldn't want to make this film?' But it turned out that lots of people didn't want to make that film. There were directors who were intrigued, and there were actors queuing up to be in it, but there were also financiers who said, 'Fantastic script, but no one wants to see a film about a man having his dick cut off.' And you think, 'Wow. You could have dressed that up a bit, but what a reality check.' So the original producers – primarily Gail Mutrux and Anne Harrison – tried valiantly for a decade to get the film made. The script didn't really change very much over that time, but I constantly thought it was going to have to, because in those ten years trans awareness really gathered pace. There was so much more interest in the territory, more research material available – and, crucially, the internet happened, which meant that previously uncollected documents in French and German started appearing online. Europe was in chaos in the period after Lili's death. The hospital in Dresden where she had her operations was firebombed by the Allies in 1945, so her medical records vanished. But gradually archives began to be unearthed and I was constantly thinking, 'Oh, Christ, some document is going to appear which will mean I'll have to completely rewrite the second act.' But mostly, when new facts emerged, we were on the right track, so there were very few revelations that surprised me. The only thing I found out quite late in the day that I wished I'd known earlier was that Gerda was considered very wild as a young woman, and her bourgeois parents were thrilled when she met Einar because he seemed so conventional and they thought he'd settle her down.

In fact, Gerda's own sexuality may have been more fluid than presented in either the film or the novel, as suggested by the erotic lesbian element present in some of her drawings and paintings.

Yes, and there were certainly conversations about including that. There's no question in my mind that Gerda would have loved to continue in a marriage with Lili, and to some extent expected that. But Lili wanted to be a 'real' girl: a conventional, heterosexual girl. So in the end societal pressure has its way with our heroines. I was much keener than others to make something of this. Gerda produced a lot of really beautiful, really witty lesbian erotica, and I was interested in including it as an expression of her sexuality and of her love for Lili, but the feeling was that we were already going as far as we could with the film. There were other things I wanted to address that fell by the wayside. One of the reasons Lili pursued further surgery was that she was interested in finding out whether or not she could have a baby, and I said that was something extraordinary that we should explore, but again the feeling was that it would be very alienating. It was a sort of madness at the time for her to think that way, but look where we are now with these issues: she was just way ahead of the curve. So I fought that corner, and I fought the lesbian corner, and in the end, even though I would like to see a version with those elements in, it became clear that the producers were absolutely right, and that if you were looking for people to actually finance a film in this territory, it was already over the line.

The fateful favour which Gerda asks of Einar – to put on women's clothing and take the place of her absent subject in a portrait she's painting – comes right at the start of the novel. You spend a little more time establishing Gerda and Einar, including their respective achievements and ambitions as artists, before you get to that scene. What were the key things you were trying to set up in the first ten pages of the script?

I was interested in it as a love story, but also a love story between two artists. Two artists in a house, there's inevitably an element of competition – and for this couple, it's also heavily gendered. Gerda was incredibly underrated as a painter, and it seemed to me that we needed to bring that out, to make it clear they knew that being a woman came at a price. We also needed to understand that this relationship was full of give and take, that they were extremely comfortable as a couple, and that Einar was happy to do this for her. In the film, it comes out of Gerda having had a difficult experience, and in that moment Einar will act the woman and Gerda can act the man and she can feel better about herself as an artist and 'he' will enable her. It's about love and art, and gender and selfhood, and release and surrender. It's about personal realisation, I suppose, and about love and art as the tools for that realisation. Stories of courage come in all sorts of guises – with guns and on horses and in refugee camps – and this happens to be a story of courage that comes in silk stockings. A story of courage and of incredible imagination.

I wrote down a line from the novel about that: 'He'd begun to think of his make-up box as his palette.' In other words, Lili becomes Einar's life's work, the ultimate form of self-expression. And, in turn, Gerda's best work comes from capturing that transformation and interpreting it in her own style.

When you first see that painting, Einar's painting, and Gerda is looking at it, there's a sense that she's looking to understand him as well as looking at the brush strokes. She's fascinated by him as an artist, but she's also just fascinated by him. She's in a relationship with him and she has questions about him, and at that point in the film those questions are not articulated, but by the end of the film she's in the landscape of that painting and, finally, she knows. She understands the person she's been in love with all these years, no matter what name or gender they have gone by. You know, before a film is released, there's always a terrible marketing meeting where they show you these charts and tell you the demographic most likely to enjoy it. And obviously, that happened with *The Danish Girl*. The first time I saw the film with an audience was in Venice at the festival, and that's a very particular industry crowd so you can't glean much from the experience. Then, when I saw it in Toronto, it was with a much older, white North American audience, and I was frankly a bit nervous about their reaction. But people found it incredibly moving.

There were a lot of middle-aged men who would not have been in our subset on the marketing diagram, and one of them came over to me at the end of the screening and said he had gone out and phoned his wife because the film had made him think about their long journey together and he wanted to hear her voice. People who had been in seasoned marriages didn't think it was about trans issues; they thought it was about a long road, about the stuff you fight through together, and the compromises you make and whether you choose to self-actualise at the expense of someone else. What are the limits of love?

One of the themes of the novel is the extent to which we are all a product of our pasts, and whether we can efface the parts of our past which we no longer identify with, and there are sections devoted to Einar and Greta's lives before they met each other. In the film, Einar's past is dealt with through dialogue, while Gerda's past is barely mentioned. Were those easy cuts to make, or did you consider including some of that material via flashback?

We had an opening sequence for a while that was in flashback, of Einar as a child in his mother's wardrobe wearing his mother's clothes after her death. It was a seductive idea, but actually not a sufficiently specific one: the little boy in the lovely clothes, and the dad beating him because he wants to be pretty, felt a bit generic. It also felt like very hokey psychology: the child who has lost a beloved mother and is now over-identifying with her. The imaginative weight of a detail like that in a film is enormous, and it felt as if we were trying to explain Lili – and I didn't want to explain her, I wanted her to explain herself. So it went. And again, I wasn't interested in the before. It's a story that takes place in the present. As painters, and in their marriage, they're in the now, all the time.

The novel ends with Lili playing hooky from the hospital in Dresden with Anna and Greta's brother Carlisle, after Greta and her lover, Hans, have got together and left for America. The film ends with Lili dying at the hospital during a visit from Gerda, then Gerda and Hans visiting the place in Jutland which forms the first shot of the film and the subject of Einar's landscape painting. Both end with an image of unfettered flight – a kite in the novel, a scarf in the film – but your

ending, in some ways, is sadder than David Ebershoff's, which is unusual in a commercial film. Again, can you talk about the interplay of fact and fiction there?

I wanted Gerda to be there at the end. I wanted them to go all the way down the road together. In reality, Gerda wasn't there at the end, she'd actually remarried – a marriage that didn't last very long, a rebound. But she and Lili were still very connected. Lili was going to come and stay with Gerda to recuperate when she came out of hospital, and there's a story – I can't remember if it's in *Man into Woman* or in another account – that Gerda was preparing the room for Lili and suddenly felt the air go cold... and she knew what had happened. So I felt that they still loved one another, that they were still taking care of one another and were still one another's primary emotional connection, and I wanted to honour that. The question of whether Lili would die in the film or not was really fraught, because on the one hand I was worried about the hetero-normative ending where the LGBT character dies and the 'straight' character gets a boyfriend, but on the other hand I wanted to be honest about Lili's courage and the fact that, even though she lived, really lived to the fullest degree, the surgery did kill her. They had friends who thought that the surgeon should have been prosecuted; who thought that she was murdered, essentially, by surgeons who had gone too far. The type of surgery Lili was going through was performed by people who learned their trade on the battlefields of the First World War, and I think she knew that she was risking her life. And in the end, I thought it would be wrong to shy away from that.

Tomas Alfredson and Lasse Hallström were attached to direct at different points before Tom Hooper came on board. You said the script didn't change much over a decade, but presumably all three of them had their own ideas about it?

I did maybe ten drafts with small changes before the different directors came in, then I did a pretty big rewrite for Tomas, until we had quite a different film – though I think we would have gone back to something more like what we'd had to begin with – then I did a less radical rewrite for Lasse, then I did a very big rewrite for

Tom, and then it kind of slipped back to where we started. When directors board a project, they're often playing catch up. If you've been working on something for ten years and someone comes in and says, 'I've had this brilliant idea about how to do it differently,' you probably have tried to do it differently and there's a good reason why it hasn't worked. There's a process of directors needing to get across the territory, to get up to their elbows in the project, and a lot of the time you're conscious that the rewrite you're working on, the pages you're showing them, are things that will never make it into the film. You have to decide how much you trust a director, or get more skilled in understanding why they're asking for a rewrite, because the risk is that you deliver something you're unhappy with – and you're then stuck with it. So we did have a very different version of *The Danish Girl*, and then Tom and Alicia and Eddie went into a week of rehearsals, just the three of them very early on, and Tom rang me and said, 'This new version is great, and Eddie and Alicia have had some ideas, and we're really looking forward to showing you what we've got.' I went in and there was this cut-and-paste version they'd come up with, and we all read it and I thought, 'Okay, it's already in a version I'm not happy about, and now the actors and director have had a go it's in a version I'm even less happy about. So what am I going to do?' But I didn't have to do anything. There was a pause at the end of the reading where we all looked at each other, then Alicia said, 'Shall we just do the script we had at the beginning?' and everyone very quickly said, 'Yes, let's do that.' So that's what happened. And it was a great and happy moment for me, as you can imagine. But those detours are important. Everyone had gone through the process they needed to go through and we reverted to something very close to the script we had begun with. There was really valuable input from various colleagues and a fair bit of fine-tuning, but what Tom shot was, in the main, the last draft I wrote independently – the last best draft.

Andrew Davies

Andrew Davies was born in 1936 in Rhiwbina, Cardiff. He has written original series and single dramas for television, plays for stage and radio, and novels for adults and children.

Since 1975 he has amassed more than 50 screen adaptation credits, including dramatisations of novels by Kingsley Amis, Jane Austen, John Banville, Maeve Binchy, Joanna Briscoe, John Cleland, Dennis Danvers, Daniel Defoe, R.F. Delderfield, Charles Dickens, Michael Dobbs, Alexandre Dumas, George Eliot, Helen Fielding, E.M. Forster, Elizabeth Gaskell, George and Weedon Grossmith, Alan Hollinghurst, Winifred Holtby, Elizabeth Jane Howard, Victor Hugo, Angela Lambert, John le Carré, Boris Pasternak, William Makepeace Thackeray, Leo Tolstoy, Anthony Trollope, Sarah Waters, Evelyn Waugh, Mary Wesley and Angus Wilson.

Four of his TV adaptations have won BAFTA Drama Serial or Single Drama Television Awards, and he was jointly nominated for the BAFTA Best Adapted Screenplay Film Award for *Bridget Jones's Diary*.

In December 2018, he was the subject of a BBC documentary, *Andrew Davies: Rewriting the Classics*.

APPROACHES TO ADAPTATION

Do you think adaptations involve a completely different set of creative gears to original screenplays?

Not entirely, but yes, substantially. I think one of the reasons I do a lot of adaptations is that actually thinking up stories is something I find quite difficult.

Do you always agree a mission statement or direction of travel with whoever has commissioned the adaptation?

No. They're getting me because either they love working with me, or they love my work, or they think it will give them a better chance of getting the thing on. I mean, of course we discuss it beforehand and confirm that we have a similar approach to the subject.

Do you usually produce an outline or treatment before you start writing the script?

Yes, there has to be one. I need one. Recently I've been working with the same people, so we have a lunch and we talk about it and someone starts batting an outline about – it might be me, it might be them – and it goes back and forth a few times – sometimes only once or twice – until I feel ready to start writing.

If you're offered material to adapt which has been adapted previously, do you take account of any previous versions when writing yours?

Yes, I do. It can be bad, but I generally find that I'm not too swayed by theirs. The thing you have to watch out for is unconscious plagiarism: you think you've come up with an original idea – and bloody hell, there it was in some adaptation by someone else that you saw years ago. So I do usually look at existing ones if I can bear to.

If the author of the source material is living, do you find it useful to have their input on the script?

Oh, yes. It's only courteous to meet them, and often I've found it extremely helpful. It's good to find out what they feel, and what they think is particularly important. Sarah Waters is a prime example, because she was writing about a world I knew little of. She's also someone who's extremely movie-literate, and understands that adaptations are not going to be literal copyings-out of the novel.

In fact, in the BBC documentary, she says that seeing your screenplays of her novels, and how you get to the heart of scenes, has been an education in terms of her own writing.

Yes. Gosh. I thought, 'That's good!' Novelists don't often view storytelling in such a ruthless way – which you have to when you're writing scripts. Elizabeth Jane Howard [*author of* Falling] was rather disappointed, I think, that I didn't use all of her dialogue and do a kind of setting-out of her book in script form.

Is it easier to navigate notes from directors, producers and script editors when you have a piece of source material to measure the screenplay against?

It can be, yes. You're more likely to understand what they're on about. Sometimes, especially if it's your own original piece, notes come in and you think, 'What on earth is going through their heads?' So yes, it is easier.

Have you ever started work on an adaptation and found it harder to adapt than you anticipated?

Almost every time [*laughs*]. Some have been more difficult than others. *Doctor Zhivago* was an exceptionally difficult one. Of course I was very familiar with the David Lean movie, which tells a wonderful story and has some wonderful scenes in it – then you read the book and you realise there are hardly any scenes in it, he just lightly refers to things. So it was a question of making up a lot of the scenes in accordance with what Pasternak must have imagined happened, and also steering clear of what David Lean did. So that was a very hard one.

Have you ever been offered material to adapt which you felt couldn't, or shouldn't, be adapted?

Well, often in the sense that I didn't think it was worth doing. But things that exist very much on the page? No. No one's ever asked me to adapt some of the more obscure Virginia Woolf things, and I'd turn them down. One of the ones I'm working on now, *A Suitable Boy*, I read ten or fifteen years ago because someone wanted me to adapt it, and I found it an absolutely lovely read but I thought, 'It's probably much better if it stays the way it is.' And then, more recently, the people at Lookout Point, who I did *War & Peace* and *Les Misérables* with, were so enthusiastic about it and said we'd have such fun doing it – and indeed that turned out to be the case. But it's such an enormous book that you can't really represent the whole complexity, the whole panorama, the vast number of characters and plots in it. What's come out is six hours, but it should have been eight, and it would have been really good at ten or more. It's going to feel very tight at six. But it's such a beautifully written book and so funny, that it was a joy to work on.

Are there any screen adaptations which you think are especially good or you particularly admire?

I can think of a couple off the top of my head. One is Christopher Hampton's script for *Dangerous Liaisons* and another is Hossein Amini's version of *The Wings of the Dove* – a terrific adaptation and extraordinarily moving. I'm not a great reader of Henry James, but it felt of its age and somehow very modern as well. I should also mention two by Tom Stoppard: *Anna Karenina* and *Parade's End*. The film of *Anna Karenina* was disappointing, but the screenplay was exemplary. And *Parade's End* was so much better than the book: incisive, sharp, funny. And some of the big old traditional things, like David Lean's *Great Expectations*. I can't remember who actually wrote the screenplay for that, but with a David Lean movie you think of him having a big input into the script. So those are a few I particularly admire.

ADAPTING FICTION

Some writers try to include as much of the novel as possible by boiling scenes down to their essence. Others are more ruthless in editing it down to a sort of greatest hits, but being true to the spirit of it. Do you favour either of those approaches?

No, not really. What I tend to do is ask fundamental questions like, 'What is this book about?' and 'Whose story is it?' and 'Who do we care about?' and 'How can they carry us through the story?'. Then I'm hoping to find stuff in the book that I can lift out and make it do the job, and if not I'm just going to have to make the scenes up. But when I do make scenes up, people don't say, 'You made those scenes up,' they say, 'That was so true to the book!'

Well, if you've got it right, they'll say that. If you've got it wrong, they're more likely to notice.

I suppose that's true, yes.

If a novel has an unusual structure, would you try to reproduce that in adapting it?

Not necessarily. But sometimes it can be something good and something that's a bit of a revelation because it's not something I would have thought of. *The Line of Beauty* has got big gaps between the three sections of the narrative, and Nick [*lead character in the novel*] almost seems to be a different person because he's in a slightly different world in each one, but of course he's not different. So the construction of the novel was very clever, and I did follow that and I think it worked.

Do you try to avoid voiceover in adapting a first-person narrative, or do you see it as another tool in the toolbox?

I do see it as another tool in the toolbox, but I know it can be used in a very lazy way by people who can't make the effort to do it in actions. One of the biggest mistakes I've seen in an adaptation – though it was a film which was very well liked – was the Edith Wharton film, *The Age of Innocence*, which has a past-tense voiceover. That immediately tells you, 'This is old shit. It's not happening now. It all happened long ago,' and holds you back as an audience from entering the story. There were some lovely performances in that film and some very beautiful cinematography, but if a movie is anything it's in the present tense. So I suppose you could call it a boldly original use of voiceover, but I just thought it was a mistake.

Do you use the language of the novel in writing the dialogue, or do you put the whole thing in your own words?

It depends. Some novelists write dialogue that plays well and some don't. Jane Austen, you can just copy out. She writes too much for a scene – she was very skilful at dialogue and enjoyed exercising that skill at length – but I think you're a fool if you don't use her language. It makes the job so much easier, really. Vikram Seth is another one who writes lovely dialogue: very funny, very apt, very neat. Other people, it seems like good dialogue when you're reading the novel, but when you put it down and imagine someone actually speaking it, it doesn't work.

Do you keep the novel beside you throughout the adaptation process, or do you try to internalise it and set it aside somewhere along the way?

I keep it pretty close. [*Sees me eyeing a battered book on the table*] That's not a novel, actually, but I'm keeping it pretty close. It's a book about the last Empress of China, by Marina Warner. Terribly hard, that, because you have the facts, in a sense, but every time I start to write a scene I have this voice inside me saying, 'You've got no idea what these people are like!' But yes, I do keep the book by me to refer to. There was a producer who was very much a mentor to me years ago, Louis Marks – I did *Middlemarch* with him, amongst other things – and he said that when you reach a problem with an adaptation, if it's a great writer then you'll find the answer in the book. I think that's true.

I was quite surprised to see the Marina Warner book there, because among your many adaptations almost none are of nonfiction.

Mr Selfridge was based on a biography, and what we could find out about his life and his business. But yes, generally I would rather adapt a novel.

Perhaps because nonfiction is closer to original material: you have to invent more of the story, which you said you find difficult.

Yes, I expect so.

How much pressure do you feel when adapting a well-known and much-loved novel, knowing that you won't be able to please everyone with the finished product?

When I first started *Pride and Prejudice* I was feeling that pressure, but not so much these days. I certainly don't want to disappoint myself, because presumably it's a book I love too, but that's really all I think about when I'm adapting it. Of course, I hope everyone's going to like it – but if they don't, I don't care.

THREE DECADES OF ADAPTATIONS: *HOUSE OF CARDS* TO *LES MISÉRABLES*

Between the late sixties and the early nineties you mainly wrote original material. Since then, you've mainly written adaptations. Do you feel that the material you choose to adapt, and the way you choose to adapt it, reflects your own voice as much as original work would?

Probably not quite as much, but it can't help doing so. It's one of those things that's easier for other people to tell me: 'This is just like you.' And you think, 'No, it's just a job I was doing.' But I was quite struck in that documentary by what Jane Tranter [*former Controller of Drama Commissioning at the BBC*] was saying about what I did. I thought, 'Oh!'

***House of Cards* and its sequels are comparatively unusual among your work in having contemporary settings – even the modern fiction**

you've adapted is often set in the past. Do you find period pieces more interesting?

No, I don't, though for the purposes of long-form television nineteenth-century fiction is often much better because there's more story to it, combined with really deep and interesting characters, and some subtlety and reflection of society. So that's the reason. I've written quite a lot of scripts that are contemporary which never got made.

So it's dictated by the market? Period pieces are more popular?

And famous books – well-known titles. They're just easier to raise money on.

Do you approach classic and modern fiction in the same way, by asking the same questions: what is this book about, whose story is it?

I think I do, yes.

You've written for the stage as well as the screen, and Francis Urquhart's monologues in *House of Cards* are strongly reminiscent of Richard III's soliloquies. Do you think there's a theatrical element in other adaptations you've done?

Sometimes. In *House of Cards* it was something I felt needed doing, and I was heavily encouraged to do that by Michael Wearing [*former Head of Serials at the BBC*] and really enjoyed going for it. Using talking to camera in television is a dangerous thing, but I come back to it from time to time. In fact, I'm doing it with this [*points to* The Dragon Empress]: she talks to us from the nineteenth century, understanding that we're in the twenty-first century. Might be great, might be a disaster. It's going to be six parts and I've written two so far and those seem to have gone over well, so fingers crossed.

You've adapted several authors more than once, but the one you've returned to most often is Jane Austen. Do you feel a particular affinity with her work?

I've always loved her work, ever since I was a boy. I just think she's brilliant. Actually, another of the things I'm working on is *Sanditon*

[*Austen's unfinished final novel*]. The ambition is to do it rather like *Mr Selfridge* and turn it into a returning series. In fact, I only found enough material in the novel for half of the first episode. It's about 100 pages, and all she does is introduce the characters and give us the setting – but what characters and what a setting, because it's such a departure for her. There's an entrepreneurial businessman trying to turn a seaside town into a fashionable resort, making plans and borrowing money and courting celebrities. There's the old town and the new town. There's a West Indian heiress with a huge fortune. Fancy that: Jane Austen, on her deathbed, writing her first black leading character. So that's the world of the novel, and I'm really excited about it.

Your approach to *Pride and Prejudice* was to tell the story as much through Mr Darcy's eyes as through Elizabeth Bennet's. How important is point of view in your adaptations?

It's very important. In *War & Peace* it was a big decision. You couldn't say there was a single person at the heart of it. I guess Pierre slightly edges it over Natasha and Andrei, but Natasha and Andrei are also important, and the people close to them are almost as important, and so on. I was consciously thinking that the ideal was to have a scene with the three of them in, but I kept each of them very much in the foreground, and if they're not in a scene it helps to have someone talking about them or thinking about them.

If I had to pinpoint the leading character, I think I would have said Pierre, and not just because Paul Dano is top billed. The way his story threads through all the rest makes him a kind of Candide figure.

That's a good analogy. No one else has said that. But it's true. He's a bit of a holy idiot, isn't he? He makes all these mistakes...

But he never stops being lovable.

That's right. Andrei can be a bit of a cold, sarcastic shit, but he loves Pierre, so you think, 'We won't dismiss Andrei, because he's got a heart.' But he's so misogynistic, Andrei.

In the book, or in the adaptation?

Well, both, really. You can't escape it. He's so contemptuous of women. He gets it from his father. I suppose, like Darcy, deep inside he's just longing for love.

I saw you interviewed at the Hay Festival not long after your TV adaptation of *Sense and Sensibility*, and in the Q&A an audience member pointed out that it opens with a sex scene, which isn't in the novel – and you said, 'No, but it's where I felt Jane Austen was heading.' It's a characteristically irreverent answer, but it reflects one of the jobs of an adapter, doesn't it, which is to dramatise subtext – even to write the scenes which the authors perhaps would have written if they could have?

There's more of a justification for starting *Sense and Sensibility* with a sex scene, because you learn late on in the novel that this happened, that Willoughby seduced a 15-year-old girl, had a great time with her in this cottage, then rode off and forgot all about her, which is a very Regency thing to do. There's lots of dark and bad sexual behaviour in Jane Austen that is always kind of there but never makes it into the scene, and I thought, 'If it happened, let's get it on the screen.' I also wanted to meet that girl again when she's had her baby – she's still hoping that Willoughby is going to come back, and Colonel Brandon has to disillusion her – because I wanted the audience to think as badly of Willoughby as I do. I think he normally gets away with it.

So you don't necessarily love all the characters you write?

He's a bit of an exception, Willoughby. Usually I do try to love all the characters, but I thought Jane Austen herself was far too gentle with Willoughby. I saw him as someone who carried a kind of seduction kit with him, with the appropriate poems and things like that: 'This one will do. This one will get this girl on her back.'

Bridget Jones's Diary is probably your most prominent feature film credit, and an appropriate one given the novel's debt to *Pride and Prejudice*. What insights were you able to bring to the former adaptation from the latter?

When I was asked if I'd like to write a draft of this – and there were many drafts – I think it was me who tilted it in the direction of romantic comedy. Helen Fielding had written a first draft and it was very funny, but she was of the view that it was a movie about the urban family and how important these friendships were. I thought that in terms of what the story was about – or should be about – her friends were an irrelevance and that it was really a comic modern version of *Pride and Prejudice*. And that's the way it went. But I don't think a single line of dialogue I wrote survived.

Another author you've returned to several times is Dickens, and your take on *Bleak House* was like a nineteenth-century soap opera: speedy, gritty, half-hour episodes, full of twists, turns, conflicts and cliffhangers. Did you have in mind the original serial form of the novel, and did you in any way try to mirror its episode structure?

Yes, we did. When I say 'we', it was principally me and the producer, Nigel Stafford-Clark, but we were encouraged by Jane Tranter, who more or less challenged us to come up with a new way of telling these classic stories. We looked first at doing it in 20 half-hour episodes, and that shrank to 18 and then to 16 – not wholly for budget reasons, it just made it tighter and stronger. So yes, we were aware of the serial structure, but we didn't try to follow Dickens' episodes, because Dickens doesn't get the story started until you're about 100 pages in, and I wanted to get the story started on page one. The director, Justin Chadwick, was also very influential in getting across the feeling we wanted.

And Susanna White, presumably, who directed the last seven of the eventual 15 episodes.

Yes. The thing is, when you're doing the later episodes you're getting into the deeper bits of the story and things coming to an absolute crunch, and she did that beautifully. But really she had to match

Justin's style, which was revolutionary for a period piece, with a lot of handheld cameras.

To what extent was that style already present on the page? Do you try to guide the camerawork via the stage directions?

Absolutely I do. Directors will say, 'I'm not going to work with this bugger,' if you try to write shots, but I do try to write what the audience will see, and I do try to write what the characters are feeling – to indicate that I don't want some great wide shot. I try to influence the director as much as I can through the script, because I'm not going to be able to do it afterwards. So my scripts do clearly indicate how you could shoot it, but I know that there are other ways – and I like to be surprised in a good way by a director.

The 30-minute, twice-weekly format remains unusual. Do you feel that British TV drama is still too much in thrall to the one-hour Sunday night slot?

No, I don't. Well, I don't know – it suits me! It suits me as an audience member as well. I preferred watching *Bleak House* in one-hour chunks.

Because the two episodes were repeated back to back on the Sunday of each week?

That's right. Now, of course, and it's happened so quickly, you've got the bingeing thing – and I binge along with the rest. But I do like going out in weekly intervals because it gives it a chance to sink in, and people – you hope – are going to talk about it – and the papers – you hope – are going to pick up on it, not just review the first episode and then forget about it. Such a lot of effort is put into making something like *The Crown*, and it's gone in a weekend if you're not able to control yourself.

Your more recent adaptations have all been in a six-part, six-hour format – though the last episode of *Les Misérables* was feature length. Is there an overarching three-act structure to that? And do you use three-act structure within episodes?

Six hours just tends to be what people can afford and what people like. Less than that is hard to sell, I think, and more starts being too expensive. But no, I've never found three-act structure very helpful. I sometimes wonder where it came from. And actually, most things that people say have a three-act structure, you could say, 'No, they're not, they're one act,' or, 'They're five acts.'

You just let the stories find their natural shape?

Yes. I mean, obviously I'm very traditional about liking a good cliffhanger ending to an episode, so you leave people thinking, 'Wow! Now what?'

***War & Peace* is possibly your most ambitious adaptation to date. A thousand-page novel, even over six hours, doesn't give you the luxury of being leisurely. Would you have liked it to be longer?**

Yes. It could have been a good eight episodes, really. It's amazing how things spread in the filming. Some lovely stuff got written and not filmed, and some lovely stuff got filmed and didn't make it in the edit.

What struck me most about it was not the big sweeping scenes but the small intimate moments, which have more impact because of the amount of time you get to spend with the characters. You get to know and care about them, and feel as if you've been on a real journey with them, which is harder to achieve in a two-hour feature film.

That's absolutely true. I guess you do get that feeling with great movies, and great movie directors take the time to just *be* with characters – and often I think the most important thing is to be with them when they're not saying or doing anything.

Do you think it will always be a struggle to condense a novel of more than 300 pages into a 120-page script? That the novel will inevitably require more radical reinvention to fit into feature length?

It depends on the novel. Some modern novels, however long, have barely enough in them for half an hour's drama. But yes, it's tricky. *Brideshead Revisited* is about 300 pages, but there's a lot in those 300 pages, and it's difficult to do as a movie – though I quite enjoyed having a crack at it. Evelyn Waugh, by the way, is one of those people who writes great economical dialogue.

And *Brideshead* is a project where you definitely have to take account of a previous adaptation.

My notion was to write a sort of counter-text: interpreting it in a way that Evelyn Waugh would have disliked strongly. My take on it was that it was about some people who had been completely fucked up by their version of the Roman Catholic religion, so the mother was the villain of the piece and I wanted Charles to be more straightforwardly atheist. I was very pleased with my screenplay, but it was a tough business and there were a lot of drafts – more than I usually care to do!

Which is how many?

About three, really. And I aim to finish up with something as close to the first draft as possible.

With more epic novels, do you employ any strategies for introducing large casts of characters? In *War & Peace*, for example, we meet a lot of characters in a single scene at a party right at the start.

That was perhaps a bit ambitious in terms of remembering it afterwards. Pierre, I guess, is the crucial character there, and people are going to realise that, but you get to know Andrei a little. But I also needed to get across St Petersburg society, which was very un-Russian and French-ified, so there was a lot to do at the same time – and you just hope that the audience is going to keep up with it.

And continue to keep up with it – which means that you as the dramatist can't afford to lose track of any one story strand for too long.

Yes. Even though Tolstoy goes in for a lot of not very useful subplots and supporting characters, he's actually very helpful in that way. You can see he has it in the back of his mind: we're going to need to come back to Natasha, or we haven't heard from Maria for a bit, so let's think of a plot twist, like an army manoeuvre, to bring Nikolai into that part of the country, and so on.

Les Misérables **is equally epic, but, initially at least, as fast and fleet as a thriller. Do you often have a particular screen genre in mind when adapting a piece of fiction?**

No. It's just that when you're doing it, it sometimes turns out that way.

There's more than just character and plot in Dickens, Tolstoy and Hugo, there's history, politics and ideas as well. How do you incorporate those things, which may be intrinsic to the author's intentions, without detracting from the story you're telling?

Well, if they really are important, they have to be important to your favourite characters, so you have to find a way of introducing them. Tolstoy's ideas, for example, are expressed to a large extent by Pierre as he's fumbling his way towards them.

How do you avoid melodrama – in other words, plot driving character, rather than character driving plot – when compressing these huge incident- and coincidence-packed narratives into just a handful of episodes?

I think by reminding myself that character is the most important thing, and by finding ways to make sure that what the characters want – or what they're trying to avoid – has led them to a certain point. There are still loads of coincidences left in *Les Misérables*. We drastically reduced them, but weren't able to do without them completely.

You have more than 50 adaptations to your credit, not counting unproduced scripts, the vast majority of those in the last three decades. Are you still learning things about the art of screen adaptation?

I hope so. It would be nice to think I was. I feel like I might still be getting better. But I may just be going into a gradual decline [*laughs*].

War & Peace **would suggest otherwise.**

Thank you. I'll keep that in mind!

Christopher Hampton

Christopher Hampton was born in 1946 in Faial, Azores. He has written nine original plays, including *Total Eclipse* (1968, filmed 1995) and *Tales from Hollywood* (1983), and numerous stage adaptations and translations, most notably *Les Liaisons Dangereuses* (1985), based on the novel by Choderlos de Laclos and filmed as *Dangerous Liaisons* (1988) from his Oscar- and BAFTA-winning screenplay.

His other screen adaptation credits include: *The History Man* (1981, novel by Malcolm Bradbury); *The Honorary Consul* (1983, novel by Graham Greene); *The Quiet American* (2002, novel by Graham Greene); *Atonement* (2007, novel by Ian McEwan); *A Dangerous Method* (2011, from his play *The Talking Cure* and the book *A Most Dangerous Method* by John Kerr); *The Singapore Grip* (2020, novel by J.G. Farrell); and *The Father* (2020, play by Florian Zeller). He also directed his own screenplays of *Carrington* (1995, book *Lytton Strachey* by Michael Holroyd); *The Secret Agent* (1996, novel by Joseph Conrad); and *Imagining Argentina* (2003, novel by Lawrence Thornton).

The case studies in this chapter, *Atonement* and *A Dangerous Method*, open with edited extracts from the Faber book *Hampton on Hampton*. When the book was published, neither film had been made (*Atonement* was subsequently Oscar- and BAFTA-nominated for Best Adapted Screenplay); the extracts therefore provide the background to those projects, while new interviews explore their subsequent development.

APPROACHES TO ADAPTATION

Do you prefer to adapt material which chimes with your own work, or material which is completely different and gives you a chance to try out new things?

I always like to feel a connection with it. So I'll accept the commissions that spark something, and sometimes – as with *Atonement* – I'll actually go out and campaign to get the job. It would be hard for me to say exactly why *Atonement* struck me so forcibly; it doesn't happen very often. I just had a very strong instinct that I wanted to do it.

Do you think adaptations involve a completely different set of creative gears to original screenplays?

Clearly it calls on different skills. It's more technical and the decision-making is in a slightly sideways compartment to what you do when you write original stuff. When you're doing original stuff, I find you've got some big ideas but you don't quite know how they're going to work out, and it's only two-thirds of the way through writing them that you start to work out why you're doing it and what they're about. Whereas, of course, with an adaptation, it's all laid out for you – though I do like adaptations that give you some leeway and freedom, *Dangerous Liaisons* being the prime example.

Do you always agree a mission statement or direction of travel with whoever has commissioned the adaptation?

They like to. I don't. I'm about to do a screenplay based on Julian Barnes's novel *The Noise of Time*, about Shostakovich, and I went to St Petersburg last year and discussed with the producers how I was going to do it. Then I found that in the contract they require a treatment – which is very puzzling, because you're adapting a novel, so what do they want a treatment for? So I said, 'Do I have to do this?' and they said, 'Oh, yes, we always have one to show the investors.' But my experience – and again, this goes back to *Atonement* – is that these things evolve as you do them and get better ideas. What I pitched to Ian McEwan to get that job bore absolutely no resemblance to the finished film.

If you're offered material to adapt which has been adapted previously, do you take account of any previous versions when writing yours?

No. I mostly take particular care not to look at anyone else's. I did see the previous version of *The Quiet American* ages ago, a film which riled Graham Greene tremendously because the American of the title was transformed into a hero – and played by a war hero – in order to say, 'This man is crusading against Communism,' not to say what the book said, which is, 'This man has misunderstood the situation and will shortly contribute to causing a massive catastrophe.'

If the author of the source material is living, do you find it useful to have their input on the script?

I would have liked to have met Graham Greene on *The Honorary Consul*, but he refused to meet me – and I subsequently discovered that was because he had written his own script and been fired. So fair enough. If I'd known that, I wouldn't have done it. Apart from that, I've had very good relationships with adaptees, Ian McEwan being one of them and Malcolm Bradbury another. On *The History Man*, I got together with Malcolm to work out new scenes that weren't in the book but I felt were necessary, and he joined in with gusto. In fact, he joined in with such gusto that he spent the rest of his life adapting novels for television. And Ian was very interesting on *Atonement*, because he was quite involved in the early stages and then gradually withdrew as it took shape. I used to think he was like the Cheshire Cat, finally just a benevolent smile – which is the ideal way for an author to be. So if they're around, I really like to have their input, but I suppose it depends on the temperament of the adaptee.

Is it easier to navigate notes from directors, producers and script editors when you have a piece of source material to measure the screenplay against?

Yes. I think you can always hold up the original and say, 'Look: this works.' Unless you can make a really good case for why we shouldn't stick with the original, let's stick with the original. I learned from reading the screenplays of Harold Pinter right at the beginning of my career that the better the source material, the closer you'd better stay to it, because why change something which is really good or that presumably inspired people to buy the rights in the first place?

Have you ever started work on an adaptation and found it harder to adapt than you anticipated?

I think that's true of a lot of them. Mind you, in a way, the degree of difficulty that something presents when you want to adapt it is an attraction for me. I like it if it's really difficult. I like the challenges.

Have you ever been offered material to adapt which you felt couldn't, or shouldn't, be adapted?

Michael Mann asked me to write *Manhunter*, which was the original Hannibal Lecter film. The book is called *Red Dragon* and I was quite shocked by it, because it felt so much more extreme than anything that had previously appeared. You might have felt the same if you'd been asked to adapt *Psycho*, and then you would have kicked yourself for the rest of your life if you hadn't. I feel slightly like that about *Manhunter*. But I did turn it down, specifically because the serial killer in it is a man who works for a photo lab developing home movies, and whenever he sees a particularly happy family he scopes out the area and then murders them all, and I thought that anyone who felt inclined to be a serial killer might think, 'That's quite a good idea.' It's absurd, but that's why I said no – and it's actually one of the few projects I've turned down that I regret.

Are there any screen adaptations which you think are especially good or you particularly admire?

There are lots. I still think Harold Pinter was the bee's knees at doing it. *The Go-Between* is one of my favourite adaptations. He really surpassed himself with that film. *L.A. Confidential*, by Curtis Hanson and Brian Helgeland, is a brilliant script, from a complicated book. *The Godfather* is pretty amazing, isn't it? And sometimes there's an adaptation that rewards studying. *Who's Afraid of Virginia Woolf?*, which is essentially the play, is so well organised, but that's almost more to do with Mike Nichols' direction. Likewise, Sidney Lumet's version of *Long Day's Journey into Night* is a textbook adaptation of a play as far as I'm concerned, because of how brilliantly he thought out every shot and turned it into cinema language without really doing anything to the text.

ADAPTING FICTION

Some writers try to include as much of the novel as possible by boiling scenes down to their essence. Others are more ruthless in editing it down to a sort of greatest hits, but being true to the spirit of it. Do you favour either of those approaches?

No, because I think every project requires a different approach. One of the jobs I've done since we did our book was an adaptation of *East of Eden*. Tom Hooper [*director of* The King's Speech] asked me if I'd do it, and I said, 'Are you insane? Aren't you aware that there's already an absolute masterpiece?' He said, 'Have you read the book?' I said no. So he gave me the book, which is about 600 pages long, and the James Dean character doesn't really appear until page 400: the first 400 pages are about the characters played in the Elia Kazan film by Raymond Massey and Jo Van Fleet, and how she came to leave him and set up a brothel in San Francisco catering mostly to sadomasochists. I realised that the 1950s *East of Eden* is an absolutely sensational adaptation. It's by a playwright called Paul Osborn, and he and Kazan obviously realised that they were already skating as close to the wind as they possibly could with it, and said, 'Let's just do this last bit of the book, which is containable.' And that was a brilliant decision, but it also meant that I could say yes and do something completely different. Needless to say, they didn't make the film, but the script is one of the ones in recent years that I'm most pleased with.

If a novel has an unusual structure, would you try to reproduce that in adapting it?

We'll talk more about this when we get on to *Atonement*, because that has an unusual structure. But I was anxious to preserve that right from the word go. What I didn't anticipate was just how closely I was going to wind up following it.

Do you try to avoid voiceover in adapting a first-person narrative, or do you see it as another tool in the toolbox?

Unless voiceover is actually built into the plot, as it is in *Sunset Boulevard* and *Double Indemnity* – Billy Wilder was very fond of it – and as it was in my original draft of *Atonement*, it always seems to me like an admission of failure. So I don't care for it. When *The Quiet American* was being edited, Phillip Noyce – who I got on with very well and I think made a very good film – asked me to do a voiceover, and I said, 'I don't think we need one.' In the end they got Anthony Minghella to do it, and on the rare occasions when I see the film it still seems completely unnecessary. Similarly, on *A Bright Shining Lie [unproduced adaptation of Neil Sheehan's nonfiction book about Lieutenant Colonel John Paul Vann and the war in Vietnam, later directed by Terry George from his own script]*, Oliver Stone demanded a voiceover when he took over, and I thought that was completely wrong because the main character wasn't a ruminative character, he was a man of action. So I refused – and later heard that Oliver said I was very uncooperative.

Do you use the language of the novel in writing the dialogue, or do you put the whole thing in your own words?

Some novelists know how to write good dialogue – and in that case, why change it? Quite a lot of the dialogue in *Atonement* comes from the novel. If you adapt Joseph Conrad, his plotting is great but his dialogue is hopeless. That's partly because he wasn't English, so all the characters talk alike and none of them sound convincing, and you've got to go in and find an appropriate language for them. Graham Greene's dialogue is good, though a touch over-explanatory. Every author presents different problems and opportunities.

Do you keep the novel beside you throughout the adaptation process, or do you try to internalise it and set it aside somewhere along the way?

I keep it beside me. I don't look at it obsessively, but it's pointless not to refer to it when you need to.

How much pressure do you feel when adapting a well-known and much-loved novel, knowing that you won't be able to please everyone with the finished product?

I don't mind that.

ADAPTING NONFICTION

When adapting a book, fiction or nonfiction, do you rely on the author's research, or do you conduct your own?

I like to do my own. For *The Noise of Time*, I've done quite a lot of research on Shostakovich. His life is very well documented, so it's interesting to know the context from which Julian Barnes has selected particular incidents, and when you're writing a dramatic scene there may be something useful in some of the letters. I enjoy all that anyway. I just love research. With *A Bright Shining Lie*, I spent about a year on it.

Do you approach a nonfiction adaptation in the same way as fiction, or does the strangeness of real events give you licence to experiment with, say, structure?

That's an interesting question. I did a script two or three years ago, based on a book called *Heart of a Soldier*, about Rick Rescorla, the Englishman on 9/11 who decided to ignore the instructions coming from the Port Authority and got nearly 2,700 people out of the World Trade Center. He was head of security for Morgan Stanley, based in the South Tower, and only a handful of people from the firm were killed, and one of them was him: he kept going back in until the whole thing came down. There was actually a TV documentary about him called *The Man Who Predicted 9/11*, because he was aware of the threat of Osama Bin Laden, and he kept trying to get people to pay attention and they wouldn't. But the book is a biography of his life and he was a bit of an adventurer. He joined the Ugandan or Tanganyika police force but balked at colonialism. He made friends with an American soldier in Africa and went back with him to America just as the Vietnam War was beginning, so he volunteered and was in Vietnam for a couple of years. Then he went back to America and was involved in all sorts of security jobs. There's a lot of incident in it. I discovered that he was at the Battle of Khe Sanh in Vietnam, and again, disregarding orders, he organised a fleet of helicopters to get people out who were surrounded and being picked off by the Viet Cong – and that seemed to set his character, really, as someone who was interested in saving people. So the film is in three sections. The first section is Vietnam, then you jump 30 years to when he first goes to work at the Twin Towers, and the last section is the day of 9/11. Of course, it's a massively expensive project, so I don't know whether anyone will ever do it, but it certainly isn't the sort of script you'd expect if you read the book.

Have you ever encountered events in a nonfiction book so strange that you couldn't use them in the adaptation because audiences wouldn't believe they were real?

No, I think you embrace all that. That's what makes it enjoyable: the things you couldn't make up.

How much responsibility do you feel towards historical accuracy when dramatising the lives of real characters?

Complete. I'm very conscientious about it. I've often had trouble in the past about this, because people say, 'Who's going to know?' Well, *I'm* going to know. It's sort of a religious feeling I have, respect for the facts.

How do you set about finding the voices of real characters, especially if there is little or no written or audio-visual research material in their own words?

With *A Bright Shining Lie*, there were boxes of tapes of John Paul Vann talking to people. The thing that concerned me – which is a slight side issue, but germane to what you're talking about – was that it was the first film I'd written with entirely American characters, and I wanted to get the language right. So I listened to him not only to hear what he was saying, but to focus on his turns of phrase and his linguistic foibles. When I handed it in, I was waiting for someone to say something about that, and eventually I said, 'Is the language all right?' and they said, 'What do you mean?' and I said, 'Well, I'm writing in American,' and they said, 'Oh, we hadn't noticed' – so clearly it worked. But I've always been a slightly ventriloquial dialogue writer. I'm not interested in imposing my style on the dialogue. I like each character to have their own vocabulary if possible, because even if audiences don't notice it, I feel it makes the characters believable.

Do you think that being based on a true story in some way gives a project more weight?

I don't, actually. But I do think the prestige of literature is such that you have a slightly easier ride with an adaptation of a well-loved novel than with a nonfiction book.

CASE STUDY: *ATONEMENT*

UK/France/US, 2007 ▪ **Directed by** Joe Wright ▪ **Produced by** Tim Bevan, Eric Fellner, Paul Webster ▪ **Screenplay by** Christopher Hampton, based on the novel by Ian McEwan ▪ **Cast:** James McAvoy (Robbie Turner), Keira Knightley (Cecilia Tallis), Romola Garai (Briony Tallis, aged 18), Saoirse Ronan (Briony Tallis, aged 13), Harriet Walter (Emily Tallis), Brenda Blethyn (Grace Turner), Vanessa Redgrave (older Briony)

My conversation with Christopher about *Atonement* formed part of a chapter in *Hampton on Hampton* which focused on his produced and unproduced screen adaptations written between the mid-1980s and the early 2000s, including a commission to adapt Deborah Moggach's novel *Tulip Fever* in 2001 (eventually filmed some 16 years later with a script credited to Moggach herself and Tom Stoppard). I started by asking whether he had found Ian McEwan's novel more difficult to adapt than the recent *Tulip Fever*.

It was technically more difficult, partly because it doesn't fall into the usual three-act structure. It's really a two-act structure, with the two acts pretty much equal in length – or, if anything, the first act a little longer than the second – which means that you have to manage a tremendous gear shift, from country house life in 1935 to the retreat from Dunkirk. I thought the best way to do that was the

THE ART OF SCREEN ADAPTATION

way *The Deer Hunter* did it, where you just go – bam! – from one world to another. I think *The Deer Hunter* is a more than dubious film, but it does have this brilliant effect in it: an extreme change of direction which galvanises the audience so that they trust you to bring the whole thing together again at the end. You also have to thread into those two acts the very short last section of the book, which reveals that it's been written by this character called Briony, who's a 13-year-old when the story starts, and that she wrote it to atone for this crime which she inadvertently committed as a girl. It's further revealed that she's been as truthful as she can in 75 per cent of the story, but, unable to come to terms with all the facts, she's invented a kind of happy ending for the lovers, which she has to confess is not what actually happened. Although this last section of the book is a real revelation, there are discussions and observations throughout about the nature of fiction which make it retrospectively logical, and you need to reproduce that so the ending doesn't just come out of nowhere. So that's the other technical difficulty.

How did you set about overcoming that?

You have to find a cinematic way of dealing with it, and my way of dealing with it was to start with this old lady and the manuscript on her desk called 'Atonement', without explaining who the old lady is. You don't know whether it's Briony or Cecilia – in fact, you're slightly misled in that respect – until halfway through the film, when you finally want to say, 'This is all seen from Briony's point of view.' In addition, I thought that this atonement of writing the book was not quite dramatically big enough, so I added the notion that she's led an entirely self-denying and celibate life to make up for what she did to her sister and her sister's lover. Everyone seems pretty pleased with the first draft, but it's early days yet. I think the thing to do is to write a second draft which is radically different in the way it deals with that particular problem, because the more different you can make the two, the more clearly people who are reading them can see which of the approaches works better.

* * *

You did ultimately write a radically different draft, after Richard Eyre left to make *Notes on a Scandal* and Joe Wright came on board in his place. But you wrote further drafts in between, working with Eyre as director and McEwan as executive producer. What form was the script in at the end of that period?

As I said, I originally had a voiceover, from older Briony, and every now and then, in the first half of the story, you'd see this old lady. For example, when Robbie is arrested and taken away, you'd cut to the upstairs window and it would be old Briony standing there. Also, the book is in four sections, getting shorter and shorter, and I'd intercut section two, the sequence in France leading up to Dunkirk, with section three, when Briony becomes a nurse, so that they happened simultaneously. That seemed to make sense, and Richard and Ian were happy with that approach. When Joe came on to the film, the first thing he said was, 'I like the script very much, but we're going to have to start from scratch.' He loved the structure of the novel, so he wanted to get back to that. And it became clear to me that, if you followed the structure of the novel, a huge problem was solved. We'd always imagined that the same actor would play Briony as a 13-year-old and Briony as an 18-year-old and that we would cast someone in her late teens. But by separating section one and section three by twenty-five minutes, or however long section two lasts, you could cast Saoirse Ronan and then come back to her as Romola Garai. I was worried about whether the audience would buy that, but of course it's the simplest thing in the world: you just give them a similar haircut and a mole. You could do it for Vanessa Redgrave as well, playing older Briony. The virtue of it was that you could do what the novel does and surprise everyone at the end, which I hadn't thought was as important as it turned out to be.

Earlier you mentioned Harold Pinter's adaptation of L.P. Hartley's novel *The Go-Between*, which I read was one of your inspirations in writing this script. Do you often have other adaptations in mind when approaching one of your own?

The three times I've directed, I've had a film that I looked at in detail. When I was doing *Carrington*, I used to watch *Jules et Jim* every weekend, because it's light and tragic at the same time and that's a very unusual combination – which I wanted to try to reproduce. When I was doing *The Secret Agent*, I was looking at *Touch of Evil*. And when I was doing *Imagining Argentina* – though by that time I didn't think *Imagining Argentina* was really like anything – I was watching Costa-Gavras's film about Uruguay, *State of Siege*, and his film about Chile, *Missing*. With *Atonement*, it was very helpful for me to think about Harold's version of *The Go-Between*. First because Ian's book, broadly speaking, is in the same family. It's about someone whose life is blighted by something that happens beyond their control as a child. Also because, if you have in your mind as a template an unconventional film that worked very well, you're not too frightened of being unconventional yourself. I just thought, 'If I can do it half as well as Harold did, we'll be quids in.'

The first half of the film – Part One of the novel – dramatises 187 pages in 47 minutes, and has to convey both the languor of a summer day and the tension of approaching calamity. How did you set about achieving that distillation and balance?

Presupposing that I did, again looking at *The Go-Between* was very helpful: the sense of heat and the claustrophobia of that house was very much in my mind. I also worked very closely with Joe. I wrote I don't know how many drafts, and then we went away for two weeks and just worked through it line by line. We had a very clear idea of the layout of the interior of the house, and who saw what through which door and when. Ian uses an interesting device in the book, where he tells you something at the beginning of a chapter, then goes through all the stages leading up to the thing you've been told. We wanted to find a cinematic equivalent of that, so we invented this device we called a flash sideways, where something would happen and then you would go back and explain it. For example, Briony goes to the window to free a wasp and sees what's going on down by the fountain, then you flash sideways and show what led up to that moment. We do that perhaps two or three times during the film, so it's not conventional in terms of its sequence of events.

Part One of the novel is told primarily from four points of view: Briony, Cecilia, their mother Emily, and Robbie. You've retained all those except Emily's, removing almost all of the chapter where she lies in bed with a migraine listening to the sounds and voices of the house and its inhabitants. Was that sort of intensely interior experience beyond the script's scope?

There was more of Emily in the early drafts, but you reach a moment where you think, 'Practically, the script ought not to be any longer than this,' and when you get to that point, you have to start throwing stuff out. You might do it in advance, or you might do it retrospectively, but you always have to subtract.

The opening of the novel is quite measured. The opening of the film is more propulsive, a quick tour of the house and introduction to some of its inhabitants, driven by the clack of the typewriter on the soundtrack. What tone and atmosphere were you aiming to establish and evoke with that opening?

We did that over I don't know how many times. The typewriter was an idea that Joe cooked up with the composer, Dario Marianelli, and once he explained it to me, and I realised where it was going, in a way that dictated the rhythm. He does direct rather musically. The sequence when Robbie is listening to Puccini in the bath and Cecilia is putting on this wonderful green dress was very much worked over because he had a musical notion about the whole thing. Also, aside from all that, I'm a great believer in getting as fast as possible to the meat of the subject.

In that image you described of Briony opening the window to let out a wasp, she looks directly into the camera as if acknowledging the audience – in other words, 'This is fiction' – and foreshadowing her on-camera appearance as an old woman in the TV interview. Was that always the intention?

That was Joe's idea, and a very good one. He worked a lot on finding reconciling images for the three actors, but I don't think that was in the script. I can't remember which of us hit on the idea of a TV interview, but it's a very good way to transition into that last section. In the book, old Briony has a conversation with her editor where she explains that she's dying and all the rest of it, so I originally had a version of that, but we weren't happy with it. I'm also a great believer in sitting down with the director; I like that process of analysing the script. At some point we realised that there was water symbolism throughout, starting with the fountain, then that scene of Briony jumping in the river and having to be rescued by Robbie, which was a tremendous issue in terms of where it was going to go: it was out and in and out and in. And in researching around the book, we discovered that when Balham tube station was bombed everyone drowned because the water main burst, which gave us the scene of the water coming down the stairs and Cecilia floating away. So the water imagery goes through all the way to the end, and was something else that we became conscious of as we were working.

There's a deleted scene on the DVD in which Briony, crying, rips the poster for the play she's written, partly because the rehearsal with her cousins didn't go well, partly because she's upset and confused by the sexually charged encounter between Robbie and Cecilia which she just witnessed from the window. There's also a detail in the novel about the romantic lead in her play being a poor doctor, obviously a character she's modelled lovingly on Robbie, who plans to go to medical school. It's almost as if, deprived of one drama, her play, she creates another, around Robbie, to make sense of events and feelings she can't understand or control. Do you think that the removal of that scene and that detail, and the consequent reduction in prominence of Briony's play in the first half of the film, make her motives for accusing Robbie more mysterious on screen than on the page?

Possibly, but you have to work back from a decision that Joe made. A different ending was shot, in which old Briony goes back to the house, now a hotel, and watches her play performed and speaks to the audience – and as she's speaking, she sees in the back row, sitting together, Robbie and Cecilia. One of the interesting things about the film for me was the willingness to re-examine what went on during the editing. In the last stages of the editing, Joe really transformed the film – and one of the things he did was to decide that the end wasn't working. So he threw it away, shot the scene on the beach that ends the film now – a more romantic ending that I think was suggested to him by Anthony Minghella – and then removed the bits and pieces that had to do with the play.

I'm interested that the scene where Briony jumps into the river so that Robbie will rescue her was in and out and in and out, because in the absence of the scenes relating to her play, it becomes the clearest explanation of why she reads his letter to Cecilia and then falsely alleges that he attacked her cousin.

Exactly. But it was very awkward to situate. It obviously couldn't go in the first section, because it happens something like two years before that.

In fact, it's placed in the film more or less where it's placed in the book, which is as a memory during the Dunkirk sequence.

Yes, I think that's right.

The France sequence in the film – Part Two of the novel – with the single, sweeping tracking shot of Dunkirk at its heart, is extraordinary, almost hallucinatory. What journey did that go on, from novel to script to screen, to arrive at its final form?

That's a perfect illustration of necessity being the mother of invention. In the script, right up until pre-production, it was a longer sequence, with the soldiers making their way through France, encountering columns of refugees, being strafed by Messerschmitts and so on. Then a few weeks before we were due to start, Working Title decided that the budget should be cut. There were whispers of, 'Are we making a 30 million dollar art movie?' and we were tasked with taking out five million. Clearly the most expensive bit was the French bit, so we focused on that and came up with this idea of incorporating as many of the things they would have encountered on their journey into one scene. It was Joe's idea to do it in a single shot. If we'd had that extra five million, I guess it would have been shot the way it was written. But we didn't have it and I think the film is all the better for it.

The scene in the film where Briony visits Robbie and Cecilia in Balham – a key moment in Part Three of the novel – contains a detail which you can convey much more clearly on screen than on the page: the fact that there's no scar on Robbie's chest, no sign of the wound he sustained in France, a visual clue that he never recovered from it, or even returned from Dunkirk.

That was probably the most rewritten scene in the entire film. Joe had an idea of what he wanted, but I couldn't grasp exactly what he meant. In fact, the scene is quite stylised, and is shot in a quite stylised way, and that was what he meant. He wanted to make it like it was a fictional scene in the middle of real scenes. That's what he was trying to do, and that's what he succeeded in doing. It's quite a strange scene, I think. But we certainly wanted to lay a couple of clues in that sequence.

How did the finished film compare to the version you had in your head when you first read the novel?

It's probably one of the projects I've done that I was most pleased with when I saw it. As we've said, you have a vague idea in your mind when you start which hopefully sharpens as you proceed, but every screenwriter is familiar with the dreaded moment where you can see it all going off the rails and heading for a different station altogether. That didn't ever happen. From the first meeting with Ian to the finished film, it was a process of travelling closer and closer to the novel, and I think that's because the novel is a masterpiece. So I was very happy about that.

CASE STUDY: *A DANGEROUS METHOD*

Germany/Canada/UK/US, 2011 ▪ **Directed by** David Cronenberg ▪ **Produced by** Jeremy Thomas ▪ **Screenplay by** Christopher Hampton, based on his stage play *The Talking Cure* and the book *A Most Dangerous Method* by John Kerr ▪ **Cast:** Keira Knightley (Sabina Spielrein), Viggo Mortensen (Sigmund Freud), Michael Fassbender (Carl Jung), Sarah Gadon (Emma Jung), Vincent Cassel (Otto Gross)

A Dangerous Method had a convoluted journey to the screen. Christopher initially adapted John Kerr's nonfiction book, *A Most Dangerous Method*, into an unproduced screenplay, *Sabina*, then turned that into a play, *The Talking Cure*. The play premiered at the National Theatre, London, in 2002, and was remounted at the Mark Taper Forum, Los Angeles, in 2004, before being turned back into the film. This section of *Hampton on Hampton* was recorded between the first and second productions of the play.

The story of Sabina Spielrein and Jung had been in the back of my mind since the late 1970s, when a book called *A Secret Symmetry* by Aldo Carotenuto gave the first inkling of this special relationship between them; but although I thought how interesting their story was and how interesting it would be to write something about psychoanalysis, perhaps the defining intellectual notion of the first half of the twentieth century, I did nothing about it. Then, in the mid-nineties, it surfaced as something that Julia Roberts' company was interested in and I went for it.

Was Julia Roberts interested in playing the part of Sabina?

Yes, she was. I was dealing mostly with her development person, a man called Pliny Porter, so things were largely filtered through him, but I had a lot of conversations with them about it, and I think Julia liked the screenplay. It was one of those projects where people said, 'We're looking forward to the next draft,' without saying what they thought the next draft should contain, so I just let it ride and didn't do another draft. Eventually, they produced a load of notes – and Fox also produced a load of notes – and, boiled down, these notes seemed to be saying that there was too much Jung in it and not enough Sabina. However, what was gradually dawning on me was the exact opposite: that the central character was Jung, because it was Jung who was torn between his wife and Sabina, and between Freud and Sabina, and that he had to be even more at the centre of it. I let various friends of mine read the screenplay and they all encouraged me to follow my instinct, which was to reorganise the material as a play, so that's what I did. [Julia] wrote me a very nice letter saying, 'Good luck with it.' In fact, both she and Fox were exceptionally generous about it.

Do you think the screenplay did things which the play couldn't, and vice versa?

The only thing I really miss from the screenplay is the sense of landscape, because there's something about the contrasting landscapes of Zürich and Vienna that tells you a lot about the characters of Jung and Freud, but I don't think there was anything essential in the screenplay which didn't make it into the play. I think the play is more effective than the screenplay – crucially the shift in focus from Sabina to Jung – but I'm actually reworking the play for America, because neither it nor the screenplay gave the Freud–Jung relationship its full weight. I want to get more of a sense of how excited they both were by their initial contact, in order to make the final split between them seem like a more momentous intellectual fracture. At the moment, their final argument is about the expunging of the names of Egyptian kings from their monuments by their sons, so the whole thing happens at one remove, and I think it would be better to have a scene where the gloves are off and they go for each other. I'm always being asked, in relation to screenplays, 'Why don't the characters just say what's on their minds?' and I usually feel that it's more interesting if you're able to see what's on their minds without them saying it, but in this case I probably erred in the direction of indirection. I think that's accurate, because I don't think Jung and Freud ever did say what was on their minds – and I was trying to respect that, because I've always been well served by being faithful to the facts – but perhaps, in this instance, I ought to respect the principles of drama more than the principles of history.

The reason I asked whether the screenplay did things which the play couldn't is that the former starts with Sabina being brought to the Burghölzli Clinic in a carriage and kicking and screaming until she gets inside the building, where she sees Jung descending the main staircase like some kind of god and immediately falls silent – a scene which, in the play, Jung simply describes, to less effect, in my opinion.

Funnily enough, the first change I've made to the play is to set the first scene, which is Jung casually discussing the case with his wife at breakfast, against Sabina arriving and being gagged and tied into a chair in the treatment room. In the production at the National, that energy went into creating a web of sound which evoked Victorian lunatic asylums, with clanking doors and people screaming, but I don't think the Burghölzli was like that, so I want to start the play in a completely different way. Another problem with the play, which I don't know how to solve, is that the first 30 pages, with their intense concentration on this one case, are so powerful that the rest of it struggles to keep up. You have the scene where the dam is breached and Sabina finally admits everything about her father, and then you have the first scene with Freud, and I don't know how to get around the sense of anti-climax and regroup.

One benefit of turning scenes which were dramatised in the screenplay into scenes which Jung describes in the play is that the character he describes them to, his wife Emma, becomes better developed and therefore a more effective rival to Sabina.

I think that's right, and I think she's the character who could stand more development on this pass and in the film.

You've solved structural problems in other plays by using mathematical devices – *Liaisons*, for example – and in this case you set up several parallels: the parallel love–hate relationships between Jung and Freud, and Jung and Sabina, and the parallel triangular relationships between Jung and Freud and Sabina, and Jung and Emma and Sabina. Was that deliberate?

Yes, whilst leaving the door open for a bit of inspiration – like showing the death of Sabina. That was an impulse which came on me in the middle of writing the play, at what was going to be the end of the first act, and you have to decide whether to give way to those impulses or corral them. The challenge is to come up with a structure that feels aesthetically right to the spectator while respecting the anarchy of real life and the spontaneity of the imagination.

Was the flash-forward from one of Jung and Sabina's trysts to her murder by German soldiers in Russia in 1942 meant to echo Jung's premonition, at the end of the play, of rivers of blood sweeping over Europe?

Yes – although, in the rewrite, the whole scene unfolds in the bedroom and a double plays her in the future, so the two scenes happen simultaneously in the same way as the two scenes at the beginning. Some people really hated that scene, but it's always the original things which people tend to hate, and it is original to say to the audience at the halfway point, 'This is what happens to her.' It means that you have that knowledge in your head throughout the second half, especially since the second half deals with issues of anti-Semitism. David Cronenberg was very interested in making a movie of it, and when I told him that the original screenplay didn't have that scene, he said, 'It's absolutely vital, and in a movie I'd put it exactly where you've put it,' which was interesting. It just seemed like the right thing to do.

How did you feel about the first production as a whole?

There's no doubt that it didn't land with the impact it should have. But then neither did *Total Eclipse* or *Tales from Hollywood* in their first productions. If you deal with a complex subject, the task is to do it in such a way that an audience, which is only going to watch it once for two hours, will grasp some of that complexity. That's a big thing to hope for, because people don't apprehend all kinds of things, so to expect a piece to land perfectly the first time out is asking too much, really. It often takes a play a while to find its way. Of course, if it doesn't make much impact in the first place it's never going to get a chance to find its way, which is something else you have to grapple with, but it can take a period of consideration and a production or two to teach you what it was you were trying to say. So I suppose I'm finally doing what I was originally asked to do, which is write another draft […] and having remounted it, I want to go on and make the movie of it, incorporating all the lessons I've learned. That's the plan, anyway.

* * *

So, did things go to plan?

Well, here's how it went. In 2004, when I was in Los Angeles fighting 11 producers over *Imagining Argentina*, I had a call from David Cronenberg, who I knew very slightly. He hadn't seen the play but he'd read it and said he wanted to do a film of it – what did I think? I said I was very pleased, because I'd always liked his work very much, but I was hoping to direct it myself. A couple of years passed, and *Imagining Argentina* was such a bruising experience that I thought it would be better to let Cronenberg do it. So I contacted him and he was still interested, so armed with the original script and the play he met me and said, 'I think the play is much better than the script and I would want to do something closer to the play.' So I started on that basis. I said, 'Do you have any advice before I embark on it?' and he said, 'I like a script to be 87 pages.' That was the extent of his advice. Anyway, I did the script – which was 103 pages – then I had another meeting with him, and of all the meetings I've ever had with directors it was the most admirably clear and direct. For example, I said before I started, 'Do we want to keep the scene from the play where Sabina is killed?' and he said, 'Yes, it's crucial, and it's very well placed in the middle.' When he read the screenplay, he said there was something about the specificness of it – perhaps that it was now so centrally about Jung – which meant that the scene didn't work, and he asked me to take it out. So I went back and did the work on it, sent it to him again, and he asked me to do one or two more things. He was interested in meeting Sabina's parents – the father who had beaten her – so I put a couple of scenes in and he said, 'I'm sorry I asked you to do that. Can you take them out again?' Then I did a bit more work on it, and then it was done. Then a few weeks before shooting, he sent me an email saying, 'I don't want you to panic' – so I immediately panicked – 'but I prefer to do the editing before I make the film rather than after, and I've taken a few things out.' I read the script and it was 87 pages. It involved a bit of rewriting where things had gone and edges had to be smoothed, but I couldn't fault it – and it was an ideal relationship with a director.

Anyone buying John Kerr's book on the strength of seeing the film is likely to be slightly surprised: the three-handed psychological drama which you carved out of it is just one strand in a dense examination of the birth of psychoanalysis. How did you arrive at the story which formed the basis of the original version of the screenplay?

Well, I did a lot of side research. I mean, the book isn't designed in that way; it just contains this very interesting story which covers a relatively small section of the narrative. Also, John Kerr's conclusion was that they hadn't had an affair. But one of the interesting things about working on this subject is that lots of stuff about Sabina has emerged in the 20 years since I was originally writing it: her letters and diaries have been published, she's become a recognised and important figure, and it's now quite clear that they did have an affair. It's also quite clear that her development as a psychoanalyst diverged from Jung in the direction of Freud. I'd sort of intuited that, but one of the things at the centre of the film version is that Jung is upset not so much by the fact that she leaves him as that she allies herself with Freud, and it's that which contributes to the strange nervous breakdown he went into at the end of this period. A lot of Jung's thinking was set off by his conversations with her, and another thing that the piece is about is how these men, these big beasts, colonised her ideas as well as her body, and drew from her in ways that Freud actually acknowledged more than Jung did.

When we talked before, you said that the facts behind *The Talking Cure* were extremely inconveniently organised. In what way were they inconvenient?

The sequence of events gets really messy after Sabina and Jung split up. I cheated a bit with their final meeting; we don't really know whether she ever saw him again. She did go to Zürich, and she probably went to his house, so she would have seen his wife. But I needed a final scene where they wrapped everything up. So in that sense it was stretching the known facts.

The opening scene we discussed, where Jung appears at the top of the stairs when Sabina is admitted to the clinic, isn't in the film; it simply

cuts from her being carried inside, to him entering the treatment room and introducing himself to her.

The first third of the play was where the cuts mostly fell in the film, and if I was dubious about one thing in the film it would be that her treatment is so abbreviated that it's almost like a miracle cure. She comes in, she's in a terrible state, and then she's better. In the play she gets better more slowly, and I think that development is useful.

I suppose the advantage of abbreviating her treatment is that you no longer have the problem of how to regroup when it ends.

Yes. Also, one of the things Cronenberg said to me was, 'We're going to need to see more of their sexual relationship,' and I could see that was something which was missing in the play. So we worked on that, and I was able to put more of it into the next version of the play, which I directed in Vienna in 2014.

In the book, you described Sabina as 'the crack down the middle of the Jung–Freud relationship. She brought them together and she drove them apart' and I suggested that she was therefore the pivotal character in the play without being the central character. Watching the film again, I wondered whether Sabina and Jung were in fact joint central characters, with Freud as a supporting character.

I think you're probably right. And maybe it's not as big an adjustment as I think it is in my head. But moving the needle from Sabina to Jung unlocked the whole subject for me. It had the same positive effect as when I decided to make *Carrington* about Carrington. It's amazing how things fall into place when you choose the right central character.

The final conversation between Jung and Freud remains almost the same in the finished film as it was in the first production of the play, with their mutual animosity channelled through their conversation about the names of the Egyptian kings. Did you decide that it was better to be indirect after all?

We obviously discussed the scene, and Cronenberg liked the fact that all the personal hostility is under the surface. But in the scene that now exists in the stage version, I more or less dramatise bits of their final furious correspondence where they insulted each other quite openly, and I actually think it works very well. It certainly did in the Vienna production.

And how do you feel about the piece now, in its final form as both a film and a play?

In terms of what Cronenberg wanted to do, I think that the film is perfectly achieved. He was totally respectful of the script, I was extremely happy with the film and I would love to work with him again. I learned from him that the physical detail of the relationship between Jung and Sabina was very useful dramatically, so that went into the play. There's also a scene in the film where Freud comes to Zürich, instead of Jung worshipping at the shrine in Vienna, and they're in Jung's boat and Freud is terribly uncomfortable, this rather inconvenient old man. I liked that very much, so a version of it went into the play and again is very useful, because it was an interesting stage in their development. I've been promising Faber for 15 years to deliver *Plays 2*, of which this would be the last, so I've got to sit down and put it in shape. But I hope someone else does the play at some point, because I think I've finally cracked it – and without Cronenberg, it wouldn't have gone through those final stages.

David Hare

David Hare was born in 1947 in St Leonards-on-Sea, East Sussex.

Among his many plays are: *Plenty* (1978, filmed 1985); *The Secret Rapture* (1988, filmed 1993); *Skylight* (1995); *My Zinc Bed* (2000, filmed 2008); *Stuff Happens* (2004); *The Power of Yes* (2009); *I'm Not Running* (2018); and his trilogy *Racing Demon* (1990), *Murmuring Judges* (1991) and *The Absence of War* (1993, filmed 1995).

His original screenplays include: *Licking Hitler* (1978); *Saigon: Year of the Cat* (1983); *Wetherby* (1985); *Paris by Night* (1988); *Strapless* (1989); *Collateral* (2018); *The White Crow* (2018); and the Worricker trilogy, *Page Eight* (2011), *Turks & Caicos* (2014) and *Salting the Battlefield* (2014), some of which he also directed.

His screen adaptation credits include: *Damage* (1992, novel by Josephine Hart); *Denial* (2016, book *History on Trial* by Deborah E. Lipstadt); and two Oscar-winning collaborations with director Stephen Daldry, *The Hours* (2002, novel by Michael Cunningham) and *The Reader* (2008, novel by Bernhard Schlink).

APPROACHES TO ADAPTATION

Do you prefer to adapt material which chimes with your own work, or material which is completely different and gives you a chance to try out new things?

I think probably what most appeals to me is the opportunity to do something different. Like a lot of screenwriters, I get sent a large number of heavyweight literary novels and I usually know within 20 or 30 pages whether they're of any interest to me. First of all, the given is respect for the book itself. I have to think that the book is a great book. And the second thing is that there's room for me to do something, that it isn't just a matter of transcribing whatever structure or ideas or, indeed, dialogue that the author has offered. There's got to be room for both of us in the bed.

Do you think adaptations involve a completely different set of creative gears to original screenplays?

Yes. I feel less implicated in the result, I don't feel it's me, and because of that, because I'm, as it were, messing around with other people's material, I'm much freer. I know at once when I read a book whether I'll be able to do it or whether I won't. It's absolutely pointless saying to me, 'Can you find a way of doing this?' When I read it the way of doing it screams at me at once, and if it doesn't scream at me I won't do it. So I turn down a lot of work, just saying, 'I don't know how to do it, and I don't want to sit for six months in panic that I don't know how to do it.' With all the ones I've done that have pleased me most, it's been screamingly obvious to me how to do them on the first day.

Do you always agree a mission statement or direction of travel with whoever has commissioned the adaptation?

It depends whether you have a director on board or not. If you take *Damage*, that was Louis Malle's film, and with a great director like Louis Malle you're simply trying to guide him towards the film he wants to make, to enable him to do what he has in mind. *Denial*, on the other hand, was developed with no particular director in mind, so I was completely free. There was no interference from the producers at all. The producers had had *Denial* for ten years and had been unable to find a way to do it. They were in Hollywood and they went to the BBC and said, 'British writers are much more skilled at this kind of political material' – and Christine Langan, who was head of BBC Films, sort of bullied me into doing it, on the grounds that if I didn't do it, no one would do it. It wouldn't get done. So because I'm fond of Christine, and owed her a favour for all the favours she'd done me, I did *Denial*, but I was given complete freedom to do exactly what I wanted with it – until Mick Jackson arrived, and once a director joins then obviously you're going to work with the director. You're crazy not to.

Louis Malle sort of bullied you into doing *Damage*, too, didn't he?

Yes. I didn't particularly want to do *Damage*: a) because I was very tired; and b) because it did seem a more than normally difficult project. So I said no, I wouldn't do *Damage*, and Louis said, 'What are you doing next?' I said, 'I'm going on holiday in the south of France,' and Louis said, 'Who are you going with?' I said, 'I'm going by myself,' and Louis said, 'Where are you staying?' And I named a hotel in Saint-Tropez – whereupon, of course, Louis moved into the hotel and ruined my holiday. He didn't, actually, but we worked for two weeks – and what pleasanter place to work than Saint-Tropez? And at the end of two weeks we had bashed out a structure for the whole film.

Why were you initially so resistant to it?

I was in a very low mood about screenwriting. I made three films in the 1980s: *Wetherby*, which was my first feature film and won the Golden Bear at Berlin; *Paris by Night*, which became ensnared in all sorts of legal difficulties not of my making; and *Strapless*, which I liked but the world liked less. I felt that artistically I was heading in the wrong direction, that each of my films had been inferior to the previous one. And I decided that it was impossible to excel in the theatre and in cinema, that all the British film directors I most admired – people like Stephen Frears and Mike Leigh and Ken Loach – were totally dedicated to film. It wasn't until Stephen Daldry and Sam Mendes appeared that you got theatre directors who could move easily between the two forms, and they remain almost the only ones who can. So I took some hard knocks with *Paris by Night* and *Strapless*, I was in despair about my screen work, and I thought, 'I don't need all the hurt that cinema is causing me.' And it was Louis who, as it were, nursed me back to self-confidence.

Do you usually produce an outline or treatment before you start writing the script?

I don't want to have to. Going back to Louis Malle, every day he would say, 'Tell me the story of the film,' and over that two week period we refined the story so that I could give an account of the film in 45 minutes. And at the end of that he said, 'Now go away and write it,' meaning that the structure was completely worked out. I generally don't do that. I have to know the ending is going to be great, so I have to know where I'm going. But everything about screenwriting, to me, is about avoiding what I call binary choices. In other words, I never want to write the kind of film in which, two-thirds of the way through, the hero or the heroine can go one way or another – where you can see a split in the road which will annoy or please half the audience whichever route you take. Any film that relies on, 'Are they going to get married?', 'Is he going to be a success?', 'Is she going to die?', 'Will this football team win the cup?' I'm bored stiff by. What I'm trying to do always is write stories where you can't see where they're going. To me, the second half of a film is infinitely more important than the first half. The first half is there to prepare for the second half, so the structuring of a film is about believing that the story is going to be fulfilled in a deeply satisfying way. And, by and large, the films you remember are the ones that have a great last 30 minutes. All films have a great first 30 minutes. But to go into something without knowing how you're going to end it is a disaster: you have to know that the end is going to deliver.

But you don't necessarily feel you have to write that in prose form before starting the script?

It depends who I'm working with. I think it was Evelyn Waugh who said, make sure you go to war with people you like, because you might as well enjoy it. My version of that is: don't make films with people you don't trust, because if you don't trust them at the beginning, by God you certainly won't trust them at the end. So a condition of my work is to work with people I like, because it just isn't worth your time to work with people you don't trust. And if you trust them, the chances are they trust you, and if they trust you and you say, 'Just give me time to work this out,' they'll structure a contract in a way that allows you to do that. If they're saying to you, 'Can you tell me in advance what you're going to write?' they're probably the wrong people to be working with.

If the author of the source material is living, do you find it useful to have their input on the script?

Oh, yes. You've got to have that.

Is it easier to navigate notes from directors, producers and script editors when you have a piece of source material to measure the screenplay against?

No, it's much harder, because of those dreaded words 'in the book'. The minute you see the book on set you bridle, because you go, 'We're not making the book. We're making the script.' You ought to be able to get everything from the script. When I showed Julianne Moore the screenplay of *The Hours*, I said, 'Do you need to know anything about this part?' and she said, 'No, everything is on the page.' And when she said that I knew she'd be fantastic in the role. So it's incredibly irritating when the book is used as a stick with which to beat the script. On the other hand, returning to the book in order to compare how the author imagined something with how you imagined it constantly deepens and enriches your screenplay. You go, 'I'd forgotten that they wrote that bit,' or, 'There's a wonderful line I hadn't noticed.' And the book, if it's a good book, will change every time you go back to it anyway.

Have you ever started work on an adaptation and found it harder to adapt than you anticipated?

I think I tend to have spotted the problems in advance [*laughs*]. For example, with *Denial*, we had to make drama out of self-denial. The essence of Deborah Lipstadt's experience of defending herself was that in court she was not allowed to defend herself. Most legal dramas, like *Erin Brockovich*, depend on a previously inarticulate person becoming articulate. Our drama depended on a highly articulate woman being silenced – and, indeed, relying on a team of men to do the job for her. So I knew that my job was to prove that her input in her own defence was decisive, even though it was not in court. That was the challenge from the very beginning.

Have you ever been offered material to adapt which you felt couldn't, or shouldn't, be adapted?

Oh, yes. The paradox is that those writers who are said to be most cinematic are actually the hardest to adapt for the cinema. Patricia Highsmith is an obvious example. Because her prose is so brilliant, she lures you into believing the plot is the engine, and it's not, mood is the engine. Graham Greene is another. There's a reason why he wrote original screenplays, because he knew his books looked cinematic on the page, but adapting them was a different matter. And Joseph Conrad is another.

Le Carré? He's in that same lineage of Conrad and Greene.

I think le Carré requires time. I've always thought that what's brilliant in le Carré is those sustained virtuoso passages, the interrogations, which is why he works so well on television. Give him six hours and le Carré is great. I've been asked to do le Carré, and if I was given six hours then yes, but people were coming to me wanting feature films, so I turned them down.

Are there any screen adaptations which you think are especially good or you particularly admire?

William Wyler had the unfailing gift of going to the centre of a subject. *Wuthering Heights*, *The Heiress* – to me, these are the absolute models. Ben Hecht and Charles MacArthur adapted one, Ruth and Augustus Goetz the other, but as a director Wyler just seems to know what the heart of a story is, what the essential drive of a story is. I look at his films and go, 'You clever bugger! How do you know?' Of contemporary screenwriters, I think Steven Zaillian is completely brilliant – he's absolutely the king of it all, isn't he?

ADAPTING FICTION

Some writers try to include as much of the novel as possible by boiling scenes down to their essence. Others are more ruthless in editing it down to a sort of greatest hits, but being true to the spirit of it. Do you favour either of those approaches?

I'm very marked by the experience of *The Corrections*, the Jonathan Franzen novel. I spent three years on that and we did 21 drafts, and at a certain point the director, Robert Zemeckis, said, 'No film can contain this whole book, so I want to make a story about just one of the children rather than all three children, because a movie has to have a point of view.' Obviously, having made *The Hours*, I didn't agree with him. On the other hand, I could see that the bagginess of a portmanteau film, which had five principal characters and five points of view, meant it was almost impossible to make. Scott Rudin, the producer, and Jonathan Franzen concluded that the answer to this was to do a television series, which I had nothing to do with and never got past the pilot. But it was true that there wasn't any way the feature film could be reduced. In the end, Scott just said to me, 'Write exactly what you want and give me your preferred version.' I wrote a version which probably lasted three hours, and he said, 'The days of *The Godfather* are gone. Cinema managers will no longer tolerate that, least of all for a literary film. Maybe a blockbuster can last three hours, but a literary adaptation can't.' So that book defeated me, and that was obviously a very painful experience.

If a novel has an unusual structure, would you try to reproduce that in adapting it?

No. But I have a reputation, rightly or wrongly, as the person who does impossible projects, and I get slightly freaked out because I can't always understand what's impossible about them. Whereas there are other things where I'm told it's incredibly obvious how you do them, and I just go, 'I don't see this.' So you have to know what it is that excites you about writing this particular thing.

Do you try to avoid voiceover in adapting a first-person narrative, or do you see it as another tool in the toolbox?

I hate voiceover. I think voiceover is a cheat. Plainly there are films – like *Sunset Boulevard* – with a great first-person narration, but it shouldn't be there to compensate for the fact that the writer can't do the job. Because the job of screenwriting is a painless, unnoticed conveying of information. When I was very young and naïve I wrote a film about the fall of Saigon, and I had a man standing in front of a blackboard, pointing at a map of Vietnam to show where the Viet Cong were. I said something to the actor about a line not being right, and he said, 'It doesn't matter what I say in this scene. If I'm pointing at a map no one is going to be listening to a bloody word.' And he was absolutely right. That is not how to convey information in a movie. You must convey information in such a way that the audience doesn't know they're receiving it. As soon as they notice information being thrown at them, they'll revolt. So I'm very against voiceover, on those grounds.

Do you use the language of the novel in writing the screenplay, or do you put the whole thing in your own words?

My own words, but there will be favourite bits of the novel. There's a wonderful line in *The Hours*: 'It had seemed like the beginning of happiness. Now she knew: it *was* happiness. That was the moment, right then.' I remember saying to Scott Rudin, 'I cannot imagine a film which does not finally include those words,' and Scott said, 'We'll see' – because he's wiser than me.

It is in the film, actually, a line of dialogue.

Is it in? I never know what's in and what isn't in the end. Okay.

Do you keep the novel beside you throughout the adaptation process, or do you try to internalise it and set it aside somewhere along the way?

Jean-Claude Carrière said you adapt a novel by reading it once and throwing it in the waste paper basket. My formula is that the only way to be faithful to a novel is by being lavishly promiscuous. By being promiscuous you will perversely be faithful, whereas if you simply write down scenes from the novel it never works. They're different media, and they have to be written differently. So I look at the novel less and less while I'm actually writing, but then I go back to it when I've finished to check what I've missed.

Between drafts, rather than during a draft?

Totally. I go back between drafts and say, 'In what way is this novel superior to what I've written?' and then I try to inject into the screenplay something of what makes the novel great. But not until I've got my own river running, so to speak.

How much pressure do you feel when adapting a well-known and much-loved novel, knowing that you won't be able to please everyone with the finished product?

Well, *The Hours* was a much-loved novel – so let's talk about that.

CASE STUDY: *THE HOURS*

US/UK, 2002 ▪ **Directed by** Stephen Daldry ▪ **Produced by** Scott Rudin, Robert Fox ▪ **Screenplay by** David Hare, based on the novel by Michael Cunningham ▪ **Cast:** Meryl Streep (Clarissa Vaughan), Julianne Moore (Laura Brown), Nicole Kidman (Virginia Woolf), Ed Harris (Richard Brown), Toni Collette (Kitty), Claire Danes (Julia Vaughan), Jeff Daniels (Louis Waters), Stephen Dillane (Leonard Woolf), Allison Janney (Sally Lester), John C. Reilly (Dan Brown), Miranda Richardson (Vanessa Bell)

In the introduction to the published screenplay, you quote producer Scott Rudin as saying that *The Hours* was perfect for you, and you also say that his reasons for wanting to make it may have been different from yours. In what way do you think they were different?

I think he very shrewdly saw that these were belting leading roles for the greatest actresses of the day, so he always knew that he would be able to cast the film up to the nines – which turned out to be true, because they were three fully realised portraits of three extraordinary women in three different periods, and how often do we get that in the cinema? Almost never. So I think that was what appealed to him. What appealed to me was that it was all interior monologue. The whole art of adaptation is to invent scenes which are the equivalent of what is in the book, but are not the book. All sorts of things happen in a film which don't happen in the book, and they happen in order to do what the book does by different means, and that particularly applies to interior monologue. It was up to me to invent scenes, because Michael wasn't trying to write scenes, he was trying to write states of mind. So, a desperate housewife and her extremely troubled relationship with her child: he gave indications of that, but I actually had to dramatise it. That's what I meant about there being room in the bed for me. And I think Michael was the happiest author I've ever worked with. He was 100 per cent happy with the film, because his attitude was that the material was created by Virginia Woolf. His book is a take on her book, *Mrs Dalloway*. My film is a take on his book, *The Hours*. He regards the whole thing as a baton being passed on, and the fact that the book of *Mrs Dalloway* went to number one on the bestseller list as a result of the film of *The Hours* was, for me, the greatest vindication of the process: we had all held the baton and passed it on.

In Cunningham's book, Virginia Woolf is in the process of writing *Mrs Dalloway*, which is then read 26 years later by Laura Brown, the character played by Julianne Moore, and then 50 years later finds an echo in the life of Clarissa Vaughan, the character played by Meryl Streep. In other words, the film isn't just an adaptation of a book, it's an adaptation of a book which is partly about books. Were you concerned that the finished film might feel too literary?

The Hours and *The Reader* are both in a genre which has vanished, which is what I call the '25 million dollar arthouse movie'. And when you make an arthouse movie for 25 million dollars, what you're trying to do is move it over into the mainstream. These films are called crossover films and there are rarely more than one or two of them a year. When I went past a multiplex in California and saw that three of the six screens were showing *The Hours*, that's the fulfilment of everything I've ever tried to do, which is to make a film on its own terms but to a high level. Twenty-five million dollars is unusual for an art film and the subject matter – the lesbian element, the suicide, everything – is art subject matter. So it is an art film, but I tried not to give it the feel of an art film, by which I mean taking itself elaborately seriously. Thanks to Stephen, it's full of life and guts and humour and warmth and fun, as well as everything else. And also it moves. A lot of art cinema is so slow. Self-consciously slow.

Did you do your own research on Virginia Woolf's life?

Yes. I had to understand the chronology of her depression. I had to know at what periods of her life she'd felt confident and at what periods she'd felt particularly low, because obviously we nip around a lot in the story. Michael always said that he was an average American teenager until, at the age of 15, he sought to impress a girl who was reading Virginia Woolf, so he read Virginia Woolf in order to be able to talk to her – and suddenly realised that there was something beyond bowling alleys. He represents Virginia Woolf as the person who opened his eyes to the world, so she'd always had this huge importance to him and he'd always known a lot about her. I didn't, I had to start from scratch.

And did you bring anything of *Mrs Dalloway* into your adaptation of *The Hours*?

I tried to make the film musical. There was a remark of Woolf's which I already knew, that all writers spend ten times as long thinking about rhythm as they do about meaning, and it was obvious to me from the start that a film with three strands would have to be rhythmically beautiful. Writing the credit sequence took me three weeks. Once the credit sequence was written, it was comparatively plain sailing. But the credit sequence announces the method by which the film is going to proceed, and it's a very unusual method. *Amores Perros* appeared the same year, and when the films were finished Guillermo Arriaga and I contacted each other and he said, 'I just want to say how much I admire *The Hours*,' and I said, 'I just want to say how much I admire *Amores Perros*,' and we both said, 'Aren't triangular structures wonderful?' – because you don't know which way they're going to go, as opposed to binary. The Nureyev film I've written actually has a triangular structure: it's about Nureyev's childhood, it's about his education in St Petersburg and it's about his time in Paris, and by putting the three together you immediately get something rich that you don't get just by flashing back to a single period in time. So I knew it had to be musical, because Woolf's writing is musical. 'Mrs Dalloway said she would buy the flowers herself.' I'm sure a poet could tell us what that is; iambic pentameter, I think. The arrival of Philip Glass's score was the oddest moment in the whole process, because I basically said, 'I've done this work. It doesn't need Philip to do it. I've already put the music in.' I'm now reconciled to it, but when I first heard it I was horrified.

How did you decide which of the three stories to cut to at any given moment?

Feeling. Pure instinct. I've always believed that each cut must progress a story. You don't cut back to someone bearing exactly the same expression on their face that they had when you left them. Every good cut in film involves forward movement, so all I was trying to do was find forward movement in each story. There are no thoughtful, contemplative, 'and now this character is staring out of the window' scenes. There's always progression in story, and that's how I put the whole thing together. In terms of which story I went to, it was only what felt right. Also, I knew I had this fabulous ending: a character from one story, which has hitherto been separate, turns out to meet a character from another story, and you don't know in advance that these characters are going to be connected.

Did you write many drafts of the script?

Countless.

So the scenes didn't necessarily land in the right order straight off the bat.

Well, when I did the publicity tour, I'd always say, 'The screenplay is totally faithful to the book,' and Scott would say, 'Have you read the book lately? The screenplay doesn't resemble it in any way!' Similarly, I'd always say, 'There was a lot of messing around but in the end all the scenes were put in exactly the same order that I'd originally imagined them.' But I haven't done the breakdown to know whether Stephen and Scott moved them around significantly differently.

Finding the right balance between the three stories must also have been vital.

I didn't want any of the three stories to be bits and pieces, I wanted all of them to have big set-piece scenes. Everyone was terrified of the scene at the railway station with Nicole Kidman and Stephen Dillane, because everyone knew it delivered the film. The film is basically about a woman's right to self-assertion, and that's when she asserts herself and says, 'Even if it's at the cost of everything, including us, I'm going back to London, because it represents life to me.' With Julianne Moore's character, it's the right to leave her child in order to survive, breaking the ultimate taboo. And with Meryl Streep's character, it's ceasing to feel responsible for Ed Harris: the acceptance of the fact that we have to let go of people and let them make their own decisions about their lives. So I was looking for big scenes with big emotions, and if all three stories had those then it would balance out.

They're not just big scenes, they're long scenes, with long passages of dialogue – which makes some screenwriters and directors nervous.

If I write eight or ten pages of dialogue, I don't even notice that I'm doing it. I'm just trying to make the dialogue as good as I possibly can, and then *nobody* will notice. Some of the greatest scenes in the history of the movies are very long dialogue scenes. And some of the greatest sequences have no dialogue at all. But dialogue is part of your weaponry. It is absolute nonsense to say film is a visual medium. It is not. Film is a medium in which words *and* images smash together in very interesting ways. One of the most memorable moments in film is Bernstein in *Citizen Kane* talking about the girl with the white parasol, and Welles doesn't cut to an image of a girl with a white parasol. He doesn't need to. He knows that this character will give you that image. *Citizen Kane* is a film richer in visual imagery than anything that came before it, but he also trusts that speech can do a job. So word and image are what you're looking for.

The book juxtaposes the three stories in chapter-size chunks. The film juxtaposes them in sequences, scenes, even single images. In other words, film gave you a chance to enhance the effect of the book. Did that strike you as you were writing it?

Very much so. When I was in Los Angeles after the film had opened, I met Almodóvar – who I didn't know, but who, like me, was in Tower Records buying DVDs – and he said, 'I tried to get the rights to *The Hours*, and I would have done it completely differently from how you did it.' And I said, 'I know you would, and it would have been great.' I would love to see Almodóvar's film of *The Hours*; I think it would be incredible. In fact, there are so many films in that book that I can imagine five different filmmakers making five different films from it, and all of them would be good. There's something in Michael's structure that offers infinite possibilities.

In the prologue of the book, when Virginia is walking to the river to kill herself, Cunningham mentions the voices in her head – presumably ancient Greek voices, which the Richard character also hears in the Mrs Dalloway strand of the novel. Did you consider including those in the film, and if not, why?

I don't know exactly what was going on in Virginia Woolf's head when she went to kill herself, and I felt squeamish about attributing to a real-life character an interpretation which was so singular and intrusive. So I was very against it. Stephen and Scott became convinced during the editing that this should be in, so they went to a Greek theatre company and recorded Greek voices to go inside her head. After a week of experimenting with these voices they told me they'd failed, but they hadn't dared tell me they were doing it because they knew it would enrage me. I said, 'Did you know that ancient Greek is different from modern Greek and the voices you were putting on were modern Greek?' They said, 'No, we didn't know that.' I said, 'Then it's lucky you didn't put them on.'

The prologue of the film – and the epilogue, looping back to the day of Virginia's death, which isn't in the book – do, however, contain the only voiceover in the film: her suicide letter to her husband.

I don't really think of a letter as voiceover.

Going back to what you said earlier, that the screenplay is totally faithful to the book; Scott Rudin may have disagreed, but actually I think it is totally faithful – as much as any screenplay can be.

Yes, I do, too.

Most scenes in the book found their way into the film in one form or another, and there's only one character of any significance who didn't make it, the writer Walter Hardy, whose scenes in the book feel almost satirical.

That's true, and I wasn't interested in satire. Michael is deeply embedded in the New York literary world, and is unapologetic about it. He reads all the novels that come out, he knows all the authors, he's a diligent and hardworking member of PEN. I'm totally uninterested in the New York literary world. I think it was explained to me who that character was 'meant to be' and that's not who I'm making the film for. I'm making the film for a general audience. I don't want it to be self-referential.

The female supporting characters are almost as rich as the leads: Miranda Richardson, Toni Collette, Claire Danes – and Allison Janney, playing Clarissa's partner, a relationship which you brought ever so slightly more into the foreground. What was your thinking there?

I think because otherwise Clarissa can seem rather haughty. Both in *Mrs Dalloway* and in *The Hours*, there's a danger of Clarissa's isolation being a bit alienating, so I wanted her to be in a fully engaged relationship. I also wanted a lesbian relationship to be credited in mainstream American cinema and treated as completely natural and not exceptional. Stephen and Scott and I all felt very strongly about this, and in fact the commercial red flags that would normally go up at that time around the representation of those relationships didn't go up on this film. We felt we'd somehow get this film into and accepted in the multiplexes, and we did, and that was great.

CASE STUDY: *THE READER*

US/Germany, 2008 ▪ **Directed by** Stephen Daldry ▪ **Produced by** Anthony Minghella, Sydney Pollack, Donna Gigliotti, Redmond Morris ▪ **Screenplay by** David Hare, based on the novel by Bernhard Schlink ▪ **Cast:** Kate Winslet (Hanna Schmitz), Ralph Fiennes (Michael Berg), David Kross (Young Michael Berg), Lena Olin (Rose Mather / Ilana Mather), Bruno Ganz (Professor Rohl)

Anthony Minghella originally intended to write and direct *The Reader*, but he ultimately produced it alongside Sydney Pollack. Do you have any sense of how differently he would have adapted it?

I read the book not long after it came out and said to my agent, 'I want to do this. I know exactly how to write a film of it.' And my agent said, 'You can't. Anthony Minghella's got it.' Minghella had the rights from the moment the book came out, and whenever I saw him I said to him, 'Come on, Anthony, give me that book.' And finally he rang me and said, 'I don't have time to do *The Reader*. You do it.' So when we set about it, this time with Stephen Daldry on board from the beginning, Anthony was more like a benign patron. The first thing to say is that the book is written in the first person, and that's a convention which is accepted in literature: the narrator has written this book in order to tell us something. There's no equivalent in film – unless you do it as a documentary made by Michael. So you start with the basic philosophical problem: why is he telling this story? I decided he must be telling it because it's hitherto been secret and he now wishes it to be known, therefore he's got to have someone to tell it to – and that's where the narrative structure with his daughter comes from. Now, Anthony said to me, 'You'll shoot that, but it'll never appear in the final film, because it's not necessary.' And I said, 'It's absolutely essential. There's no film without it, because unless you know why the story is being told, there's no point in telling it.' To me, Michael finally achieving an act of honesty with his daughter is what makes the film work, but Anthony always thought that this structure would fall away – and he died before he knew that it would stay in.

It's absolutely essential for another reason, too. Without it, the film would be completely pitiless.

That's interesting.

The film becomes about truth and reconciliation: Michael is reconciled with his daughter by telling her the truth about Hanna, but Hanna is reconciled with no one because she has no understanding of what the truth is.

That's right. There were two lines of attack on the book, and therefore on the film. The first was the presumption that the act of reading is an awakening of her moral as well as her imaginative faculty – and it is not. The film would not dare, and I would not dare, and Bernhard Schlink would not dare, to offer any sense of redemption to the character of a concentration camp guard. That would be a huge insult to people who suffered at the hands of the Nazis. We would have no moral right to do that, and if we were doing that people would have a right to be angry – but we are not. It is a deliberate misreading of the book to presume that because she is read to she develops a moral faculty whereby she understands the iniquity of what she has done. She doesn't. She doesn't in the book, and she doesn't in the film.

In the film, Michael asks Hanna what she's learned, and she says simply that she's learned to read.

Exactly. She remains morally ignorant. Their relationship has not redeemed her. She's with a young boy because he's unformed and has no real sense of history: he doesn't know what was done and isn't concerned with what was done. He thinks the relationship is mutual, but it's almost entirely on her terms. It's a relationship of control.

You mentioned two lines of attack on the book. What was the second?

The second line of attack was, is it autobiographical? From Schlink's point of view, he was damned if it was and damned if it wasn't. If it's true, 'Oh, it's just a story about your life.' If it's not, 'Oh, it's just something you made up.' At the end of it all, I have no idea. I never asked him and was never curious to find out, because it seemed to me that we had to work as if it were a true story – rather than as a true story. When I'd written it, Sydney gave me the best note anyone has ever given me. He said, 'Books get away with things that films don't, because film is a literal medium. Even if you stylise them, what's always being tested in films is plausibility: do I believe this?' So, he has an affair with an older woman when he's a student, then later goes to a trial and sees that same woman and realises she was a war criminal. He said, 'You've got to believe in that coincidence. That's your test. I can give you a hundred notes on this script, I can go through it scene by scene, but if at the end the audience don't believe that idea, you're fucked.' What a great note.

How did you deal with it?

Stephen dealt with it in the way he handled that moment. There's Kate Winslet in the dock, and in walks Michael and sees her. It's not a spine-chilling moment, because the audience sort of knows it – they've read the publicity, they know something's up – it's just an incredibly difficult moment to handle, so we spent a lot of time talking about that.

In the introduction to the published screenplay, you quote Sydney Pollack's repeated question: 'What is the metaphor of reading in the film? What is the function of literature?' What was your answer?

The film is about a woman who has lived an unremittingly ugly life, then glimpses, too late, another world – a world which can no longer operate as it might have done if it had been opened up to her when she was illiterate. Reading is her attempt to climb out of a mud of incomprehension.

There's a passage in the book: 'I thought that if the right time gets missed, if one has refused or been refused something for too long, it's too late, even if it is finally tackled with energy and received with joy. Or is there no such thing as "too late"? Is there only "late", and is "late" always better than "never"?' The ending of the film answers that question: it's too late for Hanna, but not too late for Michael.

Yes. Michael always seemed to me the central character in the film. Hanna is the flashier part, and generally people noticed Kate Winslet more than they noticed Ralph Fiennes. But actually it's Ralph's performance that holds the film together, because Michael is doing something unbelievably brave. He has lived an effectively frozen life in which he has emotionally shut down, and the film represents the moment at which he begins to come out of that. Not to take anything away from Kate, because obviously Kate is astonishing in the part, but the underlying heart of the film is held by Ralph. I feel there was a tension in the filming, which was that the producers and Stephen located the energy of the project in the figure of Hanna and I located it in the figure of Michael.

You feel that in retrospect, or you felt it at the time?

Oh, at the time. I felt that I was defending Michael, and was therefore defending the actor, Ralph Fiennes. Stephen would feel instinctively that exploring the character of Hanna was the dramatic thing to do, whereas Michael was downbeat, repressed, secretive, hidden – and, because of that, a less overtly dramatic character.

Another job that the framing narrative does – meeting his daughter, talking to his daughter, taking her to Hanna's grave – is to make the older Michael more proactive. More dramatic, in fact.

Precisely. That's exactly what I was doing. Hanna's story could never be fulfilling. His story can. The story isn't really about wartime Germany, it's about post-war Germany and how the country pulled itself together and remade itself and dealt with what had happened in the past. For that reason, I strongly resisted flashbacks to the war. I have a horror of what I call 'striped-pyjama movies', films in which well-fed actors gather together to re-enact the fate of people during the Holocaust. *Denial* isn't a striped-pyjama movie, and *The Reader* isn't a striped-pyjama movie. Many people choose to project their moral anger on to *The Reader* for its supposed redemption of a Nazi war criminal. I find it infinitely more offensive when the clichés of fiction are put on top of this experience to turn it into soapy drama. Munk's *Passenger* is great, and Resnais' *Night and Fog* is great, and *Schindler's List* is obviously great, because they're done with complete integrity and are totally convincing and seem to look the event full in the face, but I don't think you should ever use that event to hitch a ride. As a screenwriter, the toughest thing is holding the line: saying, 'You can do that, but it won't be my screenplay.' I think Christopher Hampton said, about screenwriting, that you only have power if you're willing to walk away. If you're the prisoner of a project, meaning that you go, 'I've put so much into this that I must stay regardless,' you lose all your power. If anyone had tried to shoot the war material, I would have walked away.

Going back to the point that books get away with things that films don't, Hanna's illiteracy is a good example. In the film, you have to maintain a tension between giving the audience enough information so it makes sense when they find out, but not giving them so much that they figure it out too soon.

When I said earlier that screenwriting is about conveying information, I should also have said that it's about concealing information – without the audience feeling they're being cheated. What is a cut, when you're editing a film? A cut is a jump, and it's a jump which leaves out a lot of stuff. Now, if the audience begins to feel that you're jumping over stuff which they ought to know but you're not telling them, they start to find the film dishonest. You can't just avoid the difficult scenes, you should confront them. That's another fundamental principle of screenwriting, it seems to me.

Your screenplay had already left out a lot of stuff: the draft that I read was a very tight 81 pages.

The Schlink material was so rich, and there were so many different scenes, that a lot of them got left out. And I wanted anyway to focus in on the shocking contrast between how Hanna seemed to Michael when he didn't know who she was and what she'd done, to the totally different person that he looked at with complete mystification so many years later. I also wanted the whole thing to have the feeling of a fable, like the cinematic equivalent of a novella. And above all I wanted it to be fleet. I think I failed as a filmmaker in the eighties because my films were self-consciously arty. Although *Wetherby* was hugely acclaimed, it was very much an 'Art Film', and I didn't want to work in that genre. I wanted, with Stephen, to make a genre of our own, which wasn't weighty and didn't linger.

Not only did you leave scenes out, but you also added scenes in: for example, when Hanna and young Michael go into a church she's transported by the sound of a choir singing Bach, which carries over into the framing narrative as older Michael listens to the same piece on his car stereo.

Again, that's a glimpse of a world which is completely unattainable for her – and that's the tragedy. Bernhard Schlink is asking a very brave question, which I think he deserves credit for asking, which is what was the experience like for those on the side of the oppressor? And people who have a stake in the crimes which were committed have a perfect right to say, 'I don't care. I'm totally uninterested in what the perpetrators thought and felt.' But there was an element in the reception of both the book and the film in America which seemed to me astonishingly self-deceiving, particularly people who said that the Germans were bad because they didn't stand up to Hitler and that if they'd been there they would have resisted. Anyone who knows the history of Germany in the 1930s will know that what those people are effectively saying is, 'I would have been willing to die.' And, significantly, this criticism came from people who had no experience of war at all, people who had led entirely peaceful lives. It's the moral equivalent of Donald Trump saying that the man

THE ART OF SCREEN ADAPTATION

who failed to go into the school shooting was a coward when he himself had dodged the Vietnam draft five times. I don't believe these people who say that they would have behaved so brilliantly in Nazi Germany – and Europeans who experienced occupation will know that all these things are shades of grey.

Did Bernhard Schlink like the film of *The Reader* as much as Michael Cunningham liked *The Hours*?

I don't know what Bernhard Schlink thought of the film. I never discussed it with him. In fact, I've not spoken to him since. I know Michael quite well, but Bernhard Schlink never became part of my life in the same way. I would regularly go through the script and talk scenes over with him, and he came to the shoot and was there when the film premiered in Berlin. He seemed perfectly at peace with the film, but whether he feels it represents the book or was something different from it, I don't know.

It strikes me that Sydney Pollack's question – 'What is the metaphor of reading in the film? What is the function of literature?' – could also be asked of *The Hours*. Again, what would your answer be?

So, literature exists to describe the most fundamental, elemental, profound human impulses which can't otherwise be reached except through religion, music, art. [*Long pause*]. That's about it, isn't it?

Olivia Hetreed

Olivia Hetreed was born in 1961 in Wells, Somerset.

Her screen adaptation credits include: *The Treasure Seekers* (1996, novel by E. Nesbit); *The Canterville Ghost* (1997, story by Oscar Wilde); *What Katy Did* (1999, novel by Susan Coolidge); *Girl with a Pearl Earring* (2003, novel by Tracy Chevalier); *Canterbury Tales – The Man of Law's Tale* (2003, after Chaucer); *Wuthering Heights* (2011, novel by Emily Brontë); and three novels in Caroline Lawrence's *The Roman Mysteries* series (2007).

Girl with a Pearl Earring was BAFTA-nominated for Best Adapted Screenplay.

APPROACHES TO ADAPTATION

Do you prefer to adapt material which chimes with your own work, or material which is completely different and gives you a chance to try out new things?

The opportunity to get an insight into something different is definitely part of the attraction of an adaptation for me. On the other hand, there are things I've looked at where I've thought, 'I don't have anything to add to this world.' You're quite bound in by the material and whatever research you do beyond it, so it's a question of how tight that world feels. I did an Indian adaptation recently, set at a particular moment in recent Indian history, and the book is so fantastic and expansive that I could simply go into the writer's world and it was all there. If it had been a much sparer story I would have been quite anxious about it, but the book was a brilliant guide to what I was trying to do. You can also sometimes tell a story because it's an adaptation that you wouldn't necessarily be allowed to tell if it were just a standalone piece. I'm thinking particularly of an adaptation I did of *The Man of Law's Tale* from *The Canterbury Tales*. That gave me permission to put a story about Nigerian refugees on BBC primetime which never would have got there if it wasn't pretending to be Chaucer.

Do you think adaptations involve a completely different set of creative gears to original screenplays?

No, I think it's remarkably the same. It's like building a house. If you're doing an adaptation, there was already a house there and you knock most of it down and rebuild it. If you're doing an original, you have to dig the foundations and put in the services and then build the house. So that initial work is very different because you're trying to find the story – and sometimes that's an all-encompassing, totally created world from a novel, and sometimes that's just a newspaper story – but then the actual process of writing the script is not that different.

Do you always agree a mission statement or direction of travel with whoever has commissioned the adaptation?

More and more. I didn't always realise the need for that, but it's incredibly important to know that you both want to make the same film, and I'm very keen on doing lots of preparatory work to make sure that we are, so that when they get the script they're not astonished and go, 'We didn't think it would be like this.' We've had all the difficult discussions beforehand about what's in and what's out and what perspective we're using, and there's already an outline and a treatment as a result of that, and the surprise I want them to have reading the script is how thrilling and exciting it is compared to those slightly dull documents, not, 'I never thought the story was going to be told this way.'

Have you ever had any radical disagreements with producers?

I wouldn't say I've had radical disagreements. There's been a couple of times where I'm leaning one way and they're leaning another way – particularly, interestingly, about female characters, where I feel like they're not giving that character their due – but I've never backed out of something because of creative differences. I did have a project where they didn't know where they were going. We'd set off in one direction and they'd say, 'Can you go the other way?' And then we'd go the other way and they'd change their minds again. That's the only time I've been in development hell, in that you could have gone on infinitely producing different versions.

If the author of the source material is living, do you find it useful to have their input on the script?

Certainly. It's completely up to them how much input they have, and it also depends on what kind of author they are. Tracy Chevalier, who wrote the novel of *Girl with a Pearl Earring*, was very clear that she didn't want to be the screenwriter, so it was very easy to work with her because we were just two writers working together on the best possible version. She was very open to me asking her questions about where she got this and that from, but I wasn't asking her to help me write it and she wasn't insisting on helping me write it. Whereas I've also done true stories, and that's a very different kind of relationship. That's someone who happens to have a really interesting story to tell, but isn't themselves a writer and hasn't been through this process before and doesn't have a professional detachment. It's their story, or the story of someone they know and love, so for me that's much more about them being comfortable with what's happening. Not that I'm going to tell the story to make them look wonderful all the time, but that we're going to be as truthful as we possibly can about what happened and that they understand the process as we go along. I've definitely got better at doing that, and I think it's a really complicated thing to do, because it's a huge moral undertaking to do that with someone's life. Their story will inevitably be simplified and made more exciting and characters combined and so on, and I need to feel comfortable that they really understand the whys and wherefores of that – so that when it comes to asking them difficult questions, or saying I need to talk to someone who they feel angry with or whatever, they trust that that's okay, that it's part of the process.

Is it easier to navigate notes from directors, producers and script editors when you have a piece of source material to measure the screenplay against?

I suppose it's a security blanket for everyone. You all know that this bit works in the book or that people already love this story, so they're not questioning whether anyone would be interested in the story of a girl who cleans a painter's house, but doesn't do any painting herself. Without the book, that would have been a much harder sell and you'd have been constantly defending it against people going, 'Surely the story should be about Vermeer and not about the maid?' So it's incredibly useful for that.

Have you ever started work on an adaptation and found it harder to adapt than you anticipated?

Absolutely. I must be very dim, but I often don't realise the pitfalls and then think, 'How did I not see this?' Ronald Harwood tells a story about adapting *The Diving Bell and the Butterfly* and not realising until he sat down to write it how impossible it was to be inside the head of someone who couldn't say or do anything, and I was very heartened by that. You're seduced by the story and the glory of it, and then you come down to the hard graft of, 'Where does this go?' and, 'If we take out this enormous chunk of the story how does the rest of it work?' I'd like to think I've got better at assessing that as I've done the work over and over again, but I'm sure I'll still continue to make that mistake.

Have you ever been offered material to adapt which you felt couldn't, or shouldn't, be adapted?

Yes, and I've been right and wrong about that. I've been offered things to adapt and thought, 'This isn't going to be a good adaptation because the thing that's interesting about it isn't the story, it's the way it's written or it's the witty asides or it's the 500 peripheral characters that our main character meets – which would be a terrible movie.' I've also thought that a book wasn't going to be a good adaptation because the book itself wasn't very good, but then I've seen the film and they'd achieved things with it that the book simply hadn't done successfully. I didn't feel sad or jealous or angry, I just thought, 'How wonderful that someone has taken that unpromising material and found something so fantastic in it.'

Are there any screen adaptations which you think are especially good or you particularly admire?

I think all of James Schamus and Ang Lee's adaptations are really wonderful. *The English Patient*, and Anthony Minghella's writing in general – though I would make an exception for *Cold Mountain*, which for me is an example of the thing we were just talking about. Even in the hands of a master, the things that make the book interesting weren't in the film and the things that were in the film were somehow trivial compared to the book. So even the greatest of us can get it not quite right. But I think it was fantastically interesting to see his version of Ripley when there were at least two other versions of that character which were also really good and interesting. Not only can you take something and make a great thriller of it, but you can take something that other people have already had a go at and still produce something really characteristic of that filmmaker. Possibly my favourite films in the world are both adaptations. One is *Cabaret*, by Jay Presson Allen, which I think is a flawless adaptation – again of material that's been adapted in all sorts of different ways. It's adapted from the musical, and the musical was already an adaptation of a book, but the film is so integrated that you never think about the script, you just feel it's one beautiful piece of machinery that works. And the other one I love is *The Right Stuff*, Philip Kaufman's adaptation. William Goldman, who was originally writing the screenplay, said, 'You have to choose either the space story or the Yeager story,' and Kaufman went, 'No, we need to do both,' and Goldman was right – you know, that's the correct, orthodox answer – but actually there's something so fabulous and epic and all-American about that film. I love it as an example of breaking all the rules and still making it work.

ADAPTING FICTION

Some writers try to include as much of the novel as possible by boiling scenes down to their essence. Others are more ruthless in editing it down to a sort of greatest hits, but being true to the spirit of it. Do you favour either of those approaches?

There are probably always going to be scenes, certainly in a classic or much-loved book, that have to be in the story no matter which way you slice it, but other than that I think it's my job to be absolutely ruthless with the book. I'm not there to present an audio-visual version of the book, I'm there to make the best possible film from the material – and at that point everything is up for grabs. I can take out what I want, I can add in what I want. I can do anything, because it's my version.

If a novel has an unusual structure, would you try to reproduce that in adapting it?

Not necessarily. I'd look at it and go, 'Is this central to telling the story? Is this what makes the story interesting?' If it is the thing that makes it interesting, how do I find the visual equivalent of that? And if it's not going to be exactly the same as the book, what's my guiding principle in deciding when to deviate from it? I might say to myself, 'I'm going to follow this structure except for this point, where actually we need to know less' – because a film sometimes shows you a lot more than a book does; you can withhold information in a book in a way you often can't in a film. I'd have to have a really clear idea what my rules of engagement were so that it didn't become arbitrary. The worst answer to, 'Why was that scene there?' is always, 'Because it was there in the book.' It's like with true stories: 'Why did this unbelievable thing happen?' 'Because it happened in real life.' It's just dreadful.

Do you try to avoid voiceover in adapting a first-person narrative, or do you see it as another tool in the toolbox?

I assume that I won't use voiceover, but I wouldn't say I'm never going to use it. It has to be on a case by case basis. One of the early decisions I made on *Girl with a Pearl Earring* was not to use voiceover, even though the novel is written in the first person. I knew it would put a gap between her situation and her recall of it, which would immediately make you feel safer, whereas without it you were in the situation with her. Sometimes you can play a game with that gap, where the voiceover has a different point of view to the person we're seeing, and that seems to me a really interesting and energetic way to use voiceover. I'm doing an adaptation at the moment of a true story and a lot of it hangs on a diary, and as you hear excerpts of the diary you realise that there's a divergence between what we're seeing played out and what the diary is telling us happened. The voiceover becomes a character in the drama of 'Who's telling the truth here? What version of things is this?'

Do you use the language of the novel in writing the dialogue, or do you put the whole thing in your own words?

It varies. Until quite recently I would have said that very few novelists write dialogue you can use, that all novel dialogue is just rhythmically different. And I would certainly say that about anything written pre-cinema. But when you read contemporary novels you often get a sense of the author writing down the movie they're seeing, so it's much closer now. It also depends how far away from my experience or expertise the dialogue is and what I think it needs to be achieving. With the Indian story I thought the dialogue in the novel was really rich and interesting, and I had to do a forensic examination of it to understand what the cultural and political references were. Once I understood what someone was saying, then I could make a decision as to whether they should say it in that way, or whether I should put it in some sort of context – because if I didn't understand it, another Western audience member wouldn't understand it either. But the things they were saying were so great that I was keen to hold on to them if I could.

Do you keep the novel beside you throughout the adaptation process, or do you try to internalise it and set it aside somewhere along the way?

I very much set it aside. Trying to write with the novel in your hand doesn't work for me at all, it's really inhibiting. But when I'm revising the script, particularly if I have a scene that isn't working well or isn't as good as it should be, I'll go back to the novel. There may not be an exact equivalent scene, but I'll look at the area of the novel which deals with that event or that character and go, 'What is it I've missed out?' or, 'What is it I've done wrong?' and try to reconstruct the scene in a better shape. And then before I deliver the script, particularly before I deliver the first draft, I'll sometimes go back and re-read the novel more generally and see if there are any other bits I can steal to build my house. And when the script is finally free-standing, the novel becomes an incredibly useful reference point.

How much pressure do you feel when adapting a well-known and much-loved novel, knowing that you won't be able to please everyone with the finished product?

I feel anxiety beforehand – 'Is it wise to take this on?' – but once I've decided I've got something to bring to it there's no point in being anxious about it. On *Wuthering Heights*, it really didn't bother me, because I had the version I wanted to tell and I thought it was truthful to what's in the book and I felt it hadn't been told before, so I was really clear about what my mission was in doing it. If I wasn't clear about why I was doing something, or I wasn't sure what I was bringing to it, that would be a bigger cause for anxiety. But as for worrying about whether people will be cross about it, yes of course sometimes they will be – but they can just read the book, you know? The book isn't going to be damaged by what I'm going to do to it.

CASE STUDY: *GIRL WITH A PEARL EARRING*

UK/US/Luxembourg, 2003 ▪ **Directed by** Peter Webber ▪ **Produced by** Andy Paterson, Anand Tucker ▪ **Screenplay by** Olivia Hetreed, based on the novel by Tracy Chevalier ▪ **Cast:** Colin Firth (Vermeer), Scarlett Johansson (Griet), Tom Wilkinson (Van Ruijven), Judy Parfitt (Maria Thins), Cillian Murphy (Pieter), Essie Davis (Catharina), Joanna Scanlan (Tanneke), Alakina Mann (Cornelia)

What attracted you to adapting Tracy Chevalier's novel?

I read it in proof because I have the same agent as Tracy, so I didn't have any preconceptions about it, except for my agent saying, 'You should read this. You'd love it.' And I did: I found it a thrilling read. I felt I completely understood that girl and I knew I could tell that story. I've rarely felt more confident about that. Then it was just a question of persuading everyone else, because I had no feature credits. But I was really sure I could tell it, and I was really sure it was a thriller. People kept going, 'Nothing really happens,' and 'It's all so small,' but it thrills you because those small things matter so much. It matters that Griet moves the chair in Vermeer's studio. It matters that she puts the earring in her ear. These things have very high stakes in this world. You asked earlier whether I see the complications and difficulties in things, and I absolutely didn't see the complications and difficulties of it being a subjective story and of her being an unreliable narrator; I felt those would be very easy to overcome. In terms of writing they were, but in terms of other people's perceptions they weren't.

In what way is Griet an unreliable narrator?

She's unreliable in that she thinks Vermeer is great so she gives him a lot of leeway, and dislikes his wife and always gives her short shrift, and covers up her own motives. So then you pull it apart and go, 'But what are these characters actually doing?' It was a pleasurable thought experiment to go, 'I'm Catharina, this girl has arrived and is closeted upstairs with my husband, they're doing this painting that I'm completely excluded from – how do I feel about that?' Expanding on those things was a really interesting part of exploring the book. Sometimes you feel like you're a butcher chopping the whole thing up – I've got this much steak and this many sausages – and when you chop it up you just feel like you've got a shambles. But this was one of those books where you chop it up and it all falls beautifully into the right pieces. Tracy had done such a brilliant job of constructing a narrative from the very few known facts about Vermeer and his family that it was a complete pleasure to do the dismantling.

And what was it you understood about Griet?

I understood about being a teenager and feeling a disconnect between your intellect and your circumstances; that you're being treated one way, but you feel you're something else. She's a maid, but she feels she has something to contribute and that's impossible in the world she's living in. Also, I'd always vaguely known that my family history was Dutch, but I'd never really thought about it, so when I went to Holland to do the research I had the feeling of being an adopted child who meets their birth family. I felt extraordinarily at home. Obviously the book wasn't written by a Dutch person, but there was something about Vermeer's reticent Dutch attitude to life that I found incredibly personally resonant. I just thought, 'This is so much my story.'

With the exception of the moment where she moves the chair in the studio, Griet could be perceived as a rather passive character, which is often seen as being a problem for a lead character in a film. Did that immediately occur to you?

The thing that sold the story to me is the moment where she slaps Cornelia, the wilful child. She thinks, 'If I let this kid get the upper hand here, I'm stuffed.' So she makes a choice and she slaps that child and she deals with the consequences, and I loved that choice. She proves how much she's not a passive character in that moment. Her situation is passive, but she's actually not. She doesn't wait for things to happen, she keeps moving forward to meet them. She forces the issue with Vermeer. She takes control of the relationship with Pieter. It was another brilliant thing that Tracy had done, to make her have power and agency without her ever stepping out of her proper historical position. So I really liked that about her character: she was secretly much more active than you think.

The script is very tight: 87 pages. The film is equally tight: 95 minutes. Almost an object lesson in how little exposition and dialogue is actually needed to tell a story on film.

If the room is very quiet you don't need to speak loudly to be heard, and I think that's what the film does. I come from a film editing background, so I really like things to be sparse. Through the energy of a cut or the presence of the actors you understand so much and need to say so little. What I discovered to some extent in writing that script, and certainly subsequently, was that you sometimes have to write things for people to read because they can't see what they'll see in the film. You need to explain more in a script and trust that you can let it fall away in the process. I've experimented with writing dialogue and going, 'You don't need to say this, but this is what you're thinking,' because if there's no dialogue there then the actor may not know what's going on in the scene, and having it editorialised for you on the page is quite unsatisfying. Whereas to write the dialogue and then go, 'Let's try playing the scene without actually saying those things,' can be really useful and really fruitful.

You establish a great deal very quickly in the first five pages: the class and religious differences between the Vermeers and Griet's family; her father's incapacity; and Vermeer's identity. How important is that set-up, especially with a period drama where the audience may not know that world well?

It can be very tempting to do lots of set-up: 'You don't know this world. Let me give you a guided tour.' As a writer, I'm quite keen on that stuff and you have to go, 'As a viewer am I keen on that stuff? No: I want you to get on and tell me the story and I'll find out the world as I go.' I think one of the things that's really successful in the story is that you understand her situation without anyone ever having to explain it to you. You can see where she is in the hierarchy of the family and how she relates to the kids and so on because these things just happen in front of you. There was the underlying question of how much it mattered that Vermeer's family are Catholic, and whether you have to understand seventeenth-century Dutch politics – and obviously you don't. You just have to know that there's some kind of difference between his family and Griet's, and that happens to be represented by religion: they're different from us, they're richer than us, so be careful. Then you've done your job.

It's a little way into the film before Griet and Vermeer meet for the first time, and then only briefly and wordlessly. Their scenes together have been rearranged from the script so they become longer and more intimate, and the development of the relationship between Griet and Pieter is more precisely mirrored. Did that progression emerge during the edit, or at the shooting script stage?

When I originally wrote the script, Mike Newell was attached to direct and Mike's view of the story was that the household was this little microcosm of society, and the painting emerged from all these different pressures of all these different characters on each other. It was more of an ensemble than the final film. When Peter Webber came on as director, he said, 'This is a love story, the painting is the consummation of the love story, and we need to question anything that isn't driving that forward.' So there was quite a big change of emphasis at that point, and then in the edit he was pursuing that line even further. I was seeing cuts of the film as they went along, and there was one version where there was practically nothing left of it at all, and he did bring it back from that a bit.

There was one interesting change between the script I read and the film. In the script, Vermeer and his wife come to Griet's house before she starts working for them, and he comments on her arranging the chopped vegetables in the kitchen in colour order, and you understand that she has some sort of artistic sense. In the film, that scene has disappeared and their meeting is hence delayed.

I wish I'd thought of that in the script, but actually we all felt it was fine. Then, on the day Peter shot it, he said to me, 'We're never going to use this, because as soon as you put them in the same room and he says that to her you've told the whole story.' So we were already thinking about where they would meet and the subsequent effects of that, and one of the great things about me being on set was that we could go, 'If we're not introducing them here, what are we going to do further on?' rather than going, in the edit, 'How can we cobble this together to tell the story in a different way?'

There's much less of Griet's family in the film. Why did you reduce her mother and father and brother's roles – and remove her sister completely, who dies of plague in the novel?

We wanted to isolate her as much as possible so that she felt more vulnerable. She needed to have just enough family to feel the loss of them, but not so much that she was safe and surrounded all the time. That was a very clear decision by Peter to tell a more disciplined version of the story.

On the other hand, the character of Vermeer's patron, Van Ruijven, has been considerably expanded from the novel. Did you feel that the drama needed a more overt villain?

That's pretty much exactly what I thought. I also felt like he was fun and the story is a little bit light on fun. Everyone else is very serious and earnest, so when he comes along he gets to shake things up, which seemed like a good thing in terms of the energy of the story.

The script is very deft at combining different scenes from the novel for greater dramatic effect: for example, the birth feast for Vermeer's son and the unveiling of the painting of Van Ruijven's wife. Do you deliberately look for those moments?

One of the things that became apparent once I started taking the book apart was that the story was an accumulation of hundreds of tiny moments, and that really wasn't going to work on film. So I was very conscious of looking for scenes in which you could pull those moments together, but that specific combination happened when Peter came on board. I did have those two scenes in an earlier draft, but they were doing slightly different things, and he said, 'Let's have one big party scene in which all the issues are aired.' That was a really useful note. Another combination of different bits is Vermeer's neighbours being thrown out of their house. That's a strong visual moment and we see what financial ruin looks like; we don't need it explained to us. Out goes your stuff on the side of the canal and there's no social services coming to help you. The other thing that Tracy does in the book is jump around in time – you think you're in a simple narrative, but actually, chronologically, it's quite complex – and I chose to make it completely linear. So it was a question of combining this event that happens in the present and this emotion that started it three months earlier into one moment, so we get the effect of the nonlinear narrative within the linear structure.

Do you ever feel that there are moments – not just with this novel, but in adaptations generally – where film enables you to do something better than the book?

Girl with a Pearl Earring is such a strong example of that, because the whole story is about looking and seeing, all of which you can do better on film. There are some lengthy passages in the book about her becoming aware of the effects of light and we were able to find visual ways of showing that, like the opening of the shutters in his studio and the reflection on the tray she polishes. So much of the script is actually description – much more than you're supposed to do, and much more than I'd normally do – because it's telling you what you're going to see. My intention when you read a script is always that you see the film, but usually I write just enough for you to see what's essential and preferably not a word more. But with this, it was so important that the reader understood the significance of certain objects and was confident that the silences in scenes would be explicable.

In the novel, Griet says, 'I never got to have a proper look at the finished painting.' In the film, she does see it and her reaction is, 'Oh. You looked inside me.' Why did you make that change?

Probably one of the biggest changes was that Vermeer was a less mysterious character than he is in the book, therefore she had to understand what the transaction between them had been in a more explicit way, rather than coming to that realisation years later as an adult woman looking back on it. It was really important that everything got dealt with at the end of the story.

The pearl earring itself is also put to slightly different use at the end of the novel than in the film. Just as the opening of the film is very concise, so is the ending: a 17-page epilogue is reduced to little over a page of script. Tanneke brings the earrings, a gift from Vermeer while he's alive rather than a legacy after his death – in other words, I have feelings for you that I can't do anything about, so here are the earrings instead. Then you cut to the painting. In the novel, she actually sells the earrings, which pays off Vermeer's debt to Pieter the butcher, so they and she become part of a financial transaction. So again, a deliberate shift into something more emotional and elegaic.

In the book, you never forget the financial transactions underlying everything. In the script, that was very focused around Maria Thins, the mother-in-law. She became the person who was always thinking about money, rather than everyone being driven by it. But you do have to be simpler in a film. You have this incredible visual richness, and there are all sorts of things you're saying in the way you frame and edit things, but those ambiguous moments can be a little underwhelming. Whereas with a book you sit there and savour it, with a film you want a more immediate kick.

There's a scene in the film where Griet pauses outside Vermeer's studio before leaving for the last time, and she can't go to him and he can't go to her, but they're separated only by a door. Did you want to make it clearer that he loved her? Because in the novel it seems more ambiguous, at least in Griet's mind, whether he actually cared more for her or for the painting.

That's a good question. I think in the end we felt – and I'm saying 'we' because it was very much Peter and I together – that you need to believe this love was real. You know that nothing will come of it, that they won't physically love each other, but there really was that feeling between them. It would be very cold and frustrating for us to think that she loved him, but he just wanted a painting. That's just too difficult. You'd feel cheated by it.

Difficult in that it would have narrowed the gap between Vermeer and Van Ruijven?

Exactly. They'd both have been using her. In that respect, it was a conscious decision not to completely follow the truth. Obviously I have no idea what Vermeer really thought, and this story isn't how that picture really got painted, but my reading of his paintings is that he was quite a remote person who had difficulty relating to women. He doesn't paint women in a way that suggests he was comfortable with them. He had to be in the room with them, but he puts up as many barriers as possible. In most of his paintings they're kept at a distance and framed in doorways and protected by props. And then suddenly there's this one girl staring at you and challenging you, much more intimate and physically present. It felt like there was a really important difference between her relationship with him and all the other relationships he might have had – and that was the story we were interested in telling.

You added another scene, too, where Van Ruijven finally gets his painting of Griet, but it gives him no pleasure. What was your thinking there?

It was really important to get across the sense that she had escaped all of them. He takes possession of the painting, but not of her.

And it feels absolutely right to end on the painting, because there's something so direct about her gaze that after several centuries it still endures.

Exactly. Somehow this girl still speaks to us, and even though we don't know who she was, this version is sufficiently credible that when you look at that painting, you go, 'Maybe that was her life.'

CASE STUDY: *WUTHERING HEIGHTS*

UK, 2011 ▪ **Directed by** Andrea Arnold ▪ **Produced by** Robert Bernstein, Douglas Rae, Kevin Loader ▪ **Screenplay by** Andrea Arnold and Olivia Hetreed, screen story by Olivia Hetreed, based on the novel by Emily Brontë ▪ **Cast:** Kaya Scodelario (Cathy), James Howson (Heathcliff), Solomon Glave (Young Heathcliff), Shannon Beer (Young Cathy), Steve Evets (Joseph), Oliver Milburn (Mr Linton), Paul Hilton (Mr Earnshaw), Simone Jackson (Nelly), Lee Shaw (Hindley), James Northcote (Edgar Linton), Amy Wren (Frances), Nichola Burley (Isabella Linton), Michael Hughes (Hareton)

Emily Brontë's novel has sharply divided readers since it was first published: love it or hate it. I assume you love it?

I do love it, but I first read it as a teenager and read it as a very twisted but deeply romantic story, and felt as the protagonists do that love and death were adjacent and almost equally attractive. When I came back to it many years later, and saw what an extraordinary catalogue of violence and abuse and perverse relationships is laid out for you, I was really astonished – and really impressed, because it's very unusual in classic literature to find a story that's so unflinchingly honest about being a teenager. Although some of the main characters in great fiction are teenagers, they're often not teenagers as we would recognise them. The Bennet sisters are teenagers, but they don't behave like any teenager you've ever come across. Whereas Cathy and Heathcliff are absolutely in the throes of hormonal chaos, quite apart from all the other chaos that's visited upon them, and it felt like that story hadn't really been translated into film. I didn't watch all the previous adaptations but I'd seen various versions over the years, and they seemed to me not very representative of what was most interesting in the book.

Your script is considerably stripped back from the novel, and the film is further stripped back from your script. What would you say that you, Andrea Arnold and Ecosse Films had in mind in tackling this story?

I suppose, as a producer, you look at a book like *Wuthering Heights*, and its history and heritage make it attractive in the first instance, and then you think, 'What would a version made now look like?' So they proposed it to me and I came back to them and said, 'I think this is a story about teenagers, I think this is a story in which Heathcliff is clearly not white, and I think this is a story about the damage done to you in childhood and how you can never escape that.' That isn't the way *Wuthering Heights* has usually been told, and they were really enthusiastic about that. I think part of their enthusiasm was that the *Twilight* films had just started and the first *Twilight* book is based on *Wuthering Heights*, so when I came in saying, 'This story is about teenagers,' they went, 'Teenagers. Fantastic.' Their first intention was a very commercial film, and even though we had a good time working on the script there was a certain pull towards more explanation and more romantic love than I wanted. As a screenwriter you only have a limited number of shots in your gun and you shouldn't fight battles any sooner or harder than you have to. You need to wait until you reach a point where you go, 'No: if we do this then the whole thing is pointless.' So I felt we would sort out those things in due course. But once it came to the casting, that starting point – it's about teenagers and Heathcliff isn't white – instantly became problematic. They wanted to get the film made and to support the budget that the film needed to be made at, but they felt that the casting required to achieve that budget didn't allow those things to be paramount. It was only when Andrea came on board, and we suddenly had a much lower budget and more creative freedom, that we were able to cast teenagers and a non-white Heathcliff. Although the irony is that by casting teenagers and having Andrea direct, it became a film that wasn't for teenagers – apart from very political, Gothic teenagers, who love it.

Brontë isn't precise about Heathcliff's origins, but he is described as 'a dark-skinned gypsy in aspect'. Why was his ethnicity so important to your pitch, and how did it affect your approach to the novel?

So much in the story is about prejudice, not being given a fair chance, being treated differently for who you seem to be, in looks or class. And the reaction of almost every character to Heathcliff is some comment about his 'dark-skinned looks': that he's not one of them, that he's strikingly different and therefore suspicious. I was struck in researching the writing of the book that Emily Brontë had set it at a moment when a great many former slaves were turned out of their masters' houses because slavery was no longer permitted in Britain and there was a racist panic about black vagrants, which seemed to me to resonate very clearly with the contemporary panic about 'hordes' of migrants. So it makes absolute sense that she had written this interloper, picked up off the streets of Liverpool, one of the great slave trade ports, as a person of colour. But no one who meets him in the book has any real reference for that, so they hazard a guess: gypsy, Lascar – an East Indian sailor – Chinese or plain 'black devil'. And once you see that, and get away from Laurence Olivier and Byronic dark eyes, it's hard to unsee it, and it informs all the prejudice and bad treatment that he endures and reacts against.

Would you describe the novel as a melodrama, and if so did you set out to embrace or resist that?

I think it's a combination of intense realism and Gothic melodrama, and for me the Gothic melodrama wasn't the most interesting thing about it. I know there have been versions which have gone quite Gothic and I didn't want to do that; I wanted to do something that felt very real. Some of the strongest passages in the book are her descriptions of the farmhouse and the people in it, the close relationships you have in a small household like that and how unservile the servants are towards their so-called masters. All that felt very convincing, so it was quite easy to jettison anything that seemed overblown. The dialogue is unspeakable: they never utter a single thing that you could actually say in real life – particularly Heathcliff, who carries on talking a great deal of high-flown stuff, even when he's supposed to be reduced almost to animal noises. The other Gothic element is the various layers of narration: Lockwood telling the story and Nelly telling the story and so on. Again, those have been significant elements in other versions, but they weren't the story I was interested in telling. They might be there partly because it was the first and only novel she ever got to write, so she's writing in the styles of novels she's read and working out a way of doing it, but to me they're just Gothic trappings that aren't helping you towards a better understanding of the story.

Cathy and Heathcliff aren't particularly sympathetic characters: they don't treat each other or anyone else very kindly. So why should we care about them?

I hope we care about them because we understand why they behave so appallingly. One of the things I found really interesting as I took the book to pieces was that Heathcliff is constantly referred to as devilish and diabolical and is always swearing terrible curses on people – and he does do some bad things, for sure – but mostly he just puts on a bad front and goes out of his way to make the people around him dislike him because he's such an angry, damaged person. I find something beguiling about that. Emily Brontë deals with psychological damage in a way that feels very modern and truthful, and it's obviously a book that's very heavily inflected by her own family experience of what it's like to live with someone very damaged, someone who you love but also hate. Cathy was also really interesting to me, because for most of the time I was working on the script I was the only woman in the room – and even though the men around me were very nice and sympathetic, they all disliked Cathy intensely and found her really irritating and wrongheaded. The thing with Cathy is that she has a boyfriend who's sweet and blonde and respectful – the kind of kid you could bring home to meet your parents, if you had any – and she has this other boy who's wild and dreadful and unacceptable, and she wants both of them. If that were a man and he had a sweet blonde girlfriend and a wild sexy wicked one, then it would be fine: 'Of course. What a dilemma. What can the poor boy do?' But because it's a girl we go, 'For God's sake, make up your mind, stop putting everyone through hell.' I was absolutely fascinated by how difficult that story still is. She's stuck in a horrible mess with a terrible brother; her only way out is to marry someone. She can't marry Heathcliff because he's made it impossible, so she marries Edgar. He's a decent person, it's a sensible choice. It's not romantic, but it's sensible. Then Nelly says, 'He won't want Heathcliff hanging around,' and Cathy goes, 'If he doesn't take Heathcliff he's not getting me.' She's not saying, 'I'm going to have an affair with him,' she just means, 'I need to get Heathcliff out of this awful place and rescue him as well as me, and then we can carry on as before.' And of course it's ridiculously naïve of her, but I don't think it's wicked. They're just kids, and she's trying to do the best she can under the circumstances, but the men won't have it. They won't share her, so they tear her apart.

Brontë's dialogue is dense and florid. Yours is sparser but elegant. Arnold's is sparser still and more colloquial – and more contemporary. It feels like the source material has gone on a real journey there.

When the book first came out people were horrified by it. They thought it was brutal and ugly, and that the language of it was disgusting, and I think the film has some of that too. That's not to say the film is brutal and ugly, it's beautiful in lots of ways, but it's a hard story and bad things happen in it. It's not bonnets and frocks, it's really got away from that, and I think Andrea is one of the few filmmakers who could have achieved that. You feel you're in that place, living that life – and I love that.

It's very much a northern, working-class telling of the story: both the characters and their houses are less grand than I imagined – Wuthering Heights is a farmhouse, for example, rather than a manor house.

Film often tends to push things up. You get people who are supposedly 20-something living in a palatial flat and you think, 'How the hell are they achieving that?' I wanted things to be a bit more real. It's a story that feels incredibly rooted in a particular place, and what's extraordinary about going to that place now is that it's remarkably unchanged. The feeling in the book is that the moor is a planet of its own. You have no sense of the outside world at all. And that enclosed world is clear in the film as well.

The tagline on the poster was 'Love Is A Force Of Nature', and nature certainly plays a big part in the film: the landscape, the elements, animals dead and alive. At times it feels like a collaboration between Ken Loach and Terrence Malick. How did you envisage it when you were writing it?

I just see it and write it down. It's that simple for me. I try to write down the movie I see in my head, and when the movie isn't there, I'm thinking, 'Why am I not seeing this?' Not being able to see a scene is a good indicator that something isn't quite right and I need to think differently about it. So I had a really clear idea of what it looked like. I've been to the places where it happens. I've been to the rock that they sat on, which is a real rock overlooking a real moor. And Andrea has this fantastic ability to be visually subjective, to put you right inside the sensory perceptions of the main characters. Her visual storytelling is really, really strong.

The novel is in two volumes. Your script and the film mainly dramatise the first volume, with elements of the second. In other words, a couple of hundred pages are dropped completely – including the framing narrative involving the older Nelly and the new tenant of Thrushcross Grange; Heathcliff's plot to take ownership of the Grange by marrying his and Isabella's sick son to Cathy and Edgar's daughter; and her ultimate engagement to her cousin Hareton. Were those immediate and obvious cuts for you?

It was the most agonising thing for me. I really wanted to tell that second half of the story, and the way I found to do that was to bookend the Cathy and Heathcliff story with the Catherine and Hareton story. With great toil and strain I got it down to a 24-hour framing device, in which Catherine comes to Wuthering Heights to get the doctor because her father is dying, and Heathcliff kidnaps her as he does in the book and says, 'You can't leave until you marry my son,' and while she's trapped there he effectively tells her the story. She says, 'Why do you hate us?' and his story is the explanation of why, then at the end of the Cathy and Heathcliff story you come back to Catherine and Hareton, who helps her escape and get back to her father – and in that help is implied an improved relationship which will end up with them being together. I thought that was hugely important, because the end of Cathy and Heathcliff's story isn't really an end, it's just a cessation. The end, the satisfying way of dealing with all this generational damage, is Catherine and Hareton beginning to forgive each other and being decent human beings, so you go, 'Thank God. There's hope at last. These two people can overcome all this this hatred and misery.' But what actually happened was that everyone would read the script and go, 'It doesn't get started until we get to the Cathy and Heathcliff story.' Peter Webber was originally going to direct the film, and Peter is great on script, and he said, 'I know how important this is to you, but at the moment it's not working. Why don't we just set it aside, work on the main story and put it back later?' Of course we were never going to put it back later, but it was a way of getting me off my high horse. So my feeling about my script and the finished film, is that it doesn't have an ending. I didn't find a way of solving that problem before I handed the script on and I really regret that.

The novel is about hate as much as love, and how hatred corrupts and destroys from generation to generation. There's a hint of that at the end of the film, when Hareton casually hangs a dog in the same way that Heathcliff did. But at the end of your script there's a sense that Heathcliff may treat Hareton better because of the way he was treated, rather than repeat the cycle of brutalisation. Again, can you talk me through that journey from novel to script to film?

As I said earlier, Heathcliff is constantly described as diabolical and devilish, but actually his parenting of Hareton in a practical sense is not so cruel and abusive. The thing he's done is displaced him, in the same way that he was displaced, and it's obviously a terrible injustice to Hareton that he's taken away his birthright – but he didn't steal it from him, he got it from his useless dad, and there's actually a kind of affection for him. I think at some point Heathcliff says, 'I really try to hate him, but I'm not as awful as I intend to be,' and I thought that was quite helpful, that you're not just left with this feeling of utter bleakness. Characters who are relentlessly bad aren't as interesting as characters who are contradictory and mixed up, like most of us are.

You received a screen story as well as a co-screenplay credit, which seems appropriate given that the film often follows the contours of your script, and that you chose to dramatise parts of the story which Brontë skated over. Did the story feel as much yours as Brontë's by the time you finished the script?

It's a strange hubristic thing you do in an adaptation. You do gradually take possession of it, and if you don't take possession of it that's problematic – for me, at least. Without denying for one instant that every bit of it is created or inspired by Emily Brontë, I'm saying, 'This is my version. This is what I think is important,' and I need to have a sense of ownership of the material to do that. And then, of course, it becomes the director's, and there are further versions beyond mine.

The story you told, coupled with Andrea Arnold's naturalistic shooting style and the direction she took the dialogue in, makes the film feel faithful to the spirit of the novel without being over-reverent to the letter of it. To put it another way, it's a compelling adaptation, but not a conventional one. Is that fair?

I think that is fair, and that's very much what I'd hope for it. With almost all period films, but certainly with adaptations, you get a strong sense of the time in which the film is made layered on to the original material. So when you watch a period film which was made in the 1960s, it speaks to you strongly of the 1960s. I think this film speaks equally strongly of the period in which it was made, and I don't think that's a bad thing.

Nick Hornby

Nick Hornby was born in 1957 in Redhill, Surrey.

His screen adaptation credits include: *An Education* (2009, memoir by Lynn Barber); *Wild* (2014, book *Wild: From Lost to Found on the Pacific Crest Trail* by Cheryl Strayed); *Brooklyn* (2015, novel by Colm Tóibín; *Love, Nina* (2016, book *Love, Nina: Despatches from Family Life* by Nina Stibbe); and a dramatisation of his own memoir, *Fever Pitch* (1997).

Fever Pitch was remade in the US in 2005 (released in the UK as *The Perfect Catch*). Several of his novels have also been adapted for film and television by other screenwriters, including: *High Fidelity* (film 2000/TV series 2020); *About a Boy* (film 2002/TV film 2003/TV series 2014–15); *A Long Way Down* (2014); and *Juliet, Naked* (2018). He recently scripted the Sundance TV series *State of the Union* (2019).

An Education and *Brooklyn* were both Oscar- and BAFTA-nominated for Best Adapted Screenplay.

APPROACHES TO ADAPTATION

Do you prefer to adapt material which chimes with your own work, or material which is completely different and gives you a chance to try out new things?

I don't think the nonfiction things I've done have chimed with my own work. They chime through an emotional outlook or an interest in material that I'm unlikely to generate myself. When you set out on a piece of original writing, you often think, 'This is different from anything I've done before,' then eventually you reach a point, a bit like Jim Carrey in *The Truman Show*, where you're sailing towards blue skies and – clunk! – you hit the inside of your skull: 'Oh, my God, I'm stuck here again.' But with the things I've adapted, I've found a little door out of my skull and into someone else's, and it feels incredibly refreshing.

Do you think adaptations involve a completely different set of creative gears to original screenplays?

An adaptation doesn't seem to me to require a different set of gears from writing a novel. It's just writing. I don't know how you've found it with your novel and your screenplays, but I don't feel like I become a different person when I'm doing one as opposed to the other. I'm using a broadly similar set of skills. The differences between an original and an adaptation are more practical, I think, and for all sorts of reasons connected with the industry, adaptations tend to come to the fore.

Do you always agree a mission statement or direction of travel with whoever has commissioned the adaptation?

I wouldn't put it as grandly as that. There's never anything written down. I wrote *An Education* on spec and my wife produced it, so by the time people got to see it we could pretty much say, 'This is what it is. You can see where it's going and what it wants to do, and you're either interested in it or you're not.' With *Wild*, I did go to America and talk – I wouldn't say pitch – to Reese Witherspoon and her producer, and I did have a couple of ideas about chronology, but

I think they just wanted the book adapted, really. Can we turn this book into a good film? That was our mission statement.

Do you usually produce an outline or treatment before you start writing the script?

No. I've tried to do it a couple of times, but it's really difficult if you're a prose writer, because it's deeply ingrained in you that your prose counts. I find it very hard to sit down and think, 'This is a piece of writing that will never be published, and no one is ever going to think about it in terms of its prose.' So even though I've thought I'll muster up an outline, I've given up after two paragraphs.

If the author of the source material is living, do you find it useful to have their input on the script?

It's different from case to case. I don't think Cheryl Strayed had a great deal of input into *Wild*, but she was fiercely loyal to the film – and loved it, as far as I know. With *An Education*, Lynn Barber seemed quite surprised and tickled by the whole thing in terms of it being a movie project, because what I adapted was six pages in *Granta*. We went out for lunch a couple of times to talk about it, and I remember her being helpful on period detail. The thing about adapting memoirs is I don't want to piss anyone off. It's an agonising enough process for the authors anyway, and if it makes them feel exposed or uncomfortable in a way the books didn't, then I've done something unhelpful or wrong – and I'm happy to talk to them about that, or disguise characters, or miss out a piece of the plot.

Is it easier to navigate notes from directors, producers and script editors when you have a piece of source material to measure the screenplay against?

The big capital letters answer to that is YES, both for fiction and nonfiction. One of the big problems with an original screenplay is that it only exists as a film, as it were. It's built on sand. And if it doesn't become a film, it isn't anything, really. So if a director says, 'Why doesn't this take place in the twentieth century instead of the nineteenth?' or, 'Why isn't the protagonist a woman instead of a man?' you have to think about that. But if you're adapting Dickens, it has characters, it has a shape, it has a tone, it has somewhere it's going, and those things are all enormously valuable in your battle to protect what you want to do. When it's all being spun out of the air, everyone's got equal rights to chip in.

Have you ever started work on an adaptation and found it harder to adapt than you anticipated?

Not yet. I never think anything's going to be easy, so I'm not often shocked or thinking to myself, 'My God, why am I taking this on?'

Have you ever been offered material to adapt which you felt couldn't, or shouldn't, be adapted?

There are some very basic things for me, like the length of the book. If something's 800 pages long, it's probably not a film – though it might be a very good TV series. You have to lose something like three-quarters of a book in adapting it, and at 800 pages you'd simply be losing too much to do it any kind of justice. I also don't want to write things where you have to recast the central character several times because of age. And there are lots of things I've been offered that are just too internal, where you're reading the book and the question in your mind is, 'What's actually happening here for us to look at?' and the answer is, 'Someone walking around an art gallery thinking about the past.' I tend to shy away from all those things.

If someone wants to option a book of yours, how do you decide whether to adapt it yourself – and if someone else adapts it, how involved would you be in the process?

I wanted to do *Fever Pitch* myself because it was a memoir, and I'd rather that I messed it up than someone else. But there's also a very basic reason why I adapted *Fever Pitch*, which is that when I was asked, in 1992 or 1993, I was just starting a family, I hadn't written a novel and I wasn't in the business of turning down work. So when the young director who wanted to do it said, 'Do you want to have a go at adapting it?' I said, 'Sure.' So someone paid me to do a draft, and we just kept doing drafts until someone eventually said, to my surprise, 'Okay, this is ready, we're going to make it.' By the time the film came out, in 1997, I'd written *High Fidelity* and just finished *About a Boy*, and the film rights for *High Fidelity* were sold and then the film rights for *About a Boy*, and I thought, 'This might keep happening, and I'm fucked if I'm going to spend two years writing a book and another five years taking it apart again.' While I have an idea in my head to do something else, I'm done with the last thing and I don't want to go back to it. That's just never ever appealed to me, and I've not regretted it for a moment.

What inspires you to swap the authorial autonomy of novels for the collaborative constraints of film and TV?

There are endless frustrations, as you know, and a great deal of despair, but I've made very good working relationships through screenplays with people I didn't think I'd get a chance to work with. I like the rhythm of it: I can do a draft in a few weeks. I can't do a draft of a novel in a few weeks, so I like the sense of having accomplished something that quickly. And then I like meeting to talk about it with people whose company I enjoy – and if I'm not enjoying their company, it tends not to go on too long.

Are there any screen adaptations which you think are especially good or you particularly admire?

Moneyball was really good; I was very admiring of Steven Zaillian and Aaron Sorkin's work on that. *The Godfather*, obviously, is really good. And Peter Straughan and Bridget O'Connor's adaptation of *Tinker Tailor Soldier Spy* was really good.

ADAPTING NONFICTION

When adapting a book, fiction or nonfiction, do you rely on the author's research, or do you conduct your own?

I don't think there's a consistent answer to that. With *An Education*, there wasn't enough in Lynn's piece for me not to conduct the research. With *Wild*, there was no way I was trekking off on some thousand-mile journey, so I completely relied on Cheryl. I talked to her and I watched things on YouTube, but I didn't go anywhere near the place.

Do you approach a nonfiction adaptation in the same way as fiction, or does the strangeness of real events give you licence to experiment with, say, structure?

Again, I'm not sure it makes much difference. Something either works as a screenplay or it doesn't, and the fact that things actually happened doesn't really help you in any way. I don't think it helps you to be more experimental.

Have you ever encountered events in a nonfiction book so strange that you couldn't use them in the adaptation because audiences wouldn't believe they were real?

No, but I can completely imagine that happening. The thing you've got to watch for is randomness. If a narrative development feels completely random, even if it happened in real life, that's not a good enough excuse to put it in a screenplay, which has to be organically constructed and psychologically convincing. So I can absolutely imagine chucking something out on those grounds.

How much responsibility do you feel towards historical accuracy when dramatising the lives of real characters?

It depends on who they are. Lynn isn't a character from history, she's a well-known journalist, and I was telling her story because it seemed meaningful and resonant about a particular time and place. I was using it as a way of writing about Britain at a certain point in its social history, and I felt I could write freely about what had happened to her. At the moment I'm doing some research on rock stuff. I don't know if anything will happen with it, but with that I think I have a duty to be accurate. Why not be? The facts are extraordinary enough.

How do you set about finding the voices of real characters?

With Lynn, I had perfect liberty to imagine the voice of a bright teenager in 1961. With Cheryl, I had a very strong voice in the memoir. And on the one I've been doing in the last year – another memoir about an extraordinary set of circumstances – I've been talking to the young woman concerned on an almost daily basis. But I think to a certain extent voice comes from experience. Once you have the narrative events and the character has made certain choices, then their voice starts to emerge – because it's going to be a certain kind of person who does this at this point, instead of that at that point, and you can start to fill in the corners of their soul in that way. But when I'm doing these films, I'm often asked, 'How did you get inside a woman's head?' And I say, 'I didn't have to get inside a woman's head. I adapted a book that a woman has written. That's the woman's head.' You know? Why do I have to recapture the way she thought when she wrote a book about it? That's not my job.

Do you try to avoid voiceover in adapting a first-person narrative, or do you see it as another tool in the toolbox?

It's a tool in the toolbox. If a film hasn't turned out well, people will point to the amount of voiceover and say it's the oldest fallback in the book. If they love the film, they probably won't even mention it. But it's good to make sure your screenplay is structurally sound before you start thinking about any voiceover that might be needed. The voiceover should be a flourish rather than something that's taking any narrative weight.

Do you use the language of the book in writing the dialogue and stage directions, or do you put the whole thing in your own words?

Stage directions, no. Dialogue, not immediately. You're always glad to copy something out, but it doesn't work like that most of the time. One of the reasons I do adaptations is that there are scenes where you think, 'The dialogue here is a gift,' and I get excited about the opportunity to use that. But if you're doing your job properly, actually you have very little choice about what language you use. You can't write Jane Austen dialogue when someone's had a brief period as a heroin addict. So the language sorts itself out, I think.

Do you keep the book beside you throughout the adaptation process, or do you try to internalise it and set it aside somewhere along the way?

I think you're always going to need it, even if it's just for someone's name or – with *Wild* – where they were on their journey. For that, I had a map on my pinboard to organise the material. There did come a point with *An Education* where the article was no longer any use to me. And the one I've done recently is interesting, because her memoir isn't out yet and she's been editing it. I know she's made a lot of changes to the book since I first read it, but I've stuck with her original version because I don't think whatever she's changed is going to make any difference to me in terms of what I see the essential story being. So I haven't had that beside me quite as much. When I first saw the film of *High Fidelity*, the character's name was Rob Gordon, not Rob Fleming as it is in the novel, and I said to D.V. DeVincentis, who co-wrote it, 'As a matter of interest, why did you change it?' and he said, 'I couldn't find the book.'

How much pressure do you feel when adapting a well-known and much-loved book, knowing that you won't be able to please everyone with the finished product?

I felt it a little bit with *Brooklyn*. I certainly felt it with *Wild*. That was such a phenomenon in America – number one bestseller for quite a while – and meant so much to so many women that obviously there was pressure on me because I was a bloke and I had to honour Cheryl. But whatever you've adapted, you'll meet someone whose favourite part was missing. There's a bit in *Brooklyn* which is about race, and in quite a few of the interviews I did, people who had read the book would go, 'You copped out of the race scene.' And we didn't, we filmed it. But it was a self-contained scene and when you're overlength the first thing you do is take out the self-contained scenes, especially when they're tonally jarring. It had absolutely nothing to do with race or controversy or wanting it to be a certain kind of film, it was really just the storytelling logic of it.

Of your produced screenplays, four are nonfiction – including your adaptation of your own memoir, *Fever Pitch* – and only one is fiction: *Brooklyn*. Do you prefer adapting nonfiction?

I haven't ever analysed it. Now that you say it, that's probably right. There's a social history side of me that's awoken by a certain kind of book. I read quite a lot of nonfiction and there's pretty much no nonfiction book that wouldn't make a fantastic film, even if it's just a three-page section from it. So ideas for movies do come to me more readily from nonfiction.

Do you think that being based on a true story in some way gives a project more weight?

Not to me. I'm slightly alarmed by the number of people who say, 'Oh, it's based on a true story, isn't it?' as if that somehow must mean it's worth more or is more interesting. Generally, to my way of thinking, it doesn't give it any more weight at all.

CASE STUDY: *AN EDUCATION*

UK/US, 2009 ▪ **Directed by** Lone Scherfig ▪ **Produced by** Finola Dwyer, Amanda Posey ▪ **Screenplay by** Nick Hornby, based on the memoir by Lynn Barber ▪ **Cast:** Carey Mulligan (Jenny Mellor), Peter Sarsgaard (David Goldman), Alfred Molina (Jack Mellor), Rosamund Pike (Helen), Dominic Cooper (Danny), Olivia Williams (Miss Stubbs), Emma Thompson (Headmistress), Cara Seymour (Marjorie)

Did you learn anything from adapting *Fever Pitch* which you were able to apply when adapting other people's memoirs, starting with Lynn Barber's?

No [*laughs*].

Because the stories are so different?

Yes. And because the lengths of the books were so different, and the timescales were so different, and both became fictionalised. So I guess I learned that you could fictionalise memoir, which was probably a helpful thing to know. To free myself to think, 'Just because it's a memoir, doesn't mean I have to stick to it.'

As you said, *An Education* was first published in *Granta*. If a nonfiction book is equivalent to a novel, then a magazine article is probably more like a short story. How did the length of the source material affect the work of adapting it?

An Education was really partly an adaptation and partly an original screenplay. The six pages which Lynn wrote provided me with a skeleton, but there was no flesh on that skeleton. So I had a rather nice time imagining characters more fully and inventing plot developments that fitted in with them. For example, the Peter Sarsgaard character being a cheat and a liar meant that you could make him cheat and lie about other things. I enjoyed doing all that.

In her introduction to the film tie-in edition of her expanded memoir, Barber says that the first draft of your script stuck very closely to her story – and even in its final form, *Wild* is very faithful to Cheryl Strayed's story. Is that level of fidelity always your first instinct?

It's not so much about fidelity, it's that the shape of the story is usually what's appealed to me. The ending of a book, or the midpoint crisis, has struck a chord in some way – and if I've gone away from that, it's no longer the thing I chose to adapt. With *An Education*, it took a few drafts. The first draft did stick closely to the piece, not just in terms of narrative, but in terms of Lynn's voice. Lynn is a flinty woman in her late sixties, and in the first draft Lynn was a flinty young woman in her teens, and you think, 'This isn't going to work, because she knows everything.' So you've got to chip all that away otherwise you miss the whole point of the story, which is that she's naïve enough to believe this man. But as it went on, it emerged that what I was interested in was suburban alienation and being excited by culture and wanting to get to the big city – which is also what *Fever Pitch* is about, to some extent. So I started to feel quite personally connected to the material, and felt passionately about that on Jenny's behalf. I knew exactly what it was like, that feeling of being alive because you're going to the theatre or to concerts or to clubs. But it comes at a cost for her, because she's taking a shortcut that really doesn't exist. And she's rescued by education, which is something else I probably believed.

Lynn and her older lover Simon became Jenny and David in the film, whereas their friends Danny and Helen retain the names they had in the memoir. What was your thinking there?

As I remember, it was entirely dependent on who was still alive and might recognise themselves and sue us – but it also gave me permission to go further away from the facts. I did the same thing with *Fever Pitch*, where the lead character became Paul in the film. It's a very simple thing, but the sense of freedom it brings you is much greater than the tiny change you've made.

In the film, Jenny's mother is portrayed more or less as a housewife. In reality, Barber's mother was an English teacher at a girls' school. There is an English teacher in your script, but it isn't her. Why did you change and split that character in that way?

My feeling was that having her mother working, and being an English teacher, wouldn't necessarily inspire her to feel that women could work, because everything her parents did would be dead, as my kids would say. Giving her an English teacher who's funky and inspiring and cares passionately about the arts seemed to me to do her and the script more good. And, of course, it was a time when lots of middle-class women were housewives, and I felt that young women today ought to know that often women did nothing and were very frustrated doing nothing and had to live through their kids. So the Olivia Williams character becomes an important, and very moving, example of something you can do if you go and get your education. I don't think you'd have found that if you'd used the mother.

The first half of the script is light and funny in a way that the memoir isn't, partly because the stage directions and dialogue are written in your distinctive tone. Were you aware, first, of superimposing your voice over Barber's, and second, of wanting to seduce the reader and viewer with charm and humour in the same way that David does to Jenny?

Things like stage directions are almost nothing to do with me. I've got to write them and my voice is unavoidable. I never think, 'I'd better try and do these in the voice of the author.' In terms of tone, I'm always looking for funny–sad, and there isn't that much of it out there. I'm not very interested in adapting comedy stuff, and there's an awful lot of literary fiction that hasn't got any jokes, so if I see an opportunity to create that contrast, that's a good start for me with material. The things I love most do that, where you turn on a sixpence and suddenly you're in different emotional territory. The first half of any Disney movie is light, and then it goes very dark in the second half. When you come out of those films as a kid, you feel like you've come a long way and the emotional territory you've covered is considerable. It's hard to do in a screenplay, especially over a relatively short period of time like 90 minutes, and feel you've gone somewhere by the end of the film that's different from the place you were in at the beginning – but I think tone is one of the ways you can do that. If there's some kind of emotional complexity in the tone of the film, you do feel you've been further.

It's quite a novelistic screenplay in some ways, as is *Wild*: precise descriptions of people and places, and of what people are feeling at any given moment, and even authorial comments like, 'We know now that her life can never be the same again.'

I think it causes me problems with directors. Actually, I think it makes it harder to find directors. You've got to find a director who thinks they've still got something to do, even though that kind of stuff is in there. I don't think there's anything I can do about it; it's what keeps it interesting for me. The ones that have worked have worked, and the right director has been found. I just feel that when I'm presenting a screenplay I'd like it to be read properly, rather than relying on enormous amounts of imagination from the people who are trying to think about it as a film.

Barber describes Simon as 'rather short, rather ugly, long-faced, splay-footed', which clearly isn't Peter Saarsgard, and Jenny certainly seems to fancy David more than Barber says she fancied Simon. Was that designed to make Jenny's interest in him more plausible and understandable?

I always found Lynn's description of him rather mystifying. I don't know how many 16-year-old girls would look at that character and think, 'Whoa, yeah, I'm going to get involved in this!' It seemed to add a whole level of complexity to the screenplay that didn't get us very far: you've got to spend a long time explaining why a short, ugly, splay-footed person has seduced a pretty young girl. So that's the first thing: it just simplified matters. He's got charm and that helps – and I don't think the film is a lesser thing as a result of that. The second thing is a very basic thing, which is that actors are better looking than ordinary people – that's why they're actors. Even if they're really great actors, they're also good-looking people. So every time you imagine a character being ordinary, or ordinary-ish, the person who ends up playing that part will be better looking than that, if it's a lead. If it's not, fine, but if you want your film funded, and you want to cast a short, ugly person in the lead, it's going to take a while, not least because you're trying to cast someone who by definition is not very famous. I mean, it's sort of a joke, isn't it? The relatively ordinary guy in *Fever Pitch* turns out to be played by Colin Firth. The relatively ordinary guy in *High Fidelity* turns out to be played by John Cusack. That's all you've got to work with, basically.

Similarly, Barber describes herself as having simply 'hopped in' to Simon's car when they first met, whereas Jenny puts her cello in first and walks along beside David's car to start with. Again, did you feel that Jenny would otherwise seem too silly and trusting from the point of view of a modern audience?

Yes. If you're trying to persuade people that this is a bright, complex young woman and she behaves like an idiot, even though she's only 16, then your cause is damaged. The mores of audiences have changed as well. It was interesting talking to women over 40 who saw *An Education*, because they all had an equivalent story – 'He said, "Would I like to get in his car?" and I did' – and I don't think you could show that anymore, not without an explanation. We're so sensitive about the protection of young people now, quite rightly. So we had to be careful with that and find an interesting way of delaying her getting into the car. In fact, she might have played the cello as opposed to the violin because of that scene.

Barber's headmistress refused to make her a prefect because she was a 'troublemaker', but the film gives the impression that she was initially a model pupil. Was that to emphasise the negative effect that David has on Jenny?

It was, and I also wanted her to have this hunger for culture, and it's slightly more complicated if the person with the hunger for culture is the person who's also kicking up hell at school. She wants this stuff, but it's coming too slowly and all the people around her are dim, so David becomes the conduit for things she was thirsting after as a smart, positive pupil.

At times, the memoir is more expansive than the film: Simon took Barber to Amsterdam and Bruges as well as Paris. Did you confine it for practical reasons of time and budget or, again, for plausibility?

I couldn't make head nor tail of any of that in terms of plausibility. You can imagine a huge amount of planning going into one weekend, but the idea that she jumps out of her uniform on Friday, they fly off somewhere and she comes back on Sunday – I couldn't think how I was going to sell that to a contemporary audience.

In fact, the first big trip she takes with him in the film isn't in the memoir: they go to Oxford, which is a handy way of dramatising the life she's aiming for.

Yes, and of dealing with why her parents were so credulous. He's saying, 'I've got an in with this old college professor, but never mind, next time,' and they're going, 'Oh, shit, she's going to miss out on a huge opportunity here.' It's hard work setting it up so that they're in a position where they believe it, or they're allowing it to happen, but once I started to see it through it turned out to have a lot of legs.

There are some scenes in the memoir you've bumped up and some you've downplayed. For example, Barber's discovery that Simon was married was less dramatic in real life, whereas her father's reaction was more dramatic – he went outside and kicked Simon's car.

That seemed a little absurd in terms of the way the dad had been written up to that point, and in terms of Alfred Molina's performance.

I was worried it would tip over into comedy, when the best way to play it was to show their heartbreak because they've been conned too.

Equally, Simon's wife never spoke to Barber in real life – she talked to Barber's mother, whereas Jenny sees her and talks to her directly.

I wanted Jenny to own what she'd done. I wanted her to have a very hard moment, the sort of thing that helps you grow up quick, and I didn't want her to be protected by a parent at that point.

Barber describes how, when all this was over, her parents would simply say to her, 'You know best.' But, of course, the film has the cathartic moment when her father apologises outside her bedroom. How do you reconcile the truth of real life, the lack of catharsis, with commercial cinema's hunger for tidy, redemptive endings?

I don't see the point of asking people to pay money to go to the cinema if they're left unsatisfied. *Brooklyn* was an interesting one, because a couple of people said, 'Why did you change the ending?' and we didn't change it, we extended it by about two minutes. She's made her decision. It's clear at the end of the book that she's going back to America. What we did was get her to embrace that decision as a positive thing. But there is a certain type of literary audience that prefers miserable ambiguity. Then lots of people went to see the film, because audiences were coming out in tears, grabbing people and saying, 'You have to go and see this film.' I'd rather have the second response, to be honest. I want to make it as emotionally complex as I possibly can, and I don't like cheesy redemptive endings that bear no reference to what's gone before, but I don't think the things I've been involved in have done that, actually. I wouldn't say they have happy endings. I'd say they end with some kind of doubt, or a doubt has been placed in the minds of the audience before that point.

Barber writes, again in her introduction to the film tie-in edition of the book, that in sticking very closely to her story your first draft 'cruelly exposed the fact that it had no proper ending – it reached a dramatic climax and then dwindled away'. What would you say the dramatic climax of her story is, and how did you set about creating your own

ending in subsequent drafts – and in the finished film, where the scripted ending was itself changed?

Several things happened, really. One is that we always presumed we would end with David turning up at Oxford to see Jenny, and it didn't work out. We did film it at the end of the shoot, but neither Peter nor Carey had their best day, and the big problem with that ending is that it was dramatically inert. You're just restating everything that's happened before, so it doesn't go anywhere. So it went. Another thing was that I don't think any of us expected the scene with Jenny and her father at her bedroom door to be as emotionally powerful as it was. Carey and Fred both killed it. When you're looking at it you think, 'Oh, that's probably the dramatic climax of the film, and everything from this point is a coda.' To be honest, we cobbled together an ending which we hoped worked because the thing that we hoped was going to be the ending didn't work. As I remember it, we'd been invited to Sundance and we didn't have the last scene of the film, and the idea of showing it at Sundance was to try to find an American distributor. So I wrote that final piece of voiceover and Carey came and did it, then we went to Sundance and the film was the subject of a bidding war – and Sony, who bought it, literally said, 'Carey, Best Actress nomination. Nick, Best Adapted Screenplay. And if we work, we can get Best Picture.' We've gone from not having an ending to that in about four or five weeks. This is a long way of saying that it must have worked as an ending because those responses wouldn't have been possible if it hadn't. But it was only through a mixture of bad luck, happenstance and being resourceful with the time and money we had available that we were able to come up with something which felt like an ending. That's film, isn't it? With a novel, if you haven't got the right ending, you just go off and rewrite it until you do. With a film, you've got a day of reshoots and an actress's voice, so you put that in a pot and see what you can do with it. It's not a perfect medium, it's a collaborative medium, and you have to alter things as you go. The thing we probably did right was recognising that we'd be flogging a dead horse to try to find a big, emotional moment after the door scene. That's when everyone cries. So you make a virtue of that, accept that it's your climax, and work out how you're going to negotiate the rest of the story without letting people down.

CASE STUDY: *WILD*

US, 2014 ▪ **Directed by** Jean-Marc Vallée ▪ **Produced by** Reese Witherspoon, Bruna Papandrea, Bill Pohlad ▪ **Screenplay by** Nick Hornby, based on the book *Wild: From Lost to Found on the Pacific Crest Trail* by Cheryl Strayed ▪ **Cast:** Reese Witherspoon (Cheryl), Laura Dern (Bobbi), Thomas Sadoski (Paul)

You said earlier that there was no way you were trekking off on some thousand-mile journey before you adapted *Wild*. So what drew you to it as a project?

I read a review of it in the *New York Times* by Dwight Garner, whose taste I trust, and the review was so amazing that I ordered it from Amazon and didn't really read what it was about. I just came to a paragraph where he said, 'If you find yourself in tears on the subway...' and I thought, 'I've got to buy this book.' Then, when it turned up, there's a pair of hiking boots on the front cover. I thought, 'Walking? Nature? Bollocks!' And then I opened it and read a bit and thought, 'Okay, this has got something.' This is almost too nerdy to explain, but I'm a big Bruce Springsteen fan, and to me the whole thing read like the live shows of his 1978 album *Darkness on the Edge of Town*: kind of wild and intense. I thought, 'I love this book, I want to adapt it and I think I know how to do it,' so I called my agent to find out about it and she said, 'Reese Witherspoon owns it.' I'd met Reese during award season for *An Education* and we had a very lovely and surprising connection – she was very warm about my work and particularly loved a short story she'd read in a charity anthology – and we talked about working together and nothing happened. So I emailed her and said, 'I love this book,' and she said, 'I wish I'd known, we've just asked someone else to do it.' So I was a bit disappointed. Then about a month later she said, 'We can't get a deal done with this person, will you do it?'

In her author's note, Cheryl Strayed writes, 'There are no composite characters or events in this book. I occasionally omitted people and events, but only when that omission had no impact on either the veracity or the substance of the story.' Did you try to follow the same principles in adapting it?

It got boiled down one stage further, so there were actually composite characters. But yes, pretty much the same principles. When I'd been given the gig I read the book again and was underlining stuff, and when I looked back at what I'd underlined I realised I could get a really powerful, dramatic movie out of that stuff without going anywhere near the trail, because there's so much in that book. It was like, how can I organise this material so that it reflects the walk and the backstory? Then the next level was, how can I organise this material so that you get the walk, the backstory and the sense of complete solitude that the walk gave Cheryl? Because what you're drawn to in adapting the book is incident, and quite often the incident involves other people on the trail, but that's not the point of the walk. The point of the walk was that she did it on her own, and she was frightened, and there were lots of things to be frightened of. So there was a third level to squash in, which was her silence and solitude and fear.

Wild could be called a road movie. Did you have that genre in mind, and did the fact that Cheryl's journey had a timetable and a goal help give the script a tension and a drive?

Anything that involves movement and meeting people along the way is a road movie, so I couldn't not have thought of that, but I wasn't paying particular homage to anything. I'm also very suspicious of things that have timetables and goals. It's the oldest trope in film. You've got 12 minutes to do this, or you've got 12 days to do this. Why have you? Bollocks you have. So I don't think that helps unless all the elements are right.

The book starts where the film starts, with Cheryl on the trail, losing one of her toenails – then losing one of her hiking boots, then basically losing her shit. It's an inherently dramatic, cinematic opening.

That's the bit that got me into it. But when I went to see Reese I spun the order of it, starting with the walk and spinning backwards into the heart of her crisis, because I didn't see how you could start with the toenail scene and then the mother's death, which is pretty much where the book starts. If the central dramatic moment happens in the first five minutes of the film, you're going to struggle to maintain the intensity that the book had. The image I had in my head was peeling an onion. The trail is one layer, divorce is another layer, drug addiction is another layer, promiscuity is another layer. And then right at the centre of it is this trauma of the mother's death.

And it is literally at the centre of it. Chapter 1 of the book, describing the sudden illness and death of Cheryl's mother Bobbi, becomes a series of long flashbacks in the film, culminating in a scene where she finds herself standing on the trail in the snow with only a watchful fox for company shouting 'mom' over and over. That scene falls exactly in the middle of both the book and your script. It's as if your adaptation is walking on the same path, sometimes behind, sometimes ahead, but always ultimately meeting up.

Her emotional beats are brilliant in the book, but knowing I couldn't do that because of the decision I'd made about the chronology, I had to find a parallel way. The film is probably more literal-minded, because the fox scene comes closer to the mother's death than it does in the book. Given the kind of adaptation I wanted to do, I didn't know how much spooky spirituality I could get away with, but I think it has a certain weight to it.

One of the few significant changes to the story – and one of the few deviations from Cheryl's strict point of view – is when she phones her ex-husband Paul from her motel room in Mojave, something which she had the urge to do in reality at the start of her journey but resisted. Why did you feel it was important to do that and to show Paul in his apartment with a female friend, a scene which Cheryl could have imagined, but wouldn't have seen?

The way I chose to structure the script meant that the first few minutes of the film had to do a bit of work in terms of explaining why any woman would do this, and quite a lot of that is conveyed in that scene: a relationship's ended, the guy's moved on, there's a great deal of pain involved. Him saying, 'You don't have to do this,' suggests the whimsicality of the project and stops you having to come up with a proper reason, other than her desperation, that makes her go on the walk. I thought, 'There won't be many opportunities to switch point of view from this point on, so I should make the most of this one,' and that conversation does explain things, even though what they say is quite elliptical.

Her diary, poetry extracts, snatches of songs, are all part of what she calls in the book, and you call in the script, the mix-tape radio in her head. You obviously need that because she's so often on her own, but what determined when you used it?

It was another thing I went to Reese with: the idea that there has to be this jumble. I didn't want to overuse it, but we had to find a way of externalising her thoughts without a voiceover: 'Dear Diary, today I went to blah, blah, blah.' I don't know if anyone noticed how brilliant the sound design is in the film. They found a level for that hum in her head which is between internal and external. There's a static-y quality to it which I think is great. Of course, a lot of the time, something she hears draws her back into her memory, so it was choosing the right points for the flashbacks as well.

The film starts with that moment in the middle of her journey, then flashes back to the beginning of it – then, when her journey is under way, flashes back to what motivated her to make it, even flashing back further within those flashbacks. Were your decisions about where to position the flashbacks – and what sounds and images you would use to link past and present – instinctive and immediate?

Yes, because we were on the clock. Reese said, 'I have this window next year and I'd really like to hit it,' and I said, 'I think I can do that,' but I came back in a sort of heightened state, thinking, 'Okay, this is serious.' I'd never worked with that kind of deadline before – usually there is no deadline and no one gives a shit: if it's not next year, it might be the year after that – but this was, 'I'm doing this, and I'm doing this, and I'd like to do this in-between.' I wrote the first page of the screenplay around ten months before they started shooting, so I did think more about structure than I had for previous scripts simply because it was needs must. I needed to know what I was doing before I started.

The film ends quickly once Cheryl has reached her destination, the Bridge of the Gods. You get to the point, make it, and then get out.

That was also clear to me before I started, and we knew it when we saw the cut of the film. That's the big moment.

You were known initially as a writer of men – *Fever Pitch*, *High Fidelity*, *About a Boy* – but your novels since have focused equally on women, and your produced screenplays have all been from a female perspective. What brought about that change?

An Education was a big shift in my career and my thinking. The truth is, in the urban world I write about there isn't an awful lot to stop white men doing what they want to do. It's their internal life that stops them from doing what they want to do, which is pretty much true of most of the male characters in the first three books. Women have proper obstacles, especially if it's a period piece. Historically, traditionally, they've not been allowed to do what they want to do, and there have been real barriers to stop them achieving what they want to achieve. So that was one thing: women just seem more dramatically alive to me. The second thing is the unbelievable quality of actress available to you, who don't get sent decent parts. When we cast Carey Mulligan, it quickly became apparent that we had the best actress of that age in the world. If it had been about a 25-year-old man, we absolutely would not have got the best actor in the world, because the actor would be getting paid $20 million to put on a superhero suit and would say, 'I like your little drama, but what can I do?' It makes things harder to fund and the films tend to be less commercial, but in terms of the art of it, getting to work with talent of that magnitude has got to be a huge drive for a screenwriter.

Deborah Moggach

Deborah Moggach was born in 1948 in Bushey, Hertfordshire.

Her screen adaptation credits include: *Goggle Eyes* (1993, novel by Anne Fine); *Love in a Cold Climate* (2001, novels *The Pursuit of Love* and *Love in a Cold Climate* by Nancy Mitford); *Pride & Prejudice* (2005, novel by Jane Austen); and *The Diary of Anne Frank* (2009).

She has also adapted five of her 19 novels for film and television: *To Have and To Hold* (1986); *Seesaw* (1998); *Close Relations* (1998); *Final Demand* (2003); and *Tulip Fever* (2017). Her novel *These Foolish Things* was the basis for *The Best Exotic Marigold Hotel* (2011).

Pride & Prejudice was BAFTA-nominated for Best Adapted Screenplay.

APPROACHES TO ADAPTATION

Do you prefer to adapt material which chimes with your own work, or material which is completely different and gives you a chance to try out new things?

I think I slightly prefer something different. Because I've been working for so long – 40-something years – I can get stuck in a groove, particularly a groove of domestic drama, stuff about families and children and so on. If it's something completely different, it's a bit of a stretch, and I think that's what I need at this stage.

Do you think adaptations involve a completely different set of creative gears to original screenplays?

No, I don't. I think that when writing scripts one needs completely different gears, and it's quite unusual to do both fiction and screenplays – though obviously David Nicholls and Nick Hornby and other people do it – but I don't think adaptation is by its nature that different to making up stories, it's just easier. You're moving into a house that someone else has built, and you might shift the furniture around and knock down a wall or two, but they've made the house, they've made the plot, and it's much easier rearranging someone else's plot than making up a plot of your own.

Do you always agree a mission statement or direction of travel with whoever has commissioned the adaptation?

Oh, God, no. With *Pride & Prejudice*, for example, I had no mission statement at all. Working Title just said it was time for a movie of it – it hadn't been done as a film since Aldous Huxley adapted it many years ago – and they didn't say they wanted a feminist one or a revisionist one or whatever. So I had to make up my own mind. Sometimes people do say what they want, and sometimes I agree and sometimes I don't, but it's their project, they're the ones forking out the money and making the big commitment, so you should be in tune with them before you start. But a surprising amount of times they haven't got a view; they want you to give your view, which is quite nice in a way.

That is surprising, given how much money they may have spent to option the material.

I know. But so far as outside help goes – and obviously it's a collaborative process, so it's different from writing novels – if they're intelligent and they're in tune with the project and you're in tune with them, a good script meeting can be a wonderful thing. It's such fun, because you're galloping together. In a bad script meeting, on the other hand, of which I've had many, they don't get it at all.

Do you usually produce an outline or treatment before you start writing the script?

Yes, which is loathsome. I'm sure everyone says that.

Almost everyone has said that.

They're ghastly. I don't know how people do it. There's a certain technique in reducing something to three pages or a page-and-a-half or whatever, and I don't have it. I can't boil it down. Most plots, if you reduce them to a page-and-a-half, sound banal – even *Anna Karenina* – so you fill it out because it's a sales document and you want it to sound interesting. If I do a treatment it'll be 40 pages, and I'll put in bits of dialogue as well because I want it to be readable. And by that time, you might as well write the thing. It hardly takes longer to write a script than to write the treatment. Everyone hates them, basically, but producers have got to have them because they need something to raise the funds off. Maybe if I was very famous my name would be enough, but it certainly isn't.

If the author of the source material is living, do you find it useful to have their input on the script?

That's jolly interesting. Most of mine have been dead. Jane Austen. Nancy Mitford. And Anne Frank, obviously, unfortunately. But there was a thing called *Goggle Eyes* that Anne Fine wrote, about a woman who's got children and there's a new man in her life, and the daughter's difficult relationship with her stepfather. I read the book, and it was so much what was happening in my life that I rang up Anne Fine and said, 'Is anyone doing this for television?' and she said, 'It's been optioned, here are the people who are doing it, will you ring them up?' So my agent rang them up and I got the option and I did it, and that was wonderful because Anne and I got on really well and she loved what I did and it was very encouraging to know she was there. The advantage of adapting my own work, or adapting Anne's in that case, is that you have a deeper knowledge of the characters and you can be bolder with them – and they can do more surprising and interesting things. If you just read the characters in a book of course you can adapt it, but it's really good to talk to the author about them because they'll have lived with them.

Is it easier to navigate notes from directors, producers and script editors when you have a piece of source material to measure the screenplay against?

Yes.

Have you ever started work on an adaptation and found it harder to adapt than you anticipated?

Moll Flanders. Absolutely impossible. Because Moll Flanders is impossible to understand. She's very contradictory. One minute she's weeping because her child has been taken away, the next minute she's forgotten all about it – and Defoe seems to have forgotten all about it, too. So you can't ever get a handle on her. It's very picaresque as well: it's just one damn thing after another, it doesn't actually have a shape. Andrew Davies did it in the end, and he probably did a very good job, but I had to give up. I couldn't do it.

Are there any screen adaptations which you think are especially good or you particularly admire?

Robert Altman and Frank Barhydt's *Short Cuts*, from the Raymond Carver short stories. Absolutely brilliant. They made one up and the others they wove together. Harold Pinter: good playwright, great screenwriter. His version of *The Go-Between*. A wonderful book, too. You may be talking about that later: whether it's easier to work with a good book, or with total crap.

That's a really good question, which I'm now wishing I'd asked everyone. What's your answer to it?

My answer to it is that you want a good book. If the characters are cardboard you can't put them into drama because they've got no life anyway. But if they're wonderfully observed characters, like a good book has, then they're living, breathing human beings. They'll change, because they're going to become creatures of film rather than creatures of a novel, but they already have a fullness and a life which gives them movement. They're not mannequins.

ADAPTING FICTION

Some writers try to include as much of the novel as possible by boiling scenes down to their essence. Others are more ruthless in editing it down to a sort of greatest hits, but being true to the spirit of it. Do you favour either of those approaches?

It certainly shouldn't be greatest hits, because a screenplay should have a narrative and an integrity of its own. And it's not really a question of just boiling stuff down: you may expand stuff, you may get rid of it, you may reshape it. I think it's just a different creature. Another wonderful screenplay is Emma Thompson's for *Sense and Sensibility*. She's so brilliant. She's got Jane Austen in her bone marrow. And what she did with that was dismember the baby and put it back together again with huge love and reverence. I learned a lot from reading that screenplay.

If a novel has an unusual structure, would you try to reproduce that in adapting it?

I don't think you can generalise. You'd have to see with each one. There are some novels, like *The Virgin Suicides*, where you think, 'No one can adapt this,' because either nothing happens, or it's too weird, or it's too inconsequential. But a really clever screenwriter will just 'get' it and come at it from some interesting angle: 'I'll do it all in voiceover,' or, 'I'll stick in an alter-ego,' or, 'I'll turn them into dogs.'

Do you try to avoid voiceover in adapting a first-person narrative, or do you see it as another tool in the toolbox?

Some people say it's a sign of weakness and that you're bailing yourself out. Other people, including me, think that some of the greatest movies of all time have had voiceover, from *All About Eve* onwards. You obviously don't want voiceover that just describes what's happening, but it's interesting to use it if it cuts against what's happening.

Do you keep the novel beside you throughout the adaptation process, or do you try to internalise it and set it aside somewhere along the way?

I throw it away, practically. I read it first with my adapter's hat on, watching for dramatic scenes, visual scenes – maybe underline them, maybe not – I do the first draft, which may be very literal, and then I almost physically chuck the novel away, because the first draft is what I'll then be working from. If you go back to the novel at that stage it will be regressive and will probably hit the cutting-room floor. The sea change, hopefully, will happen after the first draft: each draft will then feed off the one before and become more and more of a movie – or TV.

How much pressure do you feel when adapting a well-known and much-loved novel, knowing that you won't be able to please everyone with the finished product?

Well, I had two of the most-loved books of all time: *Pride and Prejudice* and *The Diary of Anne Frank*. It's a huge challenge and responsibility, and people are very proprietorial. So you do feel the weight of people's expectations, and you also feel the weight of all the previous adaptations. With *Pride and Prejudice*, you've got the wet shirt scene, which set female bosoms heaving the world over. And with *The Diary of Anne Frank*, there were also other adaptations, mostly rather sugary.

If someone wants to option a novel of yours, how do you decide whether to adapt it yourself – and if someone else adapts it, how involved would you be in the process?

I try to do it myself. It's poacher turned gamekeeper, but the feeling of someone else adapting your work is like being out of your house while your underwear drawer is being rifled through – very intrusive and intimate. I don't like it at all. I also think I could do a better job! I'm very ruthless with my own work, because I don't want to be thought of as precious and retentive, and I think I have the necessary distance to treat it as drama. But I may be wrong and they may not want me, and in each case where that's happened I haven't been involved at all because they haven't wanted me to be. I'd probably like to be, but someone else would come in and I'm out of it. And I really hate that.

What inspires you to swap the authorial autonomy of novels for the collaborative constraints of film and TV?

Collaborative is the word. Writing a novel is very solitary, and I'm rather sociable – and, as I said, I love a good script meeting. I love talking about work, and if you write a novel you're completely silent for a year or two years or three years. You can't talk to anyone about it, because if you let the sunlight into the room the pictures fade. But with a screenplay, because it's collaborative, you've got these other voices in your head – the director and the producer and the script editor – and if they're in tune with you, and you with them, it's really interesting. So I like that. It suits my personality.

ADAPTING NONFICTION

When adapting a book, fiction or nonfiction, do you do research beyond the book, or do you rely on the author's research?

I do some research beyond the book, but I'm very lazy so I try to get a nice researcher to do it. But I've researched the Crimean War and World War II and all sort of things.

How much responsibility do you feel towards historical accuracy when dramatising the lives of real characters?

In the case of *Anne Frank* there was a huge responsibility, because they were not only people who really lived but people who died horribly, so the responsibility was to respect that, but not to sanctify them. Sanctifying them turns them into creatures of history and I wanted to keep them as human beings. They weren't nicer or nastier than anyone else; they just happened to die in a horrible way. Young girls and boys wouldn't be able to identify with Anne Frank if she was simply a goody-goody. In fact, she was a typical stroppy teenager: fighting with her mother and obsessed with boys and all that. So that was a tightrope I had to tread: bringing to life people who actually existed and giving them a voice again without making them too cloying. In the diary, Anne is very beady and listens to people and you can use a lot of that, but some of it I had to make up. There were five episodes and I had to shape each episode, and that would mean creating stuff and having it pay off by the end, putting words into people's mouths and making up conversations. That moral responsibility towards real people who lived and died was very interesting to me – and very worrying as well. If you were adapting another nonfiction book you would to some extent have the same responsibility, but with *Anne Frank* it was particularly acute.

Have you ever encountered events in a nonfiction book so strange that you couldn't use them in the adaptation because audiences wouldn't believe they were real?

All the time. As we know, there's nothing stranger than life – but it's not as shapely as fiction, so you need fiction to shape it up.

How do you set about finding the voices of real characters, especially if there is little or no written or audio-visual research material in their own words?

I was doing a script about this chap Bernie Jordan, who escaped from his old people's home to join the D-Day celebrations. So he's a real person – he only died a couple of years ago – and I had to get a handle on him. But when I interviewed the residents of the home, no one said anything interesting about him at all, except that he liked Hobnob biscuits and wore two watches. So I put that in. But actually, in the end, we got rid of the two watches because it just made him seem odd. He's wearing two watches because he's obsessed with time, as he was in charge of a vessel that let out the troops on to the beaches and he was worried that the time wouldn't be right – or something. It just didn't work. And the biscuits I put in, but they seemed a bit feeble. So I had to get a handle on him in another way – in other words, I had to create him. His wife was also in the old people's home with him, and I didn't know anything about her attitude towards him, and whether they were in cahoots that he was stealing away. She was very passive in the first draft and people said, 'She's not interesting enough. What's her story?' So I had to go back and make up a story, but by this time I was losing the real people. In my version, she used to have a hairdressing salon, and her husband was actually traumatised by the war but he kept this down in an English way, and there will be a young helper at this place and the wife will tell her this. So I started building them up into my creatures, which is what you have to do, and they were pretty well unrecognisable by the end. And then you have the actors come in and they'll change it anyway.

Do you think that being based on a true story in some way gives a project more weight?

Yes.

CASE STUDY: *PRIDE & PREJUDICE*

UK/US/France, 2005 ▪ **Directed by** Joe Wright ▪ **Produced by** Tim Bevan, Eric Fellner, Paul Webster ▪ **Screenplay by** Deborah Moggach, based on the novel by Jane Austen ▪ **Cast:** Keira Knightley (Elizabeth Bennet), Matthew Macfadyen (Mr Darcy), Brenda Blethyn (Mrs Bennet), Donald Sutherland (Mr Bennet), Tom Hollander (Mr Collins), Rosamund Pike (Jane Bennet), Jena Malone (Lydia Bennet), Carey Mulligan (Kitty Bennet), Talulah Riley (Mary Bennet), Simon Woods (Mr Bingley), Kelly Reilly (Caroline Bingley), Rupert Friend (Mr Wickham), Judi Dench (Lady Catherine de Bourgh)

What attracted you to adapting *Pride and Prejudice*, and what did you think you could bring to it?

I wanted to adapt it because I love it – though I don't love it as much as some people do – and I thought I could bring a modern sensibility to it. It's reinvented for every generation because it's so loved, and I thought I could give it some freshness and wit. I'd just adapted Nancy Mitford and she's got a lot in common with Jane Austen – funny, lots of girls, countryside, eccentric father, animals and forensic social comedy – so I thought I could bring that. But what I most wanted to do with it was to show that it all really mattered. I didn't want it to be a frothy comedy at all. I wanted people who watched it to realise that this was pre-education, pre-Welfare State, and if one of those girls didn't marry well – because the estate was entailed – then they'd be out in the mud. I called it 'the muddy-hem version'. I wanted them to be in the same dresses day after day. I wanted them to be really young with red noses and no make-up. I wanted us to feel that outside their admittedly quite nice country home was real deprivation, and that those five young girls were going to go into a life of dependence and poverty. Maybe they'd become a governess if they were lucky; otherwise they'd be making jam all their lives. So I wanted to make it really matter that their mother had to marry one of them off – she's not just an airhead, she's actually working very hard for her girls because she knows that their period of bloom is so short – and I wanted to get inside Elizabeth Bennet's head because she's really interesting. That's why everyone loves the book: because it shows you don't have to be gorgeous to get the richest, most desirable man in Britain, you can just be funny and intelligent and true to yourself, and that gives hope to women everywhere.

You slightly lose the potency of that when you cast an attractive actor like Keira Knightley.

I know. That's another question. Casting just presumes that the heroine is going to be beautiful. But she's got very modern good looks, and Rosamund Pike, who played Jane Bennet, was much more the Jane Austen model of refined beauty. Anyway, those were some of my thoughts. I also thought that the way to get to grips with Mr Darcy, who I'd always disliked, was that he's really homesick. He's got this huge place and his darling sister, but he's always being hauled around to these house parties like a prize bull, having vapid girls thrust at him by their desperate parents. So he's not just a total snob. I also wanted to make the Bennet family as hoydenish and Hogarthian and old-fashioned as possible, because then when we move into the High Regency world of Netherfield, the world of Mr Darcy and Mr Bingley, we too would feel a bit inhibited. I wanted us to feel that the Bennets, despite their big house and their carriage, could actually be looked down on by the real posh people.

The novel could be described as a romcom. Did you ever think of it in terms of genre?

No. I tried to cut against that. But it is the archetypal romcom, the template for all that followed. There's Jane Austen, a virgin, never really been in love, and she understood the friction that's the basis of sexual attraction better than anyone. Two people think they loathe each other but really misunderstand each other; they're just about to get it together when a whole lot of obstacles are thrown in their way; and we know long before they know that they're madly in love and simply in denial. It's the perfect romcom – and the perfect plot. The plot of *Pride and Prejudice* is a beautiful thing, beautifully structured. I did have to mess about with it, but not a great deal.

Lizzie and Darcy's character arcs are perfect for mainstream cinema, but most of the other characters – Mr and Mrs Bennet, Lydia and Wickham – don't change at all during the story. Did you try to give any of them more of an arc?

Not really. I concentrated entirely on Lizzie and her interior life – though a screenplay can't do that in the same way a novel can. A novel can do hopes, dreams, fantasies, whatever. A screenplay can't. A screenplay is like a verb and a novel is like a noun, and the verb of the screenplay has to push the story along. That interior life you will only really get through watching the actors. In the scene where Lizzie bumps into Darcy at Pemberley near the end, the screenplay is completely banal. He says, 'Fancy seeing you here,' and she says, 'I'm on holiday with my aunt and uncle,' and he says, 'Are you having a pleasant trip?' and she says, 'Yes, we went to Matlock yesterday.' It's so boring you can barely say it, but what their faces are saying is, 'I completely misjudged you. I love you so much I can hardly breathe. I could be living in this house with you if I hadn't been so blinkered and snobbish and I'm so unhappy I want to die.' That's what a good screen actor is paid for: the changing weather on their face tells you their interior life.

Were there any scenes or characters which you decided to cut right away, and were there any which you had to cut reluctantly?

I wasn't reluctant to cut any of them. I cut any scene that Lizzie Bennet wasn't in, so there's no Jane in London, there's no Lydia in London. It was all through Lizzie's point of view.

The novel proceeds at a fairly steady pace. The film ebbs and flows more, from busy, bustling social scenes to moments of quiet, private reflection. Did you bring that to it, or did it emerge in the shoot and the edit?

I did several drafts, then other people came on – Emma Thompson did some, uncredited – then they called me back in and I did some more work on it. So I wasn't terribly involved in the shoot. But I am conscious when I'm writing a screenplay, whether it's an adaptation or an original, of trying to bring a rhythm to it, of trying to get light and shade and fast and slow and funny and serious. A screenplay should have a rhythm to it. It should also be a fun document to read. People love Andrew Davies's scripts because he'll write something like, in *Vanity Fair*, 'Becky thinks, "fuck it".' And Callie Khouri's script for *Thelma & Louise*, writing about Geena Davis's husband: 'Polyester was made for this man.' That's a good screenplay. The actors get it. The people buying it get it. It's totally on the button for what that character is. And it makes you laugh. That's going slightly off your question, but anyway.

Although the dialogue has been substantially trimmed, the words that the characters do say mostly come from the novel, with all the elegance and floridity of the period. Were you ever tempted to try a more modern style of dialogue?

No. There's only one line I wrote that wasn't somewhere in the book, which is when Mr Darcy says to Lizzie's uncle at Pemberley, 'The fish in the lake have been left alone for too long.' I made that up. Otherwise I just pulled a comb through Jane Austen's wonderful dialogue.

The film has a sunny, leafy, windy feel – much more outdoorsy than the novel, which seems more at home in houses than landscapes. Did you deliberately look to open it out in that way?

No, I mostly put scenes indoors because I know they're cheaper and won't depend on the weather. Sometimes I would put scenes outdoors, but I do think about what would be easier to shoot. So they did that, and found all those lovely landscapes. They were going to have a tavern scene in which I was going to be an extra, but they found this wonderful wood of gnarled oaks and decided to put the scene there. I was a bit disappointed by that, because I like being in my own work!

The novel opens with a static dialogue scene between Mr and Mrs Bennet. The film opens in a whirl of action and motion, introducing the entire Bennet family at their most typical, and setting up the equally lively dance scene that follows. Were you keen to get things moving and keep them moving?

The first opening I had was of Netherfield coming to life and all the dust sheets being pulled off, but of course it's not about a house, it's about people, so they didn't like that. Then I had Lizzie walking along a wall reading a book and going into her house, and they ran with that. The interesting thing about screenplays, which I'm still not sure I manage to do, is that you want to suggest how scenes might look or be shot, but you don't want to lay down the law, so you just have to hint at it. It's quite an art, that. If it's too technical it feels too bossy, telling people their jobs – and again, it makes the screenplay less fun to read.

The dance scene has its own three-act structure: from the entrance of Darcy and Bingley, to Darcy's dismissal of Lizzie, to Lizzie's riposte and exit. Do you consciously structure all scenes like that, or just the larger set-pieces?

The larger set-pieces are awfully difficult to write, because you don't know whether to do a great list of characters at the beginning, or feed them into the scene, or introduce them when they speak. I still don't know when to put their names in capitals; I can never understand the logic of that. I just find them really difficult. I don't think that was consciously a three-act thing, but you're always trying to shape everything, and that scene would need a beginning, a middle and an end. But Jane Austen does a lot of the shaping for you because she's so clever.

The implication in the novel is that Mr Bennet made a mistake in marrying Mrs Bennet, and therefore leaving the raising of their daughters to her was a dereliction of duty. But in the film he comes across as an affectionate, amused, comical character. Was that deliberate?

Yes, but that's also the performance of Donald Sutherland, who was marvellous, and what he brought to it was much tenderer. He finds his wife attractive, and there's a scene where they're on the bed and it looks as though they're about to have sex, and I think it makes them more human – and we respect him, and indeed her, more. She's still a bit silly and he still retreats to his study – and of course we have to have his closeness to Lizzie because she's so bright – but he's not an intelligent man who looks a fool for marrying someone ghastly.

The UK ending – Mr Bennet sitting in his study, laughing and crying at Lizzie's engagement to Darcy – is less romantic but more affecting than the US ending: Lizzie and Darcy exchanging endearments and kisses on the terrace at Pemberley. Which do you prefer?

That's jolly interesting. I didn't want to have a big wedding because it's too corny and triumphalist, so I wrote an ending where the wedding is going on, but they've stolen away at night and they're looking down the hill at the lights and they have a little conversation. But they didn't like that, and it might have been Emma Thompson who wrote a really lovely ending: it's the morning after the wedding, they're still in their night-clothes, and they steal away and he says something like, 'How do you feel this morning, my dear?' and she says, 'Oh, please don't call me that, my father calls my mother that when he's cross with her,' and he says, 'What shall I call you, then?' and they have a very tender exchange, and the dewy morning echoes the beginning of the film. Now for some reason they shot that at night, which didn't make sense at all. You couldn't work out whether they'd spent the night together, which is very important, and all those lights made it look very grand and not informal. It just didn't work. So for the English version they cut it – and ended, I think, rather well.

I think that ending is delightful. It's almost anti-climactic – except it's not, because it's so emotional.

Exactly. It's heavenly. I think lots of films should have the last scene cut! But Americans have a sweeter tooth, allegedly, so they stuck the other ending on for them.

CASE STUDY: *THE DIARY OF ANNE FRANK*

UK, 2009 ▪ **Directed by** Jon Jones ▪ **Produced by** Elinor Day ▪ **Screenplay by** Deborah Moggach, based on the book *The Diary of a Young Girl* by Anne Frank ▪ **Cast:** Ellie Kendrick (Anne Frank), Iain Glen (Otto Frank), Tamsin Greig (Edith Frank), Felicity Jones (Margot Frank), Geoffrey Breton (Peter Van Daan), Ron Cook (Hermann Van Daan), Lesley Sharp (Petronella Van Daan), Nicholas Farrell (Albert Dussel), Kate Ashfield (Miep Gies)

The Diary of Anne Frank aired on TV in five 25-minute episodes, which is a relatively unusual format for drama. Was that your decision, or the BBC's?

It was the BBC's decision, because they wanted an early evening drama to get families to watch it – because it was such an important subject. They also wanted us to follow it over one week so we're involved very intimately with the story. It's not an episode, a gap of a week, then another episode – we're living it with them. We all know what happened at the end, but we're still rooting for them.

The diary is inevitably episodic and discursive. How did you set about shaping it into a dramatic five-part narrative?

Each episode had its theme and its arc. The first one was the Franks going into the annex and the arrival of the Van Daans. One was the Franks falling out with the Van Daans. One was about religion – Anne losing her faith. One was Anne's romance with Peter. And then in the final one, we built up towards intimations of people knowing they were there. And all the way through I had stories going on among the grown-ups that Anne, however beady she was, didn't always clock. So you have the rather refined Franks and the more earthy, less sophisticated Van Daans, who in some ways were more fun than the Franks – certainly more than Mrs Frank, who was suffering hugely, and Anne's sister Margot, who was frozen with misery and subsumed herself in her studies. And you have Mr Dussel, who Anne shared that little room with and who was incredibly homesick and lonely, which is something Anne didn't get at all. Families were nearly always split up, but the Franks and the Van Daans were together there, which Mr Frank was very optimistic about, and I wanted to show that Mr Dussel was the only one who didn't have his loved ones with him.

So each episode had a theme, each episode had an arc, each episode ended on a cliffhanger. I also wanted to bring in different threats all the way through, because there were so many ways they could have been discovered: the threat when the lavatory gets blocked that the plumber will come upstairs; the threat when the building is sold that the new owners will come in; the threat when Anne falls for Peter that she will get pregnant – because she very nearly slept with him, she was very highly sexed for her age. And I needed to darken it towards the end, when they all start realising, in their different ways, that this is likely to be it for them – although always with humour, because the humour is heartbreaking, and also they weren't just sitting there terrified all the time, they were like normal people quarrelling and so on. So in each one we had a break-up and then we had them making up in some way – and at the end Anne makes her peace with Mr Dussel when her hands are trembling with fear and he helps her with her sandal strap.

The initial antagonism between Anne and Peter is less pronounced in the diary. Was that part of a strategy to enhance the conflict in the adaptation?

I manipulated their romance quite a lot, because I had to make sense of the fact that in the diary Anne picks Peter up and falls for him quite heavily, and then after a while doesn't mention him anymore. My take on it is that although she despised him for being dull and not very clever, she realised that he was as good as she was going to get. It's a horrible thought, but I think she saw that she'd better go for it, so she cobbled together this love affair with him. Then when the Dutch government in exile issued an edict, which they heard on the radio, that everyone in Holland should keep writing diaries and letters so that the world would know about their sufferings under the Nazi occupation – and her father looks at her and says, 'He's talking to you,' takes his stuff out of his briefcase and gives it to her for her diaries – that turned Anne into a writer and Peter became irrelevant. We talked to Miep, the secretary of Mr Frank who very courageously used to come and deliver stuff to them, and she said she once came in when Anne was writing and when Anne looked up she didn't recognise her. Her face was completely different, she was so absorbed in this diary. She wrote like a fury because she thought they might die, and she rewrote lots of it again and again.

One of the most striking aspects of the diary is the extent to which Anne, despite the extraordinary circumstances, remains what you described as 'a typical stroppy teenager'. You seem to have embraced that.

I embraced it because, as I said, I wanted teenage girls to sympathise with her and not consign her to history. I wanted them to think, 'What must that be like?' and, 'How would I react?' I wanted her to be a real person. We went to visit her cousin, Buddy, and watched some of it with him, and he said it was the most truthful portrayal of her – because he remembered her very well. I watched other versions and she was this cheeky, mischievous girl, and it was just ghastly. The word 'teenager', I think, was only invented in the 1940s, and she was a modern teenager – and I wanted to show that.

Given the first-person nature of the source material, was it a given that you would use voiceover?

She'd have to have a voiceover, because there are so many layers. You've got the grown-ups' stories. You've got Anne's thoughts. And you've got what Anne says, which is sometimes different from her thoughts. You've got a real stew of human emotions there. And I found it easy to write her voiceover because I felt very in tune with her – because I could remember what it was like being a teenager.

Apart from some brief scenes at the start, showing the Franks' flight from their house, the whole of the series takes place in the annex. Did you ever consider opening it out?

No. I wanted it to be claustrophobic. They reconstructed the annex inch for inch. The camera crew was stuck in there with the actors and everyone was sweating like pigs and tripping over wires. We wanted it to feel like that. There's no point in opening it out. The diary is about what happens in the annex, and if you open it out you dissipate that – and anyway, there was enough going on with the people in that annex for something ten times as long. We didn't extend it, either. Some adaptations take her to the camps, but of course the diary stops when they're discovered. I actually stole the end from another adaptation – where they're all coming down the stairs one by one and we freeze-frame and it says what happens to them – because it's such an emotional moment to have this bald little caption. 'Died of typhus'. It breaks your heart.

The last line of her voiceover is a phrase from towards the end of the diary: 'I still believe, in spite of everything, that people are truly good at heart.' Was that the underlying theme of the piece for you?

No, it wasn't. I think my underlying theme was the resilience of the human spirit. It's hard to talk about people being good at heart when the Nazis are murdering six million people. That was Anne's thought, it wasn't mine – but she did mature into an extraordinarily thoughtful young woman. That was also a theme: her maturing. She starts as this quite manipulative, difficult young girl, and she grows into someone much wiser and bigger-hearted. It was two years they were there – formative years for a young girl – and she was going through great adventures of the spirit and growing up. So although the others don't change that much, Anne does, I think.

David Nicholls

David Nicholls was born in 1966 in Eastleigh, Hampshire.

His screen adaptation credits include: *Sympatico* (1999, play by Sam Shepard); *Much Ado About Nothing* (2005, after Shakespeare); *And When Did You Last See Your Father?* (2007, book by Blake Morrison); *Tess of the D'Urbervilles* (2008, novel by Thomas Hardy); *Great Expectations* (2012, novel by Charles Dickens); *Far from the Madding Crowd* (2015, novel by Thomas Hardy); *Patrick Melrose* (2018, novels by Edward St Aubyn); and dramatisations of his own novels *Starter for 10* (2006), *One Day* (2011) and *Us* (2020).

He wrote the BBC drama *The 7.39* (2013), created and wrote the ITV and BBC series *I Saw You* and *Rescue Me* (both 2002) and contributed to the third series of *Cold Feet* (1999). His most recent novel is *Sweet Sorrow* (2019).

Patrick Melrose won the 2019 BAFTA Television Craft Award for Best Writer: Drama.

APPROACHES TO ADAPTATION

Do you prefer to adapt material which chimes with your own work, or material which is completely different and gives you a chance to try out new things?

The latter, I think. It's changed, because my own work has changed. When I first started writing, my own material was broadly romantic comedy and relationship drama, and I got sent a lot of books in that vein to adapt. It was easy to say no, even when I could see their commercial appeal, because it's less interesting to me if there's an overlap with material that I want to deal with in my own way. What I like about adaptation is that it coaxes me into writing about things I'm not necessarily confident enough to write about in an original form. To begin with, I was quite scared of original material that was outside my usual style. I would have been scared of the melodrama of *Tess of the D'Urbervilles*, which was the first thing I adapted, or the darkness of *Patrick Melrose*, or the emotional rawness of *And When Did You Last See Your Father?* Material that's different from mine serves as a sort of scaffolding which has elements of my own work, but gives me some parameters. But it would feel a little pointless to adapt a book that was too similar in style to, say, *Starter for Ten* or *One Day*.

Do you think adaptations involve a completely different set of creative gears to original screenplays?

Yes. I can adapt while I'm writing original work, but I can't write two original works at the same time. I wouldn't be able to hold two different sets of original voices and situations in my head. I get very emotionally engaged writing original fiction, because I'm drawing on my own concerns and preoccupations. Even though my books aren't directly autobiographical, they've all originated in an experience I've had, or a set of emotions I've gone through. With adaptation there's usually an element of that, something in the source material which I've responded to, but the story I'm telling isn't my own so I feel a little more distance. It's much more of an editing job, a technical, structural process.

Do you always agree a mission statement or direction of travel with whoever has commissioned the adaptation?

I think so. I mean, there's always a pitching element involved. When I took on *Patrick Melrose*, I knew there were other writers in the frame, and I had to go and meet the producers and say what I loved about the books, and what I wanted to keep and take out, and how I might augment that. Likewise, I remember my pitch for *Far from the Madding Crowd*, and how it would differ from the John Schlesinger/Frederic Raphael version. That pitch doesn't necessarily come through in the finished product, you don't always quite hit it, but the ones where my vision of the material has matched the final film are the projects that I'm happiest with. I used to work as a script editor before I was a writer, so I've been at the other end of it and I'm able to speak that language. There's a certain amount of smoke and mirrors in pitching, because you often won't find out what the source material is really about until you've spent some time with it.

Do you usually produce an outline or treatment before you start writing the script?

No, I don't, but that's probably to do with having some experience in all fields of writing. When I started out as a novelist and as an original screenwriter, I did do them and got notes on them and went back and did them again. Now, once I've made the pitch, I'll go my own way. I think I'm quite a safe pair of hands, in that I do what I say and won't submit something crazy. I won't suddenly change the ending without telling anyone, I'll talk my choices through with the script editors and producers and so on. So apart from verbally stating my intentions, I'm allowed to do what I want. The exception to that was the latter episodes of *Patrick Melrose*. As the books go on, they become less and less story-driven and more like montages of memories. There's nothing you'd call a plot in the last book, really. So with those there was a certain amount of planning and cards on the wall and story breakdowns, but that's the least story-led material I've ever worked on. With everything else there's been a great deal of discussion, but not a lot of pre-planning, except in my head.

If the author of the source material is living, do you find it useful to have their input on the script?

That's a really interesting one. No screenwriter thinks, 'I wish I was getting more notes.' So I would expect them to have input, I just wouldn't crave it coming directly to me. I'd want them to see every draft and feel free to give notes, but I'd also want those notes to be put into a pot and mediated. What you're doing is an act of vandalism. You're chopping things out and conflating characters, and undoubtedly they're going to read it and go, 'That's not what I had in mind.' On *Patrick Melrose*, I had a meeting with Edward St Aubyn, who's a writer I massively admired and, as a different kind of novelist to me, was rather intimidated by. But he's a very charming man and we had a lovely lunch; I asked him a certain number of questions and at the end he said, 'Well, we can either talk every day, or we need never talk again. It's up to you.' He completely understood either approach. If you're reading the books – and this applies to Blake Morrison's book as well – you'll inevitably think, 'We really need this scene and it isn't in the book so I'm going to have to invent it,' and the most useful question to ask the author at that point is, 'What really happened?' But in a way that's also the least useful question, because they've already given their experiences a shape which wasn't necessarily there in real life, so to ask them 'What really happened?' is a step backwards. It ruins the shape.

Is it easier to navigate notes from directors, producers and script editors when you have a piece of source material to measure the screenplay against?

I have a rule that no one is allowed to say, 'But in the book…', because adaptation means change. And of course it's a rule that's constantly broken and so not really a rule at all, but if you just go through and highlight the dialogue and copy the story, it's probably not going to work. You all have to be in agreement about what you think is important in the book, but the success of an adaptation is not necessarily how much of the book you manage to cram in, so there are limits to the extent you can use the book as evidence for your point of view. I've been on productions where we were not allowed to talk about the book, and I've been on productions where the book has been on set and people pick it up and flick through it and refer to it. I'm not crazy about them doing that, but it's okay if the adaptation is broadly faithful and we're not trying to do something different with it. I do get a little prickly if an actor says they preferred something in the book, because they're usually, quite naturally, looking at their own scene, they're not taking into account, say, the director's view or the style of the production. You might adapt Dickens or Hardy and want the dialogue to feel very up-to-date and real, and if an individual actor goes back to the book and likes the more verbose, old-fashioned version of a line, that might be more fun for them to say, but it might not fit in with the overall tone. So I am wary of the book being used as a weapon.

Have you ever started work on an adaptation and found it harder to adapt than you anticipated?

The hardest was *Patrick Melrose*, but I knew that was going to be a tough one. I've had the opposite experience, which is not that it's easier, but that it falls naturally into a certain structure. On *Tess*, for instance, we were doing four episodes and the book fell neatly into four narrative chunks with strong cliffhangers. Hardy actually originated the term 'cliffhanger', and books written for serialisation adapt particularly well to serial television. Weirdly, I found my own book, *Starter for Ten*, much harder than expected. It was inspired by a lot of films, and it had a three-act structure and a protagonist with wants and needs and various obstacles along the way, so I thought it would just be a case of picking the best scenes – but it was extremely hard to do that because of the loss of the narrator's voice. Things that were absolute highlights on the page didn't work without the irony of the narrator's point of view, so it was difficult to find the comedy in it. Actually, I think the hardest things I've had to adapt have been written in first-person voices – or what we call an indirect third person, like the *Melrose* books, where it's technically in the third person, but very much from a particular character's point of view – because you're constantly looking for ways to put thoughts into dialogue without slathering it in voiceover.

Have you ever been offered material to adapt which you felt couldn't, or shouldn't, be adapted?

Yes, I have, and I've often read books that I've loved and thought, 'This is unadaptable.' I've adapted several of my top-ten favourite books, but there are some in there that I wouldn't touch. I wouldn't touch anything by J.D. Salinger. I'd have been very wary of *The Great Gatsby*. I've been approached more than once about Ford Madox Ford's *The Good Soldier*, and I think that's unadaptable unless you throw away the point of the book, which is that you're not sure who the narrator is and what really happened. Books with unreliable narrators, books which rely on ambiguity, books where there's no objective truth, books where there's very little narrative – so a lot of modernist fiction – are all very hard to adapt. But I've been proved wrong many times. You think something can never be done, then someone does it really well.

Are there any screen adaptations which you think are especially good or you particularly admire?

There are lots. *All the President's Men*, by William Goldman, is a wonderful adaptation, probably one of the best, because it approaches Watergate in an entirely unexpected way. *The Wings of the Dove*, by Hossein Amini, is also a fantastic adaptation, of a novel I'd be very scared to adapt. I thought it was amazing that someone could deal with that material in that tone of voice. There are also celebrated adaptations that I'm not crazy about. I'm not crazy about the David Lean versions of Dickens, even though I'm absolutely sure his version of *Great Expectations* is better than ours. I love David Lean, but I don't love those.

ADAPTING FICTION

Some writers try to include as much of the novel as possible by boiling scenes down to their essence. Others are more ruthless in editing it

down to a sort of greatest hits, but being true to the spirit of it. Do you favour either of those approaches?

It depends on the project. With *Patrick Melrose*, because we were doing 800 pages of fiction in five hours, it clearly wasn't going to be a distillation of everything that happens. If you want to put things in because they're great incidents or great observations or great lines of dialogue, it's very unlikely they'll be essential to telling the story. So it was about selecting material and discarding upwards of 50 per cent of the action. The first three episodes are pretty faithful to the books, but in the last two there are great chunks missing and a story is teased out that wasn't necessarily so prominent on the page. Other times, because I've loved the material so much, I've tried to put it all in. I did that with *Great Expectations* and it was probably a mistake: I think people who have taken bigger liberties with that book have had a more successful time. There's a massive storytelling problem in the book, which is that a lot of it has happened in the past. Now you could go into flashback and dramatise it, but there's something weird about that with Dickens. Flashbacks are part of a cinematic language that sometimes feels a little strange in a nineteenth-century story. So the other option is tell the backstory in dialogue – monologue, most likely – and it starts to look like a great big slab of exposition. David Lean was much more ruthless in simplifying the plot, but I think the plot of *Great Expectations* is fantastic, so I kept a lot in. The things I chose to take out, though, I think were the right choices: a lot of the comic set pieces got thrown away because they're primarily about the tone of Dickens' prose, the wry, observational voice, and there's no way to put that on screen except using voiceover.

It also depends on the time you have available. People have said that the ideal form to adapt for a feature film is a novella or a short story, and if you try to cram a 400-page novel into two hours you're going to have difficulty. I think that's true. In a two-hour film you're either disappointed that something's not there, or everything's there but nothing really lands. The option that we didn't have open to us, even five or six years ago, was TV. When a big book came out, it used to be, 'They've sold the film rights.' Now they'll go after the TV rights, and screenwriters, and probably novelists too, are extremely pleased that they have this other, longer, equally 'cinematic' form for adaptations of their work, where the primary job of the dramatist isn't cutting stuff, it's arranging it in five or six or eight lovely chunks of material, allowing the story to breathe in the way it does on the page. If I was doing *One Day* now, and I was getting offers from film and TV companies, I would definitely go for the TV version, because it would fit much more naturally into that longer form.

If a novel has an unusual structure, would you try to reproduce that in adapting it?

That's very interesting. I did a screenplay of *Tender is the Night*, which is my favourite novel, and that has a very confusing structure for a cinemagoer. It starts from the point of view of someone who you think is the main character and they turn out to be a subsidiary character. Then it goes into an extended flashback in the middle that explains everything you saw in the first third and gives it in an entirely new context. When I adapted it, I clung to that structure and people inevitably said, 'What would happen if you told the story chronologically?' The book was actually published in two versions, the flashback version and a chronological version, and although the chronological version would probably make more sense to a cinema audience – clear central characters, forward momentum – for me it's blasphemous. The flashback structure is one of the things I love about the novel and I would find it very hard to step away from that.

Do you try to avoid voiceover in adapting a first-person narrative, or do you see it as another tool in the toolbox?

I might use it as a way in and a way out. I tend not to use it all the way through because, to continue the tool analogy, it's a bit of a blunt instrument. Voiceover rarely lands as powerfully as dialogue and gives scenes an archness that isn't always appropriate. You're always asking, 'Who's telling us this and why, and are they telling us in the moment, or are they telling us looking back?' If you think about voiceovers that really work, they're often at odds with what you're watching. There's a deliberate irony to them, or the character doesn't realise what we realise. I think that's a justification for using voiceover. But if you're using it for exposition, or to cherry-pick the best jokes or your favourite bits of internal monologue, or just to give us a taste of what's on the page, why not have a voiceover in every adaptation? With *Patrick Melrose*, we only used voiceover to suggest an altered state of mind, and that felt valid. Once he stopped taking drugs, no more voiceover. I'm a huge admirer of Billy Wilder and he uses voiceover in nearly all his films, but he uses it rather like a title card at the beginning of the film, as a way into the world, and then drops it until the end, which to me is also a valid way to use it.

Do you use the language of the novel in writing the dialogue, or do you put the whole thing in your own words?

When I've adapted Hardy, I've stepped away from the verbosity of the dialogue in the books. I love Hardy, but if you speak the dialogue off the page it's quite stilted and stiff, so I don't mind if the version in the adaptation isn't Hardyesque. There are little phrases and lines that are beautiful and memorable and of course you want to use them, but there's a verbosity, sometimes a pomposity, that I tend to simplify and condense. On *Far from the Madding Crowd*, in the scene where Boldwood proposes to Bathsheba, I'd written in the script that he says, 'Will you marry me?' and she says, 'Mr Boldwood, I cannot.' The scene was really good in rehearsal, but Carey Mulligan found the line in the novel, which was something like 'Mr Boldwood, I do not find the emotions in my heart that would allow me to say yes to your proposal.' I'd tried to simplify it, but Carey spotted that there was something in the awkwardness of it that she could use, and she did. But for the most part, I wrote a more straightforward version. Dickens, on the other hand, writes wonderful dialogue. It's also verbose and very stylised, but it's Dickens so it works. In the case of *Great Expectations*, 70 per cent of the dialogue was from the book, condensed or edited slightly, but retaining that ornate Dickensian quality.

Do you keep the novel beside you throughout the adaptation process, or do you try to internalise it and set it aside somewhere along the way?

It varies from book to book. My own books I generally know off by heart anyway. Blake's book I knew well enough not to have by my side. It's quite a short book and there's not a lot of dialogue or what you'd think of as conventional scenes, so I read it five or six times, made notes and then just wrote the script, because it was a looser adaptation. With *Patrick Melrose*, I learned the books. I went through them and annotated them, I found images in the prose that might be useful on screen, I walked around London with the audio books playing in my head. I've done the same with Dickens and Hardy. There are celebrated dramatists who read the book once and throw it away, and I've never understood that. My motive for taking on the job is a real love of the material, so I want to completely immerse myself in it and communicate that passion. The downside of this is that you can quickly grow to hate the original. I would still say *Great Expectations* is one of my favourite books, but reading it now brings back feelings of regret about the things you cut or didn't think were quite right on screen, and because you've watched scenes over and over again you can't help hearing the actors' voices in your head. So adaptation kills the thing you love.

How much pressure do you feel when adapting a well-known and much-loved novel, knowing that you won't be able to please everyone with the finished product?

More and more I feel the answer is not to adapt books that are really, really well-loved, because people don't tend to watch them and think, 'The dramatist has made an interesting choice here,' they just think, 'Sacrilege!' and that's quite inhibiting when you sit down to write the script. You're starting from a position where, if you change the material, people who love it will be disappointed, and if you stick to it, people who don't know it will be confused. The hardest experience I've ever had as a screenwriter was *One Day*, where the book became very much talked about while I was still writing the screenplay. So instead of thinking, 'How am I going to turn this book into a film?' you're thinking, 'How am I going to turn this book into a film without pissing people off?' You're no longer free to make bold choices for fear of offending loyal fans, nor are you necessarily making the best choices for people who don't know what all the fuss is about. *Patrick Melrose* was the perfect project because the books were celebrated, but we all felt they should be better known. You could introduce people to the books via the drama in a way that was good for everyone, rather than annoying five million readers.

If someone wants to option a novel of yours, how do you decide whether to adapt it yourself – and if someone else adapts it, how involved would you be in the process? Nick Payne, for example, adapted your novel *Us* for TV, but you have also written a draft of the series.

I feel a bit embarrassed about that; it's like back-seat driving. Giving it to someone else and saying, 'Here you are, run with it,' is really appealing, and Nick came in and did a fantastic job. But he has his own voice and his own take on the material, and actually I found it hard to let go of it, so I've now done a pass on his scripts. I've worked on scripts for all my books and they're the jobs I've enjoyed least, partly because when the book comes out I've told the story and it's hard to keep it fresh, partly because I've got a vision of the book in my head which makes it hard to invent new material. When I worked on *One Day*, people kept saying, 'I think we need this character, I think we need to see this scene,' and I'd already made those editorial decisions and it was hard for me to unpick them – and I'm ashamed to say that everything new I added which wasn't in the book didn't really work; Emma's parents were in it at one point, played by brilliant actors, but it was all superfluous. I lack the callousness, really, or the objectivity, to adapt my own work. At the same time, because you've invested so much, and because a truth lies behind the fiction that you want to put across, if you have experience as a screenwriter it's easy to succumb and think, 'I know I'll have to cut stuff. I know the casting might not be what I had in my head. I know the person doing the score will have different ideas to me. But I'm a screenwriter, I know how ruthless the process is,

I can do it.' And every time, even when the results have been okay, I've found it very, very hard.

What inspires you to swap the authorial autonomy of novels for the collaborative constraints of film and TV?

I saw my book agent the other day and he said, 'Why do you do it?' The novels, generally speaking, have gone quite well. There have been ups and downs, but the fluctuations have been less extreme than with screenwriting. In film, the financial risks are huge and there are so many people involved and it can seem like a much less genteel world than the world of publishing. So why *do* I do it? I really like actors. I don't spend a lot of time with them on set, but I love seeing what they bring. I love the read-through. When you see something extra brought to the dialogue, or to a scene that wasn't really working on the page, that can be really exciting and gratifying. I love the fact that it's social – until I don't love the fact that it's social. By which I mean, I love the company and I love the collaboration until the point where discussion turns into an argument. Fiction is much less scrutinised and picked apart, whereas every line of a screenplay is examined. If I write a page of dialogue in a novel it might get one or two passes, but chances are the finished version will broadly be the same as the first draft. With a screenplay, I know there's going to be ten or 15 drafts, and the director and the actors will have a view, and in the edit you'll still discover lines that were boring and unnecessary. There's a rigour in screenwriting that there really isn't in fiction, and that's both maddening and challenging. I write with great care, but I know that in every novel if I apply my edit-suite eye, there are things that can be cut. As long as the book's not dull, that's fine – the writing is the point – but I like the ruthlessness and rigour of screenplays. I like people saying, 'Do we need this scene? Is there a better way of doing it?' And other times I hate that. So that's really not a very good answer at all, is it?

ADAPTING NONFICTION

When adapting a book, fiction or nonfiction, do you rely on the author's research, or do you conduct your own?

The headline answer to this is that I almost instantly say no to biopics, or adaptations of biographies, particularly of famous people, because I know you ought to do research and explore the background and find out what really happened – and I'm not very interested in that. You're going to have to change things, and there's going to be a controversy about it – Churchill didn't go on the Tube, and Mary and Elizabeth didn't meet – and I understand why that debate happens, but as a screenwriter it isn't a debate I want to have. So whenever I've been offered something based on true events, I've nearly always turned it down. I don't want to research it, I don't want to fight about 'truth', I don't want to have an argument with a producer saying, 'I know that's not what happened, but it works better dramatically.' I also don't feel that life has a three-act structure: that you have antagonists and a series of hurdles you have to overcome. If you're Winston Churchill or Mary, Queen of Scots, do you feel that? No, of course you don't. All of that is going to be artificially stamped on to lives that were far more complicated and ambiguous and unresolved, and it can be done really well, but it isn't a form I love. In the case of Blake's book, the real events were certainly complicated and we had to flesh out the story more than it is on the page, but I didn't go through photo albums and meet the real-life versions of the characters. That may be laziness on my part, but I didn't know what I was going to gain from it. I'd chosen the material because it was great; not because it was simplistic or easy, but because it worked beautifully. What was powerful about it was what Blake had already done to it, which is that he'd brought a novelist's eye to biographical events. It isn't a biopic, it's a memoir, and memoirs often have a novelistic quality. That's why someone was compelled to write them, because they already felt like a story. So for me, the best approach, in fact the only feasible approach, was to treat it as a work of fiction and not dig around in it for further complications. There's something to be said for that kind of detective work, but it didn't feel appropriate in this case.

Have you ever encountered events in a nonfiction book so strange that you couldn't use them in the adaptation because audiences wouldn't believe they were real?

The opposite, if anything. There were some really strange things in Blake's book that we kept in and maybe we shouldn't have. There was a lot of debate about the scene where he masturbates in the bath while his father is dying in the next room, and when I read that on the page I thought it was very striking and had a confrontational truth to it. I'd never written anything as shocking as that, and describing it now it sounds quite extreme, but at the time it felt right to keep it.

How much responsibility do you feel towards historical accuracy when dramatising the lives of real characters?

I feel a certain amount of fidelity to the book but – and perhaps this is irresponsible – I don't necessarily want another person's take on it. I want it to ring true, but I also want to be true to the character – and character is a very subjective thing. Patrick Melrose isn't Edward St Aubyn, but the thing Teddy always has to talk about when he talks about his work is whether or not Patrick is him. In episode three there's a scene where Princess Margaret comes into the room, and I wrote a stage direction that said, 'Patrick remains seated.' Teddy's note was that Patrick would never do that, and I think underlying that note was, 'I would never do that,' because we were trying to impose a rebellious Republican spirit on someone who doesn't actually share the audience's antipathy to royalty and privilege. There was a similar example in *And When Did You Last See Your Father?*, which was one of the times when I was aware of the presence of a living writer. Blake was incredibly supportive during the process and I think he liked the film, but there's a scene where his father is being awful and young Blake goes into the next room and says out loud to himself, 'I hate him.' Blake felt very strongly that he would never have done that, that even when his father was at his most maddening he was always aware that he loved him, but within the structure of a film you want a moment of pure antagonism, you want to ramp things up and give them somewhere to go. There were examples in *Patrick Melrose* where we went the other way. In the books, he's unrelentingly vicious and vitriolic about his mother. But on screen, because you have a great actor playing her, and because there's a pathos in their scenes that's different from the emotion on the page, that relationship is perhaps a little more empathetic. Sometimes you have to adjust the pitch to make it work dramatically. So I feel a degree of responsibility to reality, and I wouldn't want people to feel their experiences had been misrepresented, but there will inevitably be adjustments.

Do you think that being based on a true story in some way gives a project more weight?

I think it does commercially. It's a great hook to hang the publicity on. But I must admit I do dislike biopics and 'true stories'. All I see are the wigs and the prosthetics and a sense of manipulation. I'm suspicious. I really admire *The Crown*, for instance, and Peter Morgan is a great writer, but I think, 'Are these people really that eloquent? Is the Duke of Edinburgh really that complex?' Maybe he is. Maybe I'm not being fair. There are a few exceptions. *All the President's Men* is obviously based on true events, and its great strength is its authenticity and its messiness, the fact that you don't get a pay-off and that it stops just as the story is getting started. If you made that now, people would say, 'We've got to do the next bit, not this bit. Why are we taking so much time to tell the beginning of a much bigger story?' But that's what's brilliant about it. Or *Zodiac*, which gives a real flavour of what that investigation must have been like and how frustrating it was, and communicates that frustration to the audience by not providing an answer to the case. A true story which ends with, as it were, punching the air, makes me think, 'I don't believe this.' Whereas with fiction I don't mind that. With fiction there's a permissible element of escapism, a sense of resolution that doesn't ring true to me in a true story.

CASE STUDY: *AND WHEN DID YOU LAST SEE YOUR FATHER?*

UK, 2007 ▪ **Directed by** Anand Tucker ▪ **Produced by** Elizabeth Karlsen, Stephen Woolley ▪ **Screenplay by** David Nicholls, based on the book by Blake Morrison ▪ **Cast:** Jim Broadbent (Arthur), Colin Firth (Blake), Juliet Stevenson (Kim), Gina McKee (Kathy), Sarah Lancashire (Beaty), Elaine Cassidy (Sandra), Clare Skinner (Gillian), Carey Mulligan (Rachel), Matthew Beard (Teenage Blake)

And When Did You Last See Your Father? was almost like a nonfiction dry run for Patrick Melrose: a life-and-death-spanning story of fathers and sons. Do you think they have any thematic similarities, and were you attracted to both projects for any of the same reasons?

They do share similar themes of redemption and forgiveness and coming to terms with the past. But my response to Blake's book was that it was very hopeful and humane – and very touching. Whereas my initial response to the *Melrose* books was shock and laughter – although I also find them moving, despite the hate and venom. I think they're both faithful – most of what's said and done on screen was there on the page – but I probably did introduce moments of pathos and humour in *Patrick Melrose* that aren't in the books, and the adaptation of *And When Did You Last See Your Father?* is less episodic and more eventful than the original because of how I selected and shaped the material.

The script does have a very British bittersweet tone which is all your own – which translates through to the film. Did you realise the extent to which your voice, both as a screenwriter and a novelist, had become superimposed over Blake Morrison's?

I'm aware of that with everything I've done, really, but I'm also wary of knocking the edges off things, of not being as tough as the original material is. I like writing romantic comedy and I like writing social awkwardness, and I worry that I select scenes in the source material that will allow me to do those things and perhaps neglect stuff that I'm not so good with myself as a dramatist. As I said, I'd never really dealt with darker material before I adapted *And*

When Did You Last See Your Father?, so the book gave me a leg up into writing about things that I felt a little nervous about.

The book alternates between chapters set in the past and chapters set in the present – until Arthur's death, when past and present largely converge, structure quite literally giving way. Were you aware of that effect, and did you try to mirror it in any way in your adaptation?

I was, and I think we did – but again we had to select the material, particularly in the past. It's a wonderful book, but you're always looking out for beats that are repetitive: is this yet another example of his father being a stick in the mud, or a bit embarrassing? There needs to be a cumulative quality to it, and both in the book and the film that quality comes from young Blake getting older: growing into a man himself and becoming sexually aware and wanting to move away. That's the arc in the past and you don't want to jump about, you want it to be chronological. The treatment of the past in *Patrick Melrose* was much more of a collage – dreamlike, an image from here, a line from there, something which illustrates this aspect, something which illustrates that – but with *And When Did You Last See Your Father?*, both story strands need to move towards a letting go of the past. There was a lot of good stuff in the book about him bringing back girlfriends from university, but that would have required a mid-stage Blake, which would have confused the whole issue of young and old.

The film starts where the book starts: with Arthur jumping the queue to enter a motor-racing event. But in the script, young Blake is described as 'mortified and ashamed', whereas in the film he looks at Arthur in childlike wonder and says, as an adult in voiceover, 'My father seemed to me infallible, invincible – immortal,' which sets up both his teenage disillusionment and adult grief. Can you talk me through that transition from book to script to film?

That's interesting. That feels like a response to a note. I'm almost certain that in the first draft the scene would have been as it was in the book, and the revision was probably to do with there being a journey for Blake. If we start with his father being an embarrassment to him and continue that way for 90 minutes, there's nowhere to go. It's not about imposing an arc, but about introducing variety, a change in the characters' attitudes rather than a reiteration of them.

When he's dressing for his awards dinner near the start of the film, Blake's wife Kathy jokes, 'I hope I'm going to get a mention.' In fact, she's only mentioned twice in the book, in passing. Why did you decide to make her more of a presence in your adaptation?

The book is very male. I don't mean it's a macho book, but it's pretty much a two-hander – or a four-hander, if you count their younger selves – about the father and son, then and now. At the same time, you've got these great actresses – Juliet Stevenson as Blake's mother, Gina McKee as his wife, Carey Mulligan as the young woman teenage Blake meets on holiday – so of course you want to give them something to work with. And it's necessary for the scenes to feel like scenes, for there to be more back and forth, more push and pull than there is on the page. That's not a failing of the book, because it's not the story Blake is telling, but in the book he's extremely solitary and internal, and expanding the other roles gives you a chance to vocalise that. Also – and this probably sounds pompous, but I'll say it anyway – there are sometimes female voices in source material that I feel are underserved and I want to give more of a voice and an attitude to them. In *Patrick Melrose*, he gets a lot more pushback from the female characters than he does in the novels. With *Tess of the D'Urbervilles*, I made a conscious effort to give her a wit and a curiosity that is present in the novel, but missing from previous adaptations. And with *And When Did You Last See Your Father?*, I really liked writing Carey Mulligan's scenes and the scenes with Blake's old girlfriend, played by Elaine Cassidy, and filling them out in ways that weren't necessarily in the book.

You moved the dinner from the mid-eighties to just before Arthur's illness, and show Arthur helping Blake move house at the start of his illness, rather than towards the end of it. Did you want to show Arthur fit and healthy, at his most selfish and bumptious, before the illness kicks in?

Yes. I also wanted as tight a timeframe as possible, a sense of pace and momentum. We did the same thing in *Patrick Melrose*, particularly in episode four, *Mother's Milk*. The novel covers four years; we condensed it to one month. I'd rather there be an artificial quality to the decline in his mother's health or the speed of Patrick's adultery than explain time leaps.

At the dinner, nursing his sorrows at the bar, Blake calls Arthur a 'mean-spirited, sanctimonious, narrow-minded old sod.' That's echoed later, in the flashback we talked about, where young Blake retreats to the toilet and says to his reflection in the mirror, 'I fucking, fucking, fucking hate him.' Those moments don't appear in the book, and are presumably there in the film to establish and maintain the conflict between them in a clear and dramatic way?

Absolutely. Blake found the 'fucking hate him' scene quite upsetting – and not necessarily truthful – and it's pretty unlikely he would have said the 'sanctimonious' thing either. There's two issues here. One is the age-old problem of how you express characters' thoughts. If you just write, 'Young Blake is furious,' someone reading that is likely to skip over it, so you find yourself reaching for things that are rather coarse – and sometimes you need them on screen, and sometimes, because of the things an actor can do, you don't. So one issue is the craft of it. The other issue is the truth of it. The book is very much about unexpressed feelings and the way they become a disease in themselves, and it's hard not to express that in some kind of catharsis on screen, not just for the characters, but for the audience. It's not very dramatic to watch someone getting pissed off, then getting a bit more pissed off, then getting a bit more pissed off, and not saying or doing anything about it. So I probably would have said to Blake, 'I know it's not true, but it's necessary. It's true for the character in the moment, and there needs to be some expression of fury.' You need it because there's no prose to convey his degree of emotional frustration.

You actually introduced quite a lot of conflict: in the first visit to his father's bedside, for example, Blake is at odds with both Arthur and his sister Gill. In the book, Blake and Gill are more affectionate, and she's being shielded from the extent of Arthur's illness. Did you ever hesitate about changing things to that degree?

I talked to Blake about it, and I think he talked to Gill about it – that it would be a different Gill, a fictional Gill, who didn't necessarily feel the way the real Gill felt. That's why you sometimes change characters' names: because you've written about things in a way that's partly true and partly not, and you need a character to represent an attitude or a state of mind that wasn't the case in real life.

One effect of Kathy's increased presence in the film is to emphasise Blake's misguided attempt to rekindle his sexual relationship with Sandra: it makes him seem more like his father, trying it on with another woman despite having a wife and children, but it also risks making him seem unsympathetic. What was your thinking in terms of balancing those things?

We talked a lot about that. I felt it should be less, but the director, Anand Tucker, felt it should be more, and Anand won that one – that's my memory, anyway. I thought a flirtation was okay, but there was a feeling that we might need to turn up the dial a bit if it was to be a meaningful scene. It definitely goes further than it does in the book, and I'm sure that would have been a discussion with Blake, because you wouldn't want to suggest that this was more truthful than the book. The overall tone of the book is rather melancholy and ruminative, and of course you want to get that, but you also want to feel that there's some real drama going on. We also had a very attractive actor with great charm, which perhaps takes the curse off. If we'd cast someone else, we might have got to the edit suite and thought, 'Shit, I wish we'd stuck with flirtation.' We talked about the same thing on *Patrick Melrose*. Is it clearly a midlife crisis provoked by grief and anger, or is it just a lot of excuses for shitty behaviour?

Can he really go to bed with another woman while his wife and children are asleep next door? Those are valid questions, but others are: what adjustments do you make to the sympathy dial depending on the casting, and how much charisma, warmth and humour will they bring to the performance? There are an innumerable number of variables which you're not thinking about at the writing stage. You're just thinking, 'How far do I want to push this on the page?'

Arthur's affair with Auntie Beaty is dealt with more directly in the film: young Blake first suspects something is going on during his camping trip with Arthur, and adult Blake asks Beaty about it after his father's funeral. The book contains neither that moment of realisation nor that specific conversation, but the film needs to set up and track through Blake's arc, his need to discover the truth?

Another alarm that always goes off in my head is ambiguity in a book. On the page, it's absolutely fine to have two possible outcomes, two possible truths. On screen, what are you going to do? You can't show them one after the other. You have to plump for one or the other. A good example of that is *Tess of the D'Urbervilles*. Because of the kind of writer Hardy is, and because of the complexities of Victorian morality – the conservatism of their attitudes towards sex, the euphemistic language they used, the sexual politics of the time – you read *Tess* and think, 'Was she raped or not?' Even in the 11 years since we made the programme, the language and attitudes have changed. In the unchanging, fixed text the word 'seduced' is used, but that doesn't mean there was no violence, that it wasn't what we would now call rape. So it's possible to read the book and think she was attracted to a handsome, devilish man, and she was a bit drunk and sleepy, but it was not a violent rape. It's also possible to read the book and think it absolutely was rape, that she was a rather naïve girl and very unlikely to have given consent. Neither of those things is true or false, and you can go through the book a hundred times and make arguments on both sides. But when you film it and the actor says, 'Is this a violent rape? Do I say no, am I coerced, or do I explicitly give my consent?' you have to answer those questions. You can't just say, 'Let's make it ambiguous.' So in adapting it, I'm not making a definitive statement about the book, I'm only making a definitive statement about the adaptation, and in the adaptation we've chosen to represent it as rape – and to me the story makes much more sense if it's about a shocking abuse of power rather than a 'seduction'. And in relation to Blake's book, it seemed like a mistake to have people coming out of the cinema going, 'I don't understand. Did they have an affair?' In key moments like that, the audience needs to know what's happened, and you sometimes have to ride roughshod over ambiguity to tell them.

Your dramatisation of Arthur's illness and death is, on the whole, more faithful to the facts than the flashbacks to Blake's childhood. Is that because you felt you had to be more reverent in the present-day scenes, whereas events in the past allow you more licence to change and rearrange?

That sounds about right. It's very powerfully described in the book, and such a terrible circumstance to live through, that there's not much you're required to change for dramatic effect. Since publication, other writers have been more frank and fearless about the nitty-gritty of death and illness, but at the time it felt like one of the most original and radical elements of the book. One thing we did change a lot, and argue about a lot, was the extent to which Blake leaves his father's side and travels back and forth through the different stages of his father's illness. There's a lot of that in the book, but whenever we had it in the script, whenever he was sitting on a train, it felt like there was a deflation, a loss of tension. In the context of the film, it felt like once he was there, he should stay there.

In the film, Blake doesn't cry when his father dies, and only feels the full force of his grief at the end when he remembers his father's tears on waving him off to university. It's climactic, it's cathartic, and it's also not true: in the book, Blake does cry. I imagine the challenge was finding an engaging dramatic arc for an essentially passive character through an episodic narrative?

It sounds really callous to say this, but the process of bereavement and grief is both quite slow and quite repetitive, so you have to play those cards in quite a decided and pointed way. It was also a blatant attempt to give the film a sense of climax, because it's very hard to find those kinds of climaxes in domestic stories. We felt that there needed to be a single dramatic moment where past and present collided, and it may be contrived, but it's one of those times where you have to cater to the fixed, objective rhythm of watching a film as opposed to the infinitely variable rhythm of reading a book. With the written word, you don't know whether the story will be consumed in one go or over three months. But in the cinema, the timing is the same for everyone. It's a real-time experience, so you have to shape it in a different way.

CASE STUDY: *PATRICK MELROSE*

UK/US, 2018 ▪ **Directed by** Edward Berger ▪ **Produced by** Stephen Smallwood ▪ **Screenplay by** David Nicholls, based on the novels *Never Mind*, *Bad News*, *Some Hope*, *Mother's Milk* and *At Last* by Edward St Aubyn ▪ **Cast:** Benedict Cumberbatch (Patrick Melrose), Jennifer Jason Leigh (Eleanor Melrose), Hugo Weaving (David Melrose), Holliday Grainger (Bridget Watson Scott), Anna Madeley (Mary Melrose), Sebastian Maltz (Young Patrick), Jessica Raine (Julia), Pip Torrens (Nicholas Pratt), Prasanna Puwanarajah (Johnny Hall), Harriet Walter (Princess Margaret), John Standing (George Watford)

Five novels in five, hour-long episodes. Was that always the intention?

No, it wasn't. The original idea was five 90-minute films – or possibly four, with the first two books conflated into one and flashbacks from New York to France – all of them shot by different directors. *Never Mind* would be like a Joseph Losey film, *Bad News* something like Scorsese's *After Hours*, and *Some Hope* reminiscent of Robert Altman's *Gosford Park*. It was harder to think of archetypes for *Mother's Milk* and *At Last*, but I always thought of episode five as a sort of early seventies film like *Sunday Bloody Sunday* or *The Pumpkin Eater*, something melancholy and angry in that very English way. Also, the episodes matched the chronological order of the books until quite late in the process. We all knew that would change because of the casting, but we were wary of making that change – and even after the read-through, we were talking about swapping the episodes back and starting with Patrick's childhood. So it went through all kinds of versions. It was probably three years between writing episode one and writing episode four, and episode four alone went through many different incarnations.

The novels are very sensual, in the literal sense of the word: things seen and heard, things tasted and felt, things watched and interpreted. How do you set about capturing that in a screenplay?

I think you have to be quite tough about reading the whole book. What I mean is, the drama isn't just in the dialogue or in people's actions. It's in, as you say, the sensuality: the lizard on the wall, or the rotting food in the hotel room. I had to harvest the text not just for conversations and events, but also for imagery, and to put a lot of that in the stage directions. The books are about the invasion of memory, and how past experience forms and affects present behaviour, and I think we succeeded in conveying that idea. But there's also a lot of philosophical speculation in the books, about consciousness and the self and how different characters see the world, that we couldn't really get on the screen.

Bad News and *Never Mind*

A good reason for starting with *Bad News* rather than *Never Mind* is that you introduce Patrick as an adult, played by your star, before showing him as a child. On the other hand, that means you meet him at his most extreme, which could be very off-putting. How did you reconcile those pros and cons?

We had a series of test screenings where we got people into the edit suite, and one night we played them childhood, then Patrick as a drug addict, and the other night we played them Patrick as a drug addict, then childhood, and asked them how they felt about him as a character. When we played it chronologically – i.e. *Never Mind* then *Bad News* – the second episode became a little bit boring because you knew why he hated his father and his actions seemed explicable but repetitive. When we had it the other way around, it's true that some people were shocked at how extreme it was, but at least it was compelling, and you're either going to go with that or you're not. We talked a lot about how much drug use should be in it, because that can be quite a turn-off. It's the ultimate subjective experience, and can be quite relentless for a viewer. So we thought, 'Which is the bigger gamble, this languid but harsh childhood film followed by a manic crazy hour, or the other way around?' And we felt that it was best the other way around: rather than, here's something terrible happening and here are the repercussions of that, it became, here's someone behaving in an extraordinary way and here are the reasons why. I would never, ever suggest that anyone read the books in anything other than the order in which they were intended to be read, but the benefits involved in starting with *Bad News* outweighed the risks. It's dramatically more interesting.

But you don't simply dramatise one novel then the other, you interleave them. In episode one, there are flashbacks to the young Patrick walking towards his father's bedroom door, and in episode two there are flash-forwards to the adult Patrick walking down a similar corridor. And if you showed what happened behind the door in the first episode, there would have been a danger that the audience wouldn't stick around for the second one.

We also talked a lot about how much of that there was going to be. The book is extremely shocking and upsetting, as it should be, but we always knew that we wouldn't have any of that – that actually, we would close the door. There would have been ways of doing it, but it would have been unnecessary and, I think, irresponsible.

The second episode opens with a recap, as does the third, but it's more than just 'Previously on *Patrick Melrose*...', you actually incorporate it into the drama: the phone call where Patrick learns of his father's death, viewing David's body, the coffin being closed and then cremated, the box of ashes on which Patrick takes out his anger. It puts you firmly in Patrick's head.

That sequence was always in the script, the phone call then the cremation, as if you were now following David Melrose's story too, watching his ultimate fate then flashing back. But initially, after the phone call, there was not a single glimpse of Benedict Cumberbatch in episode two. That was a studio note. The execs were nervous about Benedict not being in the second episode at all, and also, because it has a different style, that you'd turn on and feel like you were watching a different show, rather than a continuation of the same story. So the idea of dropping in one or two beats of Patrick going through cold turkey, almost hallucinating the flashbacks, came quite late and was shot rather grudgingly. It was one of those notes where you think, 'I don't want to do that,' then you do it and find you probably need it. The cry of the screenwriter is, 'Why won't they leave me alone? Why do they give me these ridiculous notes?', but actually the people giving them are often on to something.

In episode two, we see clearly how similar Patrick and his mother Eleanor's reactions are to the different kinds of abuse they both suffered – obliterating their sorrows in drugs and drink. In episode four, it's equally clear that he's now turning into his father: the cigar, the dressing gown, the bitterness and betrayal, the casual callousness towards his own children. Do you think the language of film sometimes gives you a chance to do things more simply, more directly and maybe better than the book did?

Yes, although I also worry about overstating things. When you put the imagery of a novel on screen, it becomes images in a much more literal way. Things that were mentioned in passing now shout, 'Look! They've got the same body language and they're in the same spot saying the same thing!' You can't do any of those things in prose, and there's a danger when you do them visually that you make them too on-the-nose. So you have to make judgments, both in the writing and in the editing, about how heavily to underline things. But you do sometimes feel with an adaptation as if you're giving a note to the author. There's a scene in *Far from the Madding Crowd* where they're dipping sheep, and Bathsheba is watching rather loftily and criticises them, and Gabriel says, 'If you know better, you come down and do it,' and she does. She gets into the trough with the workers and dips the sheep herself, and it's a little step in her mellowing. That's not what happens in the novel, but I like to think that if Thomas Hardy could see the film he might say, 'That's a good idea.' With *Patrick Melrose*, the novels weren't conceived as a saga and Edward St Aubyn doesn't feel the obligation to make it work as one, so there are characters who appear in one book and never come back. Patrick's ex-girlfriend, Julia, is only in *Mother's Milk* and *At Last*, but there are other characters in *Bad News* and *Some Hope* who are very like her, so conflating those characters and giving Julia an arc and exploring her relationship with Patrick actually works quite well. Similarly, his father's terrible best friend, Nicholas, isn't in *Bad News*, but he's one of the most interesting characters and it's a very interesting time to see him, when Patrick's strung out in New York, so of course he's got to be there. When you're exploring a family in slow decline, it doesn't hurt to draw out those saga elements and provide the viewer with recurring characters, so that they can see them getting older as time goes on.

Some Hope

Episode three clearly has a theme: escape. Were you aware of the other episodes having individual themes too?

I had some experience of that on the first show I ever wrote, *Cold Feet*. There used to be quite a strict formula for those nine o'clock TV shows: you have the ongoing story and the story of the week and a little comic plot, and they all reflect each other and are often linked by a theme and will always collide at some point. It was a bit like three-act structure in films, and you really did have to learn it. I didn't feel the same compulsion to do that with *Patrick Melrose*, but of course the books have very clear themes which were brought into the show and elaborated. I think that's why I found episode five particularly difficult, because the question I got asked most often was, 'What it's about?' It's an irritating question to be asked, but if you're not able to answer it, that may give you a clue as to why something isn't working.

It's two and a half episodes – two and a half hours – before Patrick says or does something likeable: the sympathy he shows towards Bridget's

daughter during her embarrassing encounter with Princess Margaret. Were you aware of that being his first moment of kindness, and did you ever wonder whether the audience would stick with him for that long?

I was aware of it, because it touches on childhood and kindness to children. It was clear to me as a reader, and I thought it would be clear to the audience, that people who suffer monstrously often become monsters – but his monstrousness, if it was entertaining, would be acceptable. There's a touch of Withnail in Patrick. In *Withnail and I*, Withnail's vulnerability isn't really explicit until the last minute of the film. Until then, the pleasure has been from the irresponsibility and extremity of that character. I certainly never got the note, 'Can you make Patrick more likeable?', but that was partly because my instinct was to do that anyway. I didn't think I was censoring the character, but there were times when I thought, 'We've got enough of that.' Enough of Patrick the snob, or Patrick the misogynist, or Patrick patronising people. Enough that it didn't need to be overstated – although perhaps other dramatists would have written harsher versions of the material. It's also possible to imagine it being played by someone else and not having the pathos that Benedict brings to the part. So a lot of it is in the performance rather than the script.

The pivotal scene in episode three is Patrick's confession to Johnny that he was abused by his father, a confession which comes at a different point and in a different location in the novel. How did you arrive at the final structure of that episode?

Some Hope was always my favourite book, and I thought that everything in it was good and strong, but there was no real climax to it. The climax of the novel – George having a heart attack and being taken to hospital – happens again in episode five, to Nicholas. You can forgive that if you're reading the books over the course of 20 years, but in a TV show you can't have two major elderly characters die of heart attacks at social events within two weeks of broadcast. So we had to cut that scene from *Some Hope*, which meant there was a certain amount of action missing from the latter half of the episode. Also, Patrick and Johnny aren't at the party until very late in the novel. Patrick's confession happens halfway through, in the pub, and for the rest of the book he has this series of lovely, wise conversations with various characters about forgiveness: whether he can ever forgive his father and, if he can't, whether it's possible just to be indifferent to what's happened to him. All of that existed in early drafts of the script, but was a bit dramatically flat. You felt you could take out any of it and it wouldn't make much difference to the story of that episode. So putting the confession late in the episode was extremely helpful. It was a big change, but I think it was a good change.

Mother's Milk

Some Hope ends with Patrick on an up. By the time you get to Mother's Milk, he's come down again. It's quite a jarring gear shift reading them back to back.

It is jarring, and also his dynamic as a 40-year-old man needs to be different from his dynamic in his twenties; he no longer has the alibi of youth. His response to things has to be different and the tone of it has to be different. He's a family man with responsibilities, and drinking himself into a stupor and letching after young women could have become tiresome. The last two books were both problematic to adapt, and at one stage I pushed quite hard just to do the first three. Even though I love all five, the first three have an arc to them, which is the father's story, and then you have to ramp things up again for the last two to tell the mother's story. Patrick's problem isn't solved at the end of the third book, but he's at a moment of peace and reconciliation, so why not stop there? I'm glad we did them all in the end, but at the time I found the fourth book very hard.

It's easy to see why. It's the longest of the five novels, it's told from multiple points of view, and it spans four years rather than a few days.

When you sit down to do Mother's Milk, you're immediately confronted with Patrick's son Robert being born – seen from Robert's point of view. So that's not going to work. Then you get to the stuff about the nanny being sacked, which is really funny, but you're introduced to a character who's immediately discarded in a way that makes Patrick look quite mean. So you cross that out. And you keep going like that until you get to something you feel you can't live without, which is him being dispossessed by his mother and the dispossession being the catalyst for his breakdown – and once we decided that was what it was about, it was fine. I worked very closely with Edward Berger on that episode; it's the most input I've ever had from a director on a script. It was originally much more faithful to the middle of the book – the summer where Patrick really starts drinking and his affair with Julia kicks off, and there is a series of visitors to the house and they all have conversations with him – and condensed into an hour it was a bit boring. I'm actually pretty pleased with the finished version. It's not my favourite episode, but I always thought it was going to be a disaster, and it was rewritten a lot right up to the read-through.

What were the most obvious cuts and what were the hardest?

I found it very hard to lose the conversations with Johnny, because when you're adapting material, close friends are invaluable, even more so if they're therapists. There's no contrivance in confession, so they're the perfect sounding boards. There are a lot of passages in the book where Johnny says, 'So how are you feeling?' and Patrick tells him: my memories of childhood are this, and my feelings towards women are this. But I was constantly getting the note to take out Johnny, because having them walk around the grounds and confide in each other for pages and pages stopped things dead. The last section of the book, where they come back to London and Patrick starts to think about the euthanasia of his mother, also got cut back, because the episode is about dealing with her death, rather than dealing with how she might die. It was an interesting moral issue, but once Edward Berger came on board he said, 'It's about a family man falling apart and fighting not to turn into his father, and anything that's not serving that you've got to cut.'

Patrick's children, principally Robert, play a big part on the page – especially in this book, given its title – but a small part on screen. Why was that?

Because kids are a nightmare in dramas that cover a long period of time. Irrespective of the actor's ability, irrespective of what works in the script, you always have to be aware of the practicalities of production, of one face morphing into the next and not being able to show intermediate stages. One of the strongest alarms that goes off when I'm reading something with an eye to adaptation is the highest possible age of the young actor. In *Great Expectations*, Pip doesn't leap in the book from being eight to being 21, but when you put it on screen you have to bunch up the action on either side and cut the bit in the middle so that you can jump from one actor to the other. The same with Blake's book. There are scenes where he has encounters with his father in his twenties and thirties, but we didn't even attempt to make the young actor look like Colin Firth and just cut the intermediate versions. That's an easy choice. There was a third incarnation of Patrick in certain drafts of the script, because there was some great stuff in the novel about the teenage Patrick going to see his destitute father and finding the confidence to taunt him for the first time, but it was exhausting just thinking about casting a midway Patrick. So the material you select is often determined by practical considerations.

At Last

The final episode struck me as being very silent and still. Was that quality in the script, or was it in the way it was shot?

Again, Edward Berger had a lot of input. He wasn't around for the initiation of the project, so he was less involved in the writing of the first three, but he did a lot of thinning out of the latter drafts of four and five. We knew that the early drafts were too faithful and that we'd need to cut some of the chatter that's in the book and replace it with essential beats that weren't. In the book, there's a lot more jumping around between different groups at the mother's funeral, and also a lot missing. You don't see the break-up of Patrick's marriage in the book; it's all happened in the past, so that had to be invented. There's no scene in the book where Patrick breaks down, and no scene with his mother where they both acknowledge David's crimes, so they had to be invented. It didn't feel acceptable for his anger with his mother to be that internalised, so there's a lot of speechifying, which is the most sustained piece of invention in the five episodes. I feel it's necessary and I think it's extremely well acted, but it's the stuff I'm most nervous about because it's not entirely in tune with Edward St Aubyn's vision, which is less cathartic. So it's slightly out of character, but you have to weigh up the change in style against the demands of the audience.

I was going to ask you about the scene where Patrick finally tells his mother that his father abused him. It's a short but devastating scene, and I didn't remember it in the novels.

It's referred to glancingly in *Mother's Milk*, but it's not a scene, it's just a sentence, in the passage where he's complaining about the egotism and selfishness of his mother, and how everything always has to be about her, and that he has been locked all his life in a competition with her as to who suffered most at the hands of his father. It's a great passage, but it's quite violently anti-Eleanor, and we felt we had to see a more sympathetic version of that. But you're right, it is devastating, because he doesn't know how to react and the scene just stops. In the writing process we would ask, 'What would happen if we kept the camera running? Is he angry? Does he reveal more? Does she say anything else?' and every time we tried to answer those questions we got into trouble. We didn't want the sentimental version where two people who have suffered greatly give each other a big hug and say, 'I love you.' Nor were we comfortable with the version where he goes, 'For fuck's sake, at least let me have this,' and storms off, because that's extremely unsympathetic. So in a way, the short version is the only version that works. You feel both sympathy for the suffering Eleanor has undoubtedly experienced and a little of Patrick's shock at her response. It isn't quite what's in the book, but I don't think it's a betrayal. And again, when you make characters flesh and blood they're often more touching or more maddening than they were on the page, and you can't predict that.

The final episode is the one where I noticed the humour most. How important was humour to you in adapting such dark, difficult subject matter?

In a way, it's what drew me to the material. I read the first book when it came out in 1992: I was working in a bookshop and picked it up off the table and read it on my lunch breaks and thought it was amazing. It seemed to be part of a British fiction tradition that I loved, the tradition of Evelyn Waugh, especially the Waugh of *A Handful of Dust*. So the humour was absolutely essential to me, and I'm hugely relieved that it comes across. If it had fallen flat it would have seemed incredibly unpleasant, a frivolous approach to the most serious subject matter imaginable. Most of the best jokes are Teddy's, though; if I've invented dialogue, it's often been more emotional stuff. I'm very proud both of the scripts and of the finished show, but I'm also very aware of it being an editorial contribution rather than lots of invention on my part. I've just given a more conventional shape to books that don't have that – and why would they? It's not what the novels set out to do.

Sarah Phelps

Sarah Phelps was born in 1966 in Kingston upon Thames.

She has written 100 episodes of *EastEnders*, and her other television work includes episodes of *No Angels* (2004/2006) and *Dickensian* (2015–16). She also created and wrote the BBC series *The Crimson Field* (2014).

Her screen adaptation credits include: the Dickens serials *Oliver Twist* (2007) and *Great Expectations* (2011); *Falcón* (2012, novel *The Silent and the Damned* by Robert Wilson); *The Casual Vacancy* (2015, novel by J.K. Rowling); *Dublin Murders* (2019, novels *In the Woods* and *The Likeness* by Tana French); and four novels and a short story by Agatha Christie: *And Then There Were None* (2015), *The Witness for the Prosecution* (2016), *Ordeal by Innocence* (2018), *The ABC Murders* (2018) and *The Pale Horse* (2020).

APPROACHES TO ADAPTATION

Do you prefer to adapt material which chimes with your own work, or material which is completely different and gives you a chance to try out new things?

I would say that I prefer to do work that's outside of what I would write. But when I adapt something I do a very thorough adaptation, so even if it's way outside what I would write about, it becomes my own work anyway. Sometimes even though a novel is really popular and everyone thinks they know it, when I've read it I've found something completely different in it. The usual way of perceiving *Oliver Twist* is that Nancy is a victim and Bill Sikes is a thug. But in the book that's not true. He's incredibly tender to her. There's a bit in the book when she has a gin-soaked seizure while they're all arguing about the lunatic plot, and Sikes picks her up and puts her down very gently on some ratty straw-filled mattress in the corner and says, 'She'll be all right now.' And after he's murdered her, when he tries to get out of London into the country, wherever he goes he sees her face. That's not a thug, that's a man with a conscience who's aware that he's snuffed out the one pure light in his life – and unable to bear it he returns to London to be chased across the rooftops, fired up by that ghastly man Brownlow shouting that there'll be a reward for anyone who hunts him down. It's a horrible sequence in the book; there's a blood-letting quality to it which is really repugnant. In my version, I sent him down into the sewers to kill himself, so it wasn't a public accident, it was a private covenant with the terrible thing he had done. He had broken his own heart. And it was also his circumstances: the poverty of it, the terror of it, the not knowing if you're going to end the day alive. It was really important to me to tell that story. So someone else might have adapted the novel one way, and I adapted it my way.

Do you think adaptations involve a completely different set of creative gears to original screenplays?

It depends. There's a difference between working with an author who's long dead and been adapted a million times before – like Dickens – and working with an author who's been adapted before, but is very much alive – like J.K. Rowling – and working with an author who's also long dead, but has an incredibly vigilant estate and whose works are so popular that there's a kind of cosy familiarity about them. People often ask me, 'Did you ever think when you were writing *EastEnders* that you'd end up doing this?' And I'm like, 'Of course.' I mean, no, but there's no difference in my mind between writing a piece of original work and writing for something like *EastEnders*, which is a huge factory, and turning my attention to either a familiar or unfamiliar piece of work and trying to do something different with it. Because what it comes down to, all of it, is character and storytelling. If you haven't got that root-and-branch DNA, then you haven't got anything, regardless of what the project is.

Do you always agree a mission statement or direction of travel with whoever has commissioned the adaptation?

I don't generally agree a mission statement; I say what I'm going to do and people either like it or they don't. I'm not going to pitch how I want to tell the story and then have someone say, 'You know what, can you make it a bit more like this?' Obviously when you're working on something, especially if it's a long project, it goes through changes, and ultimately whatever you do is a collaboration between you, the producers, the director, the actors, not just from the point of view of being in line with – sounding rather poncey – your 'vision', but also what's achievable in terms of budget and schedule. A lot of the time when you're writing, after your first draft, you're dealing with problems like, 'This is great but we can't afford it.' *Oliver Twist* was one of the first big adaptations I did, and I don't think anyone thought, 'Let's ask Sarah Phelps because she's really got her finger on the pulse of Dickens.' I think someone else had dropped out and they needed someone who could write scripts fast, which I can do because of turning scripts around for *EastEnders*. And in one of the first meetings they said, 'We can't afford a rooftop chase!' – which never occurred to me anyway, because I wouldn't have wanted to do it. So their vision for the book was partly predicated on the fact that they couldn't afford a rooftop chase and we had to find something else, but that gave me something else for Bill Sikes and helped me tell the story I wanted to tell.

When I went in for *And Then There Were None*, Mathew Prichard [*executive producer*] said, 'I think it would be great if we did it like *Big Brother*,' and I said, 'That's a terrible idea. Why would you do that? Everyone's going to fuck up, no one's going to have any fun, and you can't tell a satisfying story. I want to tell it like this,' and then talked until they felt so battered by this tsunami of verbiage that they meekly agreed. It was the same when I went up to meet Jo Rowling to talk about *The Casual Vacancy*. It was a nervy sort of meeting with quite a few people in there; Jo is obviously surrounded by people who manage her affairs, because how many hours in the day has the woman got, she's busy. She's also excellent, by the way. So I said, 'This is the story I want to tell. This is how I want to tell it. I want to do this, this, this and this to make sure we serve the story that I think you want to tell – which is the story of what happens to a teenage girl who no one gives a shit about: *Tess of the d'Urbervilles* in a modern-day setting.' There was a silence, because it was quite a hard-core pitch, but as we left we got a phone call saying, 'Yes, do it.'

I think if you've read a piece of work and you don't at some gut level have a passion for what you want to do for it, then you shouldn't be doing it, because ultimately you're the writer and your script has got to lead everything: 'There's something in this book that hasn't been seen before and that's what I'm going to tell.' With adaptation, you're changing a lot. You're going to get inside the book and beat it up, and shake it and see what comes out, and find the passionate heart at the centre of it – and if you're not leading the charge on that, then seriously, go home.

Do you usually produce an outline or treatment before you start writing the script?

Not if I can help it. I'll sometimes write potted histories of the characters, so I know why they think the way they do and walk the way they do, but I hate outlines and I hate treatments. I really, really can't bear them. When I was new in my career and people would say, 'Can you write a treatment?' I was like, 'No. Why don't you just commission a script? What's the matter with you?' How the hell is reading four pages – or beat by beat, or scene by scene – going to tell you how a script works? A script works in a completely different way from how prose works – although I am very prose-y and write endless, very descriptive stage directions which probably annoy people – and if you're having to spend hours and hours writing paragraph after paragraph of what's in the room and how the sunlight falls, it's a killer. I always feel desperately anguished on behalf of writers who are asked to do another pass on a treatment. You just feel your soul die. I'm working with writers who are coming in to work on shows with me, and sometimes they want to do an outline, but I like to go straight into script. I think most people feel released and trusted when you say, 'Let's do a first draft and see how you get on.' Prose doesn't reflect the muscularity of how dialogue works. When you're into a scene and characters are opening their mouths and speaking, everything changes. It just becomes a different beast.

If you're offered material to adapt which has been adapted previously, do you take account of any previous versions when writing yours?

I've got a rule, and it's a really firm rule, and it's been there since I started doing adaptations, which is that I don't watch any other adaptations when I'm working. I didn't want to see David Lean's classic adaptation of *Oliver Twist*. The same with *Great Expectations*. All that mattered to me was the novel. There have been countless iterations of *Oliver Twist*, and I just wasn't interested in them – apart from the musical, which my mum took me to see when I was little and I completely fell in love with Oliver Reed and filthy London and the back streets. Every time Oliver was in the Brownlow house I thought, 'That's boring, why can't he go back to Bill and Nancy and Fagin?' When I wrote my version, I wanted to fill the Brownlow house with danger and give the world of Fagin a sense of safety – and give the characters surrounding Oliver, like Fagin and Dodger, a humanity and a dignity. Fagin's lair is the first time Oliver gets a suit of clothes, it's the first time he gets a bed for himself, it's the first time anyone is actually kind to him; there's a comfort there which he'd never found before. And I wanted it to be not just where Oliver found a home, but where Dodger found a home, and to show Dodger's love of Fagin and his love of Nancy, so that by the end, when Dodger has lost everyone, all the people he loved – Fagin, Nancy, even Sikes – we realise that something beautiful has been broken by the cruelty of the state and that Dodger is going to suffer, and that he will now be more dangerous than Bill Sikes ever was.

If the author of the source material is living, do you find it useful to have their input on the script?

No. When I was doing *The Casual Vacancy*, Jo stood right back from it. Obviously she read drafts, but she was very good at making sure her input didn't intrude on me writing. She's got grace when she's working with other writers, which is much appreciated. When it comes to working with the Christie estate, they're representing the views of the estate, not of Agatha Christie, so that's an interesting tightrope to walk. We don't know what she thinks, so you can only go on what the books offer up.

Is it easier to navigate notes from directors, producers and script editors when you have a piece of source material to measure the screenplay against?

No. There's this whole thing about, 'Well, in the novel this happens,' and I go, 'Yeah, but that's the letter of the novel, and if we do the letter of the novel we're going to have 37 hours of TV and every single hour is going to make you want to open your wrists.' Because the book is different, and it's not what we're working on anymore. We're working on what I've written, which is its own beast. So unless I've gone way off base and suddenly introduced an elephant or something, it's absolutely pointless to go back to the book. The dialogue is all different, some of the motivations are different, even some of the ways I've represented the characters are different. *Witness for the Prosecution* contained some overtly sexual scenes that weren't in the short story, but why shouldn't they be there? In that situation, of course they would be. I'm quite an argumentative person, so if someone says, 'We can't do that.' I say, 'Yes, we can.' But I've also made them believe the story I'm telling. I've told it with all the heart and the guts that I can, and I've really owned it and made it compelling. If people aren't compelled to follow the narrative you're telling, of course they'll go, 'I don't know about this.' But if you've put everything into those early drafts and gone, 'It's this twist and then this turn,' then people will buy it and trust you. People have got to trust you. The audience has to trust you, the actors have to trust you, and the people who are making your show have to trust you.

Have you ever started work on an adaptation and found it harder to adapt than you anticipated?

Oh, yeah, I've been sacked. Well, not sacked – 'gone our separate ways'. Sometimes that's about personalities and power politics, and sometimes it's because I like to take more licence than people want me to take, and sometimes it just doesn't work and everyone agrees that I'm not the right person for the project. My friend Tony Jordan says, 'Never underestimate the power of no.' So, yeah, I've left projects because I'm not the writer they need. They thought I was, and I thought I could do it, and then everyone goes, 'This is a nightmare. Let's just call it quits,' and I go, 'All right. Bye-bye.'

Are there any screen adaptations which you think are especially good or you particularly admire?

There are ones which I think transcend the original books. *One Flew Over the Cuckoo's Nest*: I can't bear the book, it's loads of blokes thinking they're great and hating women, but I remember being profoundly moved by the film and it being a really important part of growing up. *Midnight Cowboy*, by Waldo Salt, is a phenomenal adaptation. *Precious Bane*, which Maggie Wadey adapted for the BBC ages ago, was fantastic. It was a Christmas treat, and me and my mum sat down to watch it, and my brothers, who were just great big lumps, were like, 'We ain't watching this bullshit,' and by the end of it they were like [*mimes wiping tears away*]. Good job! I loved *The English Patient*: so hard to do, but done amazingly. Rachel Bennette did a brilliant job of Zadie Smith's *NW*, I thought. Nick Dear's adaptation of *Persuasion* is wonderful: sparse and very funny and really emotional – and people get dirty. Emma Thompson's *Sense and Sensibility* is also wonderful and gets rid of that chocolate boxy thing. You'd be amazed how people still want things to be chocolate boxy and clean. It's difficult enough to keep clean in the twenty-first century; imagine what it would have been like then. All that stuff has to be laundered by hand, and if you haven't got servants you're doing it yourself. That's the kind of thing I like to think about when I'm writing these things: who's emptying the chamber pot?

ADAPTING FICTION

Some writers try to include as much of the novel as possible by boiling scenes down to their essence. Others are more ruthless in editing it down to a sort of greatest hits, but being true to the spirit of it. Do you favour either of those approaches?

There are always things that you've got to have. Oliver in the orphanage. Pip in the forge. But you're going to have to be ruthless. You're going to have to slice people out. So with those great big novels I always try to have a little rubric which informs how I respond to it, otherwise I'll end up going down various highways and byways. With *Great Expectations* it was, 'A boy sells his soul and buys it back by becoming a man.' That keeps you focused on the internal drive, on what the story is. The Marshes are the story. Magwitch is the story. Satis House is the story. London is the story. So I don't think about how I'm going to ruthlessly edit it down or how I'm going to make it a greatest hits, I just think about how I'm going to tell the central story. And sometimes I'll entirely shift the focus of the storytelling.

If a novel has an unusual structure, would you try to reproduce that in adapting it?

That's quite a difficult question, because I've never been in the situation where someone's handed me something that looks really groundbreaking and unconventional on the page. If it was something really important to the way people responded to the story, I would absolutely try to represent that in the way I told the story. The way the story is told *is* the story, as it were.

Do you try to avoid voiceover in adapting a first-person narrative, or do you see it as another tool in the toolbox?

I'm not keen on voiceover. I always think it's a white flag of surrender. I don't like being told things. Unless it's about that unreliable first-person narrator, but most first-person narrators are unreliable – that's the definition. Or unless someone is telling you a story and you suddenly realise you're not getting a voiceover, you're getting something else. I'm writing something at the moment where you think you're going to get a voiceover and it turns out not to be, but whether I can play with form like that and get away with it remains to be seen. Otherwise, I'm not keen on it. [*Dramatic voice*] 'And there I was, all alone in the world, lost and desolated…' Don't fucking tell me – show me!

Do you use the prose from the novel in writing the dialogue and stage directions, or do you put the whole thing in your own words?

Prose, no. Once I've got the characters and the story, it's my world and I say what happens. Dialogue, no, because once you've decided to frame the story in a particular way there's no point replicating the dialogue. I might use a familiar phrase to give the audience a feeling that they're watching an adaptation of their beloved book and not something I've completely bastardised and made up. With *Oliver Twist*, there were two things I picked out from the book: one was Fagin's 'my dear', and the other was that they call Oliver 'Nolly'. That's not really well known, so that was my nod to the source material. With *Great Expectations,* the phrase I picked out was Mrs Joe's, where she's constantly complaining about raising the boy 'by hand', and that was my nod.

Do you keep the novel beside you throughout the adaptation process, or do you try to internalise it and set it aside somewhere along the way?

Keeping the novel beside me: I've just got this image of someone with a really tidy desk and the novel sitting there full of post-it notes so that they can refer to it – and that's not what my desk is like at all! What I tend to do is, I've read it and it's in there, but the images I've got, and the characters I've got, have superseded it. So it's always somewhere in the room, but there's a very strong chance that unless someone puts a gun to my head I won't pick it up again, because I'm just looking at my script.

How much pressure do you feel when adapting a well-known and much-loved novel, knowing that you won't be able to please everyone with the finished product?

I couldn't give a shit. But it is fascinating to me how passionately people feel a sense of ownership over a novel. They've had this relationship with it at some point in their youth, or they picked it off the shelf when they had mumps and were comforted by its rhythms, even though it's the darkest story about death you can possibly imagine. So it's not just how we read a book that's important when it comes to adaptation, it's how we *remember* how we read a book. *Great Expectations* seems to really chime with a lot of people, and particularly chime with people who imagine themselves to have been betrayed by a girl, like Pip – so that was their experience of reading it. I remember my brother saying something like, 'Estella is all the girls who ever blew you out.' I said, 'She's a stolen child!' He said, 'What?' I said, 'Why are you reading it like that, where it's all about your experience and it's not about anything else?' My brother sort of went, 'Oh, yeah,' but a lot of people become really defensive about novels: 'You've done it wrong!'

People reacted really badly to the casting of Gillian Anderson in *Great Expectations*: 'Miss Havisham is way too young.' Well, show me the page where it says how old she is. 'She's always been like that.' Yes, because we always like to think that women soaked in grief are grotesques. But if you make her a grotesque, why does Pip fall under her spell? If you make her a grotesque, then what's happening in that house, the obscenely sexualised education she's giving to Estella to get her revenge, doesn't have the power it should have. I thought Gillian was fantastic and played the role exactly as I'd written it, as this strange arrested child with this slightly Mandarin quality to the way she speaks, so you're never quite sure what it is she's saying. It's couched in a layered secrecy, so poor Pip thinks he hears one version and Estella knows another was intended. You need someone that dangerous to infect these children's lives. People were also very angry – people with minimal conceptual grasp or understanding of history – about the fact that we cast Sophie Okonedo in *Oliver Twist*: 'BBC box-ticking, no black people in Victorian England, blah, blah, blah.' I never think about actors when I'm writing, I just think about the character, but the minute I started writing Nancy I knew I wanted Sophie, for that grace and that fire and that glorious complex humanity.

So, yeah, people get very involved in their personal responses to particular novels, so much so that when they see something that doesn't represent their ideal version, their reaction is wildly disproportionate. I did a panel once about adaptation and Dickens, and a woman shot her hand up and said to me, 'I got up really early and got a coach to London just to tell you that you RUINED this book! You ruined it for me and I can never read it AGAIN!' To be honest, the Christie fandom can be pretty strange, too. Have you ever been to a Christie festival? I went to one in Dorset or somewhere, and when I walked into the hotel where I was staying I saw two Poirots sharing a pack of barbecued beef crisps. Really odd.

CASE STUDY: *GREAT EXPECTATIONS*

UK, 2011 ▪ Directed by Brian Kirk ▪ Produced by George Ormond ▪ Screenplay by Sarah Phelps, based on the novel by Charles Dickens ▪ Cast: Douglas Booth (Pip), Ray Winstone (Abel Magwitch), Gillian Anderson (Miss Havisham), David Suchet (Jaggers), Tom Burke (Bentley Drummle), Shaun Dooley (Joe Gargery), Vanessa Kirby (Estella), Susan Lynch (Molly), Jack Roth (Dolge Orlick), Claire Rushbrook (Mrs Joe)

You've dramatised two books by Dickens: *Great Expectations* and *Oliver Twist*. As an adapter, what attracts you to his work?

I never liked Dickens the man until I read Claire Tomalin's biography of him, when I realised something that made my heart break for him a little bit and made me understand him a whole lot more: he was bipolar. He soaks his head in iced water because he can't sleep, and he walks and walks and walks and walks, and he's either manic or he's so depressed he can barely get out of bed. The thing that always fascinated me was the way he treated his wife, which was appalling – and I kept wondering why. He wouldn't have been the first man to run two households, and it's not as if he made his relationship with

Ellen Ternan public – in fact, he went to ludicrous lengths to keep it secret. But he went to equally ludicrous lengths to break up his household, to print terrible things about his wife, to refuse to speak to his children if they carried on a relationship with their mother. I was thinking about this for ages, and thinking about the way his brain would teem with life and then just stop, and I realised that he broke up his household for one reason and one reason only: because he needed chaos to write. And what comes out of that appalling time is all the later novels – *Great Expectations*, *Dombey and Son* – the great novels of grief and loss and desperate need for forgiveness.

There's a part of him that was always writing the same story – how we try to find tenderness amidst cruelty – but if he'd written *Oliver Twist* at the same time as he wrote *Great Expectations*, I think he'd have told that story in a very different way. It would have been much more about what it means to be brave, not to be done to, but to do. Everything in *Oliver Twist* is being done to: he's always crying and it's very sentimental. Obviously it was the first time, more or less, that a child had been the focus of a book, and you can't deny Dickens' crusading zeal, but Oliver does collapse under the weight of his own story and he is a whining little sod. There were points where I got really frustrated with the book – every time Dickens describes Fagin as a repulsive wizened Jew, you want to say 'Fuck off' and throw the thing across the room – then on the next page he hits you with some amazing piece of description and you go, 'You absolute bastard, I'm going to have to tolerate you.' But you're watching a young man finding his way as a writer, I think, and by the time you get to the other end of his life you can see a different level of achievement.

My dad loved Dickens and loved *Great Expectations* – so much so that we used to call him the Aged P – and he encouraged me to read it because of Magwitch and because of everything Magwitch is trying to make better for that moment on the marshes. The orphan Pip has these two extraordinary fathers in Joe Gargery and in Magwitch, and it's so moving because you watch him lose and regain his soul. You watch him change from being obsessed with Estella and obsessed with Bentley Drummle and obsessed with money, to being ashamed of Joe and ashamed of Magwitch and disgusted by the money, to looking down the river and seeing the danger coming Magwitch's way and knowing he has to save him. I defy anyone not to be moved by Magwitch's death, and by Pip holding his hand and saying, 'I know your daughter, and I love her,' and Magwitch dying with that knowledge, and with that promise. And by Pip walking over the hillside and finding Joe alone in the forge and saying, 'I'm so sorry,' and Joe putting his arm around him and forgiving him after everything. What a miracle.

Before it became a title in its own right, 'Dickensian' was the word used to describe Dickens' fictional world and its screen representations, suggesting a cosy, familiar, pantomime reduction of his novels' complexities. What does that mean to you in terms of your approach to adapting him? I already get the sense that it's a concept you would run...

...a million miles from. It's like 'Austenesque', where everyone is wearing Empire-line dresses and no one ever gets muddy. I find it intensely problematic, because I think it stops being about the books and starts being about the perceived world of the books, which to me feels less like storytelling and more like marketing. The authors get lost. I feel the same way about the Christie world. Writers don't care if they sell fudge. Writers want to be read and to feel like what they've got to say is important. Christie, Dickens, Austen, the Brontës, they've become these huge great shibboleths of themselves, and you've got to strip away the heritage trail and the tea towels and all the other extraneous bollocks surrounding them and say, 'What's the story about?' I actually wrote a load of episodes for the series *Dickensian* and loved doing it. I even wrote an episode which the *Daily Mail* approved of, which made me feel pretty dodgy. But again, one of the pleasures of it was, 'You think you know these characters? Well, what if we do this with them? What if we tell their origin stories?' Like, how did Lady Dedlock become Lady Dedlock, what happened to make her this character? And that's a buzz, because you're lifting it out of that world of, 'This is the way it's always been and always must be,' which is simply a stranglehold that stops you inventing. 'That's not Dickensian. That's not Austenesque.' Who cares?

Great Expectations **was another three-part adaptation, though the book itself seems to demand that, breaking down into three distinct acts: the marshes and Satis House; Pip coming into his expectations; and the final reckoning. Was there ever any question that it would be anything other than three parts?**

It does naturally split into three, but it all has to have a thread – and when everything hits you at the end, you want it to hit with the impact of when it first happened: the moment that little boy unwraps the pie and says, 'I thought you might be hungry.' Again, I changed that from the book. In the book, Magwitch asks Pip to bring him food and a file. In my version, he gets away from the prison boat and has to get the shackles off and what he puts in his belly is low down his list of priorities. That kid has got just one mission, and that's to get him a file. But Pip, out of the goodness of his heart, sees a man starving and thinks, 'I've got his file, but look, there's this pie.' It was a bit like *Oliver Twist*. In the book he's bullied into asking for more, but in my version he does it because he's brave, because he knows it's the right thing to do – which makes us love him and believe in him. I wanted Pip to be the same: we have to believe in him. We're going to follow him down a very dark path and he's going to make us question him, so we've got to remember that his heart is good. When Joe welds Magwitch's shackles and the soldiers try to give him money, he says, 'It's a poor job and I don't want paying for it.' He sees a soul in pain and he responds, and I wanted Pip to be enough of Joe's boy that he would do the same, because that would mean that wherever Magwitch went he would carry that little boy's face with him. He'd be sent to the other end of the world, make an absolute fortune and still go, 'That kid. That kid.' The thing that powers Magwitch is grief over his lost child and trying to fill the gaping maw of that loss, and when Pip holds out that piece of pie on a shaking hand you can see that this is his new child. That feels right to me, that feels right to me about Dickens. Not Dickensian, but Dickens.

Great Expectations **contains fewer characters than some of Dickens' novels, but still more than a three-hour drama can encompass. How** did you decide which ones to keep and which to cut? Why Orlick, for example, but no Biddy – and no Aged P?

Why would you have Biddy? Biddy is always hauling Pip over the coals and wagging her finger and being really pompous. Then Pip thinks he'll marry her but she's now married Joe, which makes me feel differently about Joe, and that wasn't the way I wanted to write Joe. In the book, Joe just rolls with the punches, so I changed him and gave him a very different intelligence, which I felt was more dignified in terms of his relationship to Pip. So Biddy was neither here nor there. Orlick was more important for me because I wanted Orlick to really hate Pip, and the reason Orlick really hated Pip was that he really loved Joe. Joe was like a dad and Joe was kind. I wanted my Orlick to be beside himself when he was sent away and uprooted, so that by the time he betrayed Pip there was a reason for him to do it. Why no Aged P? Couldn't fit him in. It would have been nice, but it takes you out of Pip's world and takes you somewhere else. That's all well and good if you've got to fill a load of instalments in a paper and then read them to an audience who want a few laughs, but in this it would have been a distraction. Someone said to me, 'You've taken all the humour out of it.' Well, Christ almighty. Lies, betrayal, a broken heart, a stolen child, an obscenely sexualised education and a man who's going to hang. Tell me what the fucking joke is. Because Dickens doesn't get it and neither do I. He tells a joke to keep people listening. It's a palate cleanser. It's a glass of water between the dark cups of coffee. But I don't have to do that because I've only got three hours and I don't think it's funny. I want to find the beauty and the tenderness in it more than I want to find some pointless joke.

Given all the familiar scenes and characters you had to – or chose to – cut, it's noticeable when you put something new in: the scene where Drummle takes Pip to a brothel, for example, which feels like the sort of scene Dickens might have written had he been allowed to.

In the book, Bentley Drummle doesn't really exist beyond what people say about him, which is that he's spoilt and violent and that Estella is going to marry him. I wanted to write something different. When Pip looks at Drummle he sees a rock god – he sees what he wants to be. But when Drummle looks at Pip he sees a rival – and does what all bullies do, which is to find his weak spot. Drummle is going to go to a brothel, he's going to take Pip, and Pip is going to be very embarrassed – and realise that he's not like this person. Pip tries to impress Drummle, but will always be out of step with him, because Drummle is clothed in privilege and Pip will never understand entitlement. Drummle is a man who can sit back and say, 'I'll have her, her and her,' because he believes that flesh, women's flesh, is a commodity to be bought and sold – which makes him really dangerous to Estella. Also, because *Great Expectations* is about sex and about taking revenge through sex, I wanted to sexualise their adult life as men and to equate the Victorian euphemism for ejaculation, 'spend', with what Pip does with this new money that isn't his: he spends it, to pass in society. And when they go to that brothel, none of the women are white, which is a nod to the way the Victorians felt towards the world at large: it's ours and we'll pay a farthing and we'll do what we like and walk away. So it's about money, it's about class, it's about gender – it's about saying that Estella has absolutely no power whatsoever. You hear Jaggers say later, 'We hope the lady will come out on top,' and you know that's not what's going to happen. She's sold into a terrible marriage with a violent man that is absolute hell, and for what? Nothing. That felt like a much more potent way to tell the story.

Dickens changed the original, downbeat ending of his novel to bring Pip and Estella together, albeit in a way which makes you doubt whether they'll stay together. What were your thoughts in approaching the ending and its subtle ambiguities?

I really wanted to honour what was at the heart of that book, which is damage: the damage to Miss Havisham and how it impacts so massively on everyone, and what happens when she becomes theatrically in love with that damage. In the book, she sets fire to herself by accident, and I have her do it on purpose when she realises that she could have been happy, she could have had a house full of children. All she had to do was fall out of love with her vengeance – but now it's too late. It's a really important moment when Estella says, 'I am your blade. You cannot now complain if you also feel the hurt.' Having created this cold little woman and deprived her of the opportunity for happiness, there is no joy in it, only the savage realisation that you have destroyed yourself with your self-obsession and sent your daughter out into the world to be brutalised. So I found the two endings really intriguing, and I always preferred the one in which that fracture cannot be overcome. But when I came to writing my ending, because I'd written Miss Havisham and Joe and Magwitch in a particular way, I wanted Pip and Estella to feel that they could step out of that damage and live.

Our set designer did a brilliant thing for Miss Havisham's dressing room. There was this lovely chinoiserie jewellery box with little open drawers, and in the top one was coiled a tiny string of seed pearls with a golden clasp. The camera never saw it, but we all knew it was there. And it was as if Miss Havisham had stood in front of the mirror getting ready for her wedding day, and had put her hand in there to pick up these pearls that an adoring, long dead parent might have given her on a significant birthday, and she would put them around her neck so that they were with her when she was happy, when she got married, and just as she was about to pull them out the letter arrived and they were dropped back in and they never moved again. That kind of detail just thrills me, because it gives the story heart and meaning and significance and makes the suffering real. This really happened and her heart broke, and her humiliation was so intense that she said to Jaggers, 'I want a child,' and Jaggers found her a child, and this is what came out of it. I wrote a scene that never went in – which didn't matter, because I knew it was there – where you had this carriage bucketing through the night and this man holding still a little bundle on the seat, and the carriage draws up outside a house and the man lifts down this struggling bundle, drags it down cobwebbed corridors, through the green baize door where the servants enter, into this hallway lit with candles and swagged with wedding flowers, where this strange woman stands on the stairs in her wedding gown. She pulls back the blanket from this child, covered in dirt and bruises, hair snarled and spitting like a wildcat, and takes the child's chin and tilts it to the light and sees how beautiful she already is and says, 'Very well. You'll do.'

There's a scene from the book that also never went in, but really informed my reaction and my adaptation, which is where Pip is exploring the back of Satis House and wanders into this brewery and looks up and thinks he sees Miss Havisham hanging in her bridal dress – and it's not her, it's hop sacks. It's a really arresting image. And the other image that really informs the cruelty and sadism that thrums below the surface of the story is of Jaggers' servant, Molly. Jaggers and all those unbearable, entitled, Boris Johnson-style young men are sitting around the table having dinner and Molly is serving them, and he grabs her hands and drags them into the light and her arms are covered in scars: 'They were trying to take my life.' The mother of Estella. The mother of a stolen child. That's the story I wanted to tell. That's the story that matters. What it means to lose what you love.

CASE STUDY: *AND THEN THERE WERE NONE*

UK, 2015 ▪ **Directed by** Craig Viveiros ▪ **Produced by** Abi Bach ▪ **Screenplay by** Sarah Phelps, based on the novel by Agatha Christie ▪ **Cast:** Douglas Booth (Anthony Marston), Charles Dance (Justice Lawrence Wargrave), Maeve Dermody (Vera Claythorne), Burn Gorman (Detective Sergeant William Blore), Anna Maxwell Martin (Ethel Rogers), Sam Neill (General John Macarthur), Miranda Richardson (Emily Brent), Toby Stephens (Doctor Edward Armstrong), Noah Taylor (Thomas Rogers), Aidan Turner (Philip Lombard)

First Dickens, then Christie. Again, is there something about her style or her stories which particularly attracts you?

I'd never read any Agatha Christie before I read *And Then There Were None*. I always thought they were just cosy parlour games. There's a body on the floor and no one really cares; it's just a catalyst for someone to come in and be incredibly clever. Now, it's interesting that the someones who come in are all outsiders. Poirot is an outsider, Marple is an outsider – she's a spinster, he's a refugee. But the point is that they come in and they make everything safe and they restore your equilibrium and they return you to a sense of Englishness. What shocked and surprised me about *And Then There Were None*, which was the first one I did, was just how cold it was. It felt like Greek tragedy, because it's remorseless: action begets action begets action begets action. You're going to be ended because of the thing you did back there – and everything that's happened from that point on has led you here. So in some ways it is a parlour game – the judge, the general, the butler, the playboy, the mercenary, all in this closed-room murder mystery – but you can also look at it from other perspectives. You could see it as a portrait of a psychopath, or you could see it as a disquisition into the nature of guilt, or you could see it as a thoroughly subversive portrait of Britain as it stands on the edge of being calamitously pitched into another world war: all these people on this rock cut off from the mainland, and all they have is each other and the mores they live by, and coming towards them across the sea like the unblinking eye of God is their death.

The book was written and published in the summer of 1939 and I really wanted to set it at that time, because I thought it was a great way to write about what war does to people and how it changes everyone. Here you all are in this time of national crisis, when you should stand together and say, 'We know who you are because you speak with this accent and you fulfil this role, which is how society is ordered and what we are all fighting for, and because we know who you are, we know who we are.' And then you find out that they're all murderers. These people who you should trust have all done something terrible and not one of them has suffered. If it wasn't for this moment right here, right now, all of them would carry on living. So it felt like a really subversive way to say, 'You think you know Englishness? You think you know nationality? You think you know identity? You don't.' It was really exciting when we cast an Irish actor as Philip Lombard, because in that world if someone in the house has a gun and that person has an English accent, even if they are a mercenary and have been doing God knows what in the dark places of the world, you might imagine that they'd be on your side. But an Irishman with a service revolver in 1939 is a completely different kettle of fish. What's he been doing? Who's he been a soldier for? I wanted to show that the world was changing, that the past is not watching people through the wrong end of the telescope, gesticulating. It's now, it's us, without Wi-Fi. It's that simple.

I also wanted to write something terrifying: where you're terrified of the thing you've done, but there's a reason you did it, and doing it seemed totally reasonable to you at the time. You can regret it, but it came out of passion, it came out of loathing, it came out of jealousy, it came out of being angry that you were vulnerable. It felt like a thrilling way to write about what happens to us when the lights go off. A lot of what I write is about what happens to us when the lights go off, when everything drops away. When you flip a switch and it's not working, when you turn a tap and the water doesn't come out, when you pick up a phone and it's dead. What happens to us then? So I loved that remorselessness: you're going to get hunted down and you're not going to get away. There is no plea, there is no mitigation, there is no agency with which you can barter for clemency. It's death, that's it, here it comes – brace your fucking self.

Was it your decision to adapt the book in three episodes and was it always clear where those episodes would fall?

I like threes. Beginning, middle, end. Thesis, antithesis, synthesis. It's a really satisfying way to write a drama, and a really satisfying way to watch a drama. Once you start going into people's backgrounds there's so much material, and once you start building a world you could build it for hours. *Witness for the Prosecution* was two episodes, but there were times when I thought, 'I could do with another hour of this.' Endlessly self-indulgent. With this, I decided where the breaks would come in the scripts, but they came out differently when it was done, especially between episodes one and two. Sometimes, for whatever reason, the way you've written something hasn't been impactful on screen, hasn't given you that 'Ooh!' moment, so you play around with that in the edit. But I was always aware of where and how I wanted to leave things, and what was going to move the story on to the next phase.

And did you try to give each episode its own three-act structure?

I don't think like that. Loads of people have tried to make me think like that and it's a waste of time. Someone once said to me, 'What's the inciting incident?' I was like, 'Don't ever say that to me again.

Fuck off.' And they were like, 'I was just trying to help.' And I was like, 'But now I hate you. How is that helpful?' I sometimes go and talk to people who are doing writing courses and they talk like that, and I just think, 'This is horrible.' I never think about structure like that. The story tells you what the structure is. I'm working with another writer at the moment who thinks in terms of a five-act structure for an hour's worth of script, and I think, 'But that only gives you ten minutes per act.' I cannot make myself think like that. It infuriates people, but I can only think the way I think.

Christie is better known for her plots than her dialogue, and you've been noticeably more faithful to the former than the latter. There's swearing, for starters.

Sometimes even the plots make you go, 'Really?' I don't write anything which is just plot, because just plot is nothing. It's empty figures transitioning from one position to another. So I felt, with this, the plot will only work, and work satisfyingly and frighteningly and in a new way, if you have pumped your characters full of blood, pumped them full of the things they have been trying to keep secret from themselves – like the surgeon's trembling hand and his PTSD from having been in a front-line field hospital in World War I. They sit there all barbed and polite with their lies fizzing beneath the surface, but once a few people have died they get dirty and they get nasty. It's what happens when people are scared. It's what happens when they start to unravel. It's part of the downward spiral. If you think someone is trying to kill you, you're going to start to swear, surely? I would. Do you want to hear a funny story?

Absolutely.

I've got to the end of the scripts, I'm very proud of them, everyone's very excited by them. We've got a brilliant cast and a really great director and we're at the read-through. It's a huge room and it's crammed full of people and the last line I'd written for Philip Lombard – before Vera Claythorne shoots him, when she's holding the gun on him – was for him to come really close to her and reach out and take the gun and say, 'The safety catch, you stupid cunt.' And you thought:

he will kill you. It doesn't matter that you've had sex. It doesn't matter that you've danced cheek to cheek. He will kill you. Later on, a researcher came back and said service revolvers didn't have safety catches, but that's beside the point. It read brilliantly and it got a shiver around the room. So then we had the read-through notes, and the BBC exec said, 'I've got one note. You've got to take "cunt" out.' I was absolutely livid: 'What are you talking about? Don't be ridiculous! It's completely character-driven. It's a huge moment in the script!' Ranting and raving for about 15 minutes. And this poor guy went, 'Sarah, it's Christmas. You can't have "cunt" at Christmas.' It was brilliant. Thirty people in a room all crying with laughter. And I was like, 'Fine. I'm not going to argue with you anymore. Because I lose the line but gain one hell of an anecdote.'

The opening scenes introducing the characters, some of them receiving instructions and payment from a seedy intermediary, have a jauntier tone than what follows. Was there a sense of giving the audience a little of what they expect before the darkness draws in?

I didn't even think about it like that. I just wanted the uneasiness to coil inside you and the significance of that character to come out later on. It had a levity which was just going to be destroyed. Initially, when Vera says, 'I suffer because that little boy died in my care,' you want to believe her, so that later you go, 'Jesus Christ, she planned this, she calculated it down to the last moment.' And when she says she's not a woman who enjoys being looked at, she *is* a woman who enjoys being looked at. The first image I had when I read *And Then There Were None*, the first thing that stuck in my mind, was of this white-limbed woman in a red bathing suit in front of a white, folded geometric house, lifting her head and catching the eye of this man, and you realise: she's been lying about who she is and there's no end to her deviousness – and she nearly gets away with it. I love that last line I gave to her: 'They'll believe me. They believed me last time!' A few of the others waver: the policeman, Blore, feels guilt; the soldier, Macarthur, feels guilt. Vera doesn't. She's sorry she lost her lover. She's sorry her plan didn't work. But she's not sorry about that little boy. That's an exciting way to write women. Not sorry. No guilt.

Most of the characters' backstories, the crimes they're called to account for, you've lifted intact from the novel, but some you've made changes to. How did you determine which ones to change?

It was the ones which were confusing or weren't impactful. Vera's is pretty much intact. I changed the tone and inference of others. Blore's was the one I really changed around. In the book, Blore has lied to send someone to prison, and I thought, 'You don't want that, you want something direct,' so in my version we see him kick a young man to death, and that young man is gay. Everyone was like, 'He's obviously a self-hating gay man.' Now, there is a self-hating gay person in my version, but that's Emily Brent, and that's why she throws that girl out, because she's got pregnant, and Emily Brent can't bear to think of her housemaid, whose pricked finger she takes to her lips, being ridden. She throws her out not because of religion, but because of violent and confused sexual emotions, but no one seemed to pick up on that. With Blore, it's because he saw someone more vulnerable than he was, and more lonely, and he found it unbearable, so he had to kill him to feel better. I wanted it to be something that you would feel such guilt over, such hurt. That you do things you don't even understand and carry them around as a burden. You sit on your allotment and eat your radishes and wish for catharsis, but it's not going to come.

One of the biggest changes is to the ending: no baffled police, no message in a bottle explaining the plot. Why did you eliminate all that?

Because it's boring.

But doesn't it leave a question about how the murderer knew all of the victims' backstories?

You do get Wargrave explaining, don't you, the fact that he's a judge who gets to oversee all these sorts of things? I just didn't want to drag on about it. It's like that thing about voiceover. You've got to make it happen in the moment. You've got to make it happen in that final conversation between Vera and Wargrave. You know, 'Left all alone, he went and hanged himself and then there were none.' We've set up the thing about Wargrave taking painkillers and the doctor,

Armstrong, recognising him because the guy he shares a clinic with is a cancer specialist, so you know he's been incredibly ill. But the big thing, of course, is that you've got to make people believe that he's dead, so when he walks through the door you go, 'Fucking hell!' That's really important. I did play with the idea of the police turning up, but it became a little bit Agatha Christie and a lot less shocking. There's so much cruelty and calculation in what Wargrave sets up, it's all so solipsistic and self-aggrandising, that for there to be a kind of, 'And now I'm going to explain how I did it,' would have made it a bit pathetic. I thought that actually this was Wargrave's gift to the audience: 'I know, and you know, but they will never know, and it will drive them mad for years.' And it's a hell of a way to end a Christmas show, isn't it, someone's brains running down the wall? Happy fucking Christmas!

Index

INDEX

INDEX

About Us

In addition to Creative Essentials, Oldcastle Books has a number of other imprints, including No Exit Press, Kamera Books, Pulp! The Classics, Pocket Essentials and High Stakes Publishing
> oldcastlebooks.co.uk

Checkout the kamera film salon for independent, arthouse and world cinema **> kamera.co.uk**

For more information, media inquiries and review copies please contact **> marketing@oldcastlebooks.com**